Steve Neal

HST

HST

MEMORIES OF THE TRUMAN YEARS

EDITED BY Steve Neal

FOREWORD BY Clifton Truman Daniel

Southern Illinois University Press CARBONDALE

Copyright © 2003 Board of Trustees,
Southern Illinois University
Printed in the United States of America
06   05   04   03   4   3   2   1

Designed by Richard Hendel

Library of Congress Cataloging-in-Publication Data

HST : memories of the Truman years / edited by Steve Neal.
　　　 p. cm.
　　　 Includes bibliographical references and index.
　　　　 1. Truman, Harry S., 1884–1972.   2. Presidents—United States—
Biography.   3. United States—Politics and government—1945–
1953.   4. Truman, Harry S., 1884–1972—Friends and associates.
5. Interviews—United States.   I. Neal, Steve, 1949–
E814 .H76 2003
973.918′092—dc21
ISBN 0-8093-2558-6 (alk. paper)   2003010463

Printed on recycled paper.

The paper used in this publication meets the minimum requirements of
American National Standard for Information Sciences—Permanence of
Paper for Printed Library Materials, ANSI Z39.48-1992. ⊗

For PAUL SIMON and DAN ROSTENKOWSKI

CONTENTS

ILLUSTRATIONS

FOREWORD

One of the great things about my grandfather was that he always said what was on his mind — even when there was no one around to listen. Most presidents leave a paper trail of official speeches, public pronouncements, and formal correspondence, as well as more mundane but often more revealing items like diaries and personal notes. No one but Grandpa, however, wrote down so much of what he was thinking and feeling. Often, when faced with a major decision, he took a couple of pads of notepaper, went off by himself, and wrote it all out, pro and con, so he could look at the problem objectively. As a result, we have page after page on which he poured out his heart and mind, leaving us with a much better understanding of Harry S. Truman than of any other United States president. That's the way he wanted it. He believed Americans should understand the presidency.

In that vein, almost forty years ago, the Truman Library in Independence, Missouri, began recording the words of my grandfather's contemporaries, the men and women who worked for him and with him, who had been his friends and colleagues, and who had even taught him at school. The goal of these oral histories, in keeping with Grandpa's stated desire that the library be about his presidency, not a monument to him, was to preserve forever the perspective of those who had shared his life and times and, in many cases, helped him shape the world.

It was from the oral histories that I first discovered what a unique child my grandfather had been. One of his grade-school teachers recalled that during recess, while the other children were chasing a ball or each other, Grandpa was down on his hands and knees in the dirt, building a replica of Hadrian's Wall across a corner of the schoolyard. This went a long way toward explaining why, when I was four and my brother, Will, was two, Grandpa deemed it appropriate to sit us down in an armchair and read to us from the Greek historian Thucydides. If my mother hadn't interrupted us, we might have moved on to building Roman fortifications in Central Park.

Sifting through thousands of vignettes buried in hundreds of transcripts and pulling twenty of them together to shape a coherent and compelling book is no mean feat. It takes someone every bit as dedicated to recording and preserving history as my grandfather was.

Like Grandpa, Steve Neal was an unusual child. I don't know whether he liked Thucydides or Hadrian, but he knew early on that he liked politics and wanted to spend his life writing about it. After a couple of decades as the *Sun-Times*'s political columnist, you'd think he'd be jaded, that the muck stirred up by the players in the world's second-oldest profession would have gummed up his sensibilities. Not Steve. His enthusiasm for the machinations of public office and the people who do the machinating is astounding — and more than a little infectious. If you could put him and Grandpa in a room together, you might as well play solitaire for all the input you'd have.

What Steve has assembled here are, in effect, conversations, all of them fascinating and all of them, I'm sure, conversations that Steve himself would have wanted to have. He has selected them with an eye toward painting a thorough, engaging picture of my grandfather and the events of his presidency. He has also made sure that each interview reveals not only its subject's role but his personality as well. You can hear the humor in the words of my grandfather's best friend, Tom Evans, as he recalls his wife giving Grandpa hell for washing his own socks on the campaign trail. You may be surprised, as I was, to learn that the Eastern-educated secretary of state Dean Acheson spoke just as plainly and bluntly as his friend and boss, the former Missouri farmer.

You have some illuminating conversations ahead of you, courtesy of Steve Neal. When you're done, you may feel as though you had been sitting in a room with Acheson, General Omar Bradley, Clark Clifford, Averell Harriman, and a host of others, chatting about Harry Truman, his personality, his decisions, his family . . . and his dirty socks.

They may have been giants and they may be gone, but it doesn't feel like it.

Clifton Truman Daniel

ACKNOWLEDGMENTS

I am most grateful to Robert H. Ferrell, Distinguished Professor of History Emeritus at Indiana University, for sharing his vast knowledge of the Truman era. When I began going through the transcripts of oral history interviews at the Truman Library, Professor Ferrell could not have been more helpful. As the author of a dozen volumes about the subject of this book, he is familiar with the entire oral history collection and pointed out some of the more valuable interviews.

Clifton Truman Daniel, President Truman's first grandson, has generously given his time and shared his memories of Harry S. Truman (HST). I can't thank him enough.

Thanks to Michael Devine, director of the Harry S. Truman Library in Independence, and his deputy Scott Roley and archivist Amy Williams. Elizabeth Safly, the reference librarian, encouraged me to edit this collection and generously shared her perspectives on the oral history program. The archivists Dennis Bilger and Randy Sowell were also quite helpful. I am most appreciative to Anita M. Smith, coordinator of interlibrary loans, for making interview transcripts available to me on a regular basis. Thanks also to Pauline Testerman, audiovisual archivist, for providing photographs from the Truman years.

Closer to home, I am indebted to Susan McNeil-Marshall, Janet Widdel, and Diane Brooks of the Hinsdale Public Library's reference department; the late Terri Golembiewski, Judith Halper, Virginia Davis, Ziggy Ulmanis, Herb Ballard, Dale McCullough, Ron Theel, and Ted White of the *Chicago Sun-Times* reference staff; and Charlotte Ulmanis of the *Sun-Times* editorial department.

Thanks to my editors at the *Chicago Sun-Times*, Michael Cooke, John Cruickshank, and Steve Huntley. I am grateful to Rick Stetter, director of the Southern Illinois University Press. Finally, thanks to my wife, Susan, and daughters, Erin and Shannon.

Introduction The Man of Independence

There was never any doubt about where he stood. Harry Truman was a leader of uncommon courage and character. When faced with tough choices, he was never afraid to lead. "A President is either constantly on top of events or, if he hesitates, events will soon be on top of him," he wrote in *Years of Trial and Hope.* "I never felt that I could let up for a single moment."

His decisions were often unpopular. As he left office, his approval ratings were at a low point. Yet he never worried about his place in history. "Do your duty," he said in 1948, "and history will do you justice." Before the end of his long life, he would gain recognition as one of our greatest presidents. With his thick glasses, double-breasted suits, and salty vocabulary, he has become part of American folklore. Though his success astonished nearly everyone, it was no accident. The former World War I artillery captain and chief judge of Jackson County was a shrewd politician with a sense of history. It was partly because of his modesty and Franklin D. Roosevelt's long shadow that he was often underestimated.

By any measure, his accomplishments were extraordinary. Truman led the Western alliance to its final victory in World War II. He shortened the war by dropping the atomic bomb on Japan, a controversial decision that Truman believed saved a half-million lives because it resulted in peace without an invasion. More than anything else, his foreign-policy leadership has earned him a place on the very short list of important presidents. He responded to the challenge of Soviet expansionism with the Truman Doctrine, the Marshall Plan, the Berlin airlift, and history's most successful alliance, the North Atlantic Treaty Organization (NATO).

At the beginning of the cold war, he was confident about the outcome. "The Communist world has great resources, and it looks strong," he declared in the final week of his presidency. "But there is a fatal flaw in their society. Theirs is a godless system, a system of slavery; there is no freedom in it, no consent. The Iron Curtain, the secret police, the constant purges, all of these are symptoms of a great basic weakness — the rulers' fear of their own people. In the long run the strength of our free society, and our ideals, will prevail over a system that has respect for neither God nor man."

In what he described as his most difficult decision, Truman used military force to thwart Communist aggression in Korea. Upholding the principle of civilian control of the armed services, he fired General Douglas MacArthur for insubordination. Though he was vilified for this unpopular action, Truman acted in the public interest.

On domestic issues, his most enduring legacy is in civil rights. No other chief executive since Abraham Lincoln did more to promote racial equality. By executive order, he ended the segregation of the armed services. With the stroke of his pen, he also ended discrimination in the federal government and launched the modern civil rights movement. With his encouragement, the Justice Department fought discrimination against African Americans in housing and public schools. He viewed himself as a man of the people. "The president has to look out for the interests of the 150 million people who can't afford lobbyists in Washington," he once declared.

This book is about Truman, both the man and his presidency, as remembered by the people who knew him. The Truman Library was among the pioneers in the field of oral history. Nearly all of the former president's close friends and associates were interviewed for this project. Since the library's first director, Philip C. Brooks, launched the oral history program in 1961, more than 460 people have been interviewed.

The memoirs in this volume have been excerpted from full-scale oral history interviews, most of which are available in transcript form and are open to researchers. In choosing selections for this collection, I have sought to include a diversity of voices: a renowned artist, two generals and a journalist, the president's best friend, senior White House assistants, and the men who worked with Truman in changing the direction of the postwar world.

From their collected memories, a portrait of Truman emerges. Averell Harriman talks about how the president shunned self-promotion and gave others credit for his work. Earl Warren, the 1948 Republican nominee for vice president, gives the inside story of that historic election. General Omar Bradley recalls the commander in chief's firing of Douglas MacArthur. Dean Acheson discusses the early cold war period and wryly dismisses the bipartisan foreign policy as a myth. Richard L. Strout explains why reporters liked Truman. Judge Samuel Rosenman recalls working with Roosevelt and his successor. Thomas L. Evans describes Truman, as the 1944 Democratic nominee for the vice presidency, washing out his socks in a Boston hotel room.

It was during the Truman presidency that the Columbia University historian Allan Nevins started the first organized oral history program. In writing a biography of one of Truman's favorite presidents, Grover Cleveland, he was disappointed to learn that Cleveland and his associates had not been interviewed for posterity. To make the past come alive for future generations, Nevins called for an organized effort "to obtain from the lips and papers of living Americans who have led significant lives, a fuller record of their participation in the political, economic, and cultural life of the last sixty years."

In May 1948 he began conducting interviews for the Columbia program. Among the projects undertaken by this office were the New Deal, Dwight D. Eisenhower, and Adlai E. Stevenson.

Truman supported the oral history movement because he wanted to leave a comprehensive record of his administration. In working on his two-volume White House memoirs and his 1960 book, Mr. Citizen, he was interviewed by his collaborators. The transcripts of those sessions are available to scholars and are invaluable. After the former president's death, the novelist Merle Miller wrote Plain Speaking, which he described as an "oral biography." Robert H. Ferrell, the dean of Truman scholars, has exposed Miller as a fraud. Miller made up quotes and attributed them to the former president. During his lifetime, Truman took legal action to prevent Miller from publishing excerpts from an interview. "I am not in favor of such articles, especially this one which has so many misstatements of fact in it," he wrote Miller in 1963.

In founding his presidential library, he vowed that it would "belong to the people of the United States. My papers will be the property of the people and be accessible to them. And this is as it should be. The papers of the presidents are among the most valuable sources of material for history. They ought to be preserved, and they ought to be used." So should these memories of the Truman years.

Dean Acheson

Kansas City, Missouri   February 18, 1955

Interviewed by William Hillman and David Noyes;

edited by Francis Heller

Dean Acheson (1893–1971), secretary of state from 1949 until 1953, was Truman's partner in shaping the postwar world. He was among the key architects of the Truman Doctrine, the Marshall Plan, and the North Atlantic Treaty Organization. His elegantly written memoir, *Present at the Creation,* is the definitive history of postwar foreign policy. Even though they came from different worlds, the son of the Missouri horse trader and the son of the Anglican bishop of Connecticut had a special relationship. "I wish I could sit and talk with you for an hour, or thirty minutes, or even for five minutes," the former president wrote his friend. Truman ranked Acheson as the most important secretary of state of modern times. An *American Heritage* poll of diplomatic historians in the early 1980s ranked Acheson below John Quincy Adams but ahead of Thomas Jefferson and Daniel Webster. It is questionable that Truman would have approved of the recent decision to put his name on the State Department Building. There is no doubt that he would have preferred honoring his favorite associate.

Acheson: This is probably unique in American history. I don't think it ever happened before. Driving in this morning I mentioned something to the president on this. He was talking about Douglas Freeman. He said he admired him very much but that something had happened. He didn't know what it was. I said I didn't think it was much. Douglas Freeman wrote the introduction to the book you have right there, by Mac [McGeorge] Bundy, about my speeches. He says that American history will show that there was no other secretary who so identified himself with the personality of the president and his policies as I had. I wrote and thanked him for it. It is a nice introduction. In it he said that one of the reasons I got into trouble was that I showed contempt for the contemptible. That was a very unwise thing to do. I wrote and thanked him for this, and I said I thought what he said was only half the picture about my relations with the president. This thing worked both ways.

I don't think there is any example of a president who so stood by his secretary as Mr. Truman had me. I said that the important thing about it is that the two men should completely understand their roles and not get them mixed up. It's an easy thing to do, to get them mixed up. A secretary should never have the illusion that he is president of the United States. They have, you know, but they would not quite admit it. They think *he* lives in the White House, but *I* really am the guy who runs things. And a great many presidents have been under the illusion that they were the secretary of state. FDR was the latest example of it. They are not and cannot be, and they will get into trouble indeed if they try. Therefore each fellow has to understand his role, keep his role, and stay within it exactly.

The function of the secretary of state is to be the president's personal adviser on foreign affairs. He is running a department which is skilled and experienced and very good. He must use that department so that he gets the best information it is possible to get on any subject or problem. He gets the very best advice from people who live with this thing which he must present to the president of the United States. The president of the United States must recognize that that is the role of the secretary of state. He must not go off on little frolics of his own. FDR knew that if he told [Cordell] Hull about something, Hull would get a lot of people in the department working on it, and he would have to change it; so, he would go off on his own and get everyone in trouble. He had enough to do without doing that technical role.

It was a great thing between Mr. Truman and me. Each one understood his role and the other's. We never got tangled up in it. I never thought I was the president, and he never thought he was the secretary. He never took any action, except one, without going over the whole thing with me. You have to do that from the very beginning of a problem, because it becomes more and more complicated. That was partly at the root of the president's differences with Jimmy Byrnes. It does no good to go ahead with a matter until it has reached a quarter to midnight and then go and say to the president, "Here's the whole thing. It has to be signed in the next three minutes." What can the president do? The only thing he can decide is what you want him to decide. You put him in a hole. A good deal of Jimmy's trouble came from that. He was never vicious, but he just didn't want to bother him about it until it was all wrapped up.

An important part of my role was to pull together everything that these five or six thousand people who were working for me knew and get that to the president. Also, I had to get to those five or six thousand people the president's general thoughts on the whole field of foreign affairs. Foreign affairs is a part of the total policy of the United States. There's no line between the Treasury's policy, economic policy, political policy, or military — it's all part of one thing, which is what the government of the United States does. And the whole is wrapped up in taxes — it's the life and death of a lot of people in the country. Therefore, what I had to do was to be in close touch with the president's program — his thoughts, the things he wanted developed. And I had to be close to my colleagues and continually guide the department so that they would not be taking a different road than the president's. There was a constant exchange of thought between us.

These appointments I had two times a week, but I must have seen the president five or six times a week. For a long time we had cabinet luncheons on Mondays, but this didn't go all the way through the thing. I forget why. That gave you a long time to talk with the president. Then I had these appointments on either Monday and Thursday or Tuesday and Thursday — from 12:30 to a quarter past one. I think it was Monday because we used to walk to luncheon together. A lot of business can be transacted in fifteen minutes. There were a lot of things to tell him about — questions which were just sticking their heads over the horizon, that would come up in six weeks or six months. And we would talk back and forth, discuss the things. I had to get an idea of how he approached it. If it was very bad, I would argue like hell about it, but we would come together. Whatever he made up his mind on, that was the line. We took that, right or wrong, good or bad.

I would take this back to the department, never as what the president said but as what I thought. One of the great ways to cause trouble in an organization like the United States government is to be a hero to your own people and set up your boss as the one who causes all the trouble. You can go over with a fine program and then come back and say, "I did the best I could, but you know, fellows, I guess we'll have to do it this way." And they mutter about that fellow in the White House. That's a sure way to ruin things. That gets found out right away and causes trouble, suspicions. It was clear to me that the president's ideas were my ideas. If he changed something, I would say to my people, "I thought it over last night, and I think we have been on the wrong track. This is the way to do it." They would argue with me, and I would say, "What you say just doesn't convince me." No one could ever say that Acheson thinks this and the president thinks that. It was one thought. There were a lot of differences between me and the president. It wasn't a sweet and easy life, but to anyone outside that room there was but one person, one thought. That is very important.

One thing I see at the present time which I see being done wrong in the State Department is that the department really doesn't function. I operate it very much the way it did under Jimmy Byrnes. There were three or four fellows who were closer to the secretary, and the great majority, they would say, "What's the use? Don't break your neck on something. You're wasting effort." No man who has not grown up in this business can extirpate information from his own mind; you have to get that from the department, and that you get by encouraging everyone, making everyone feel that what he is doing is important, by having meetings with everybody, down through the desk officer. The thing is to let them talk; you listen more than you talk yourself. You ask questions, bring out inconsistencies in their thinking, get them straightened out. It encourages them to go to work. Bert Marshall was working on a speech for the president, and he felt that something which had been agreed on was the wrong line. He talked with me on it. Bert's a very able fellow; he was on our policy planning staff. I said, "I just think you are wrong, but after all, this is a very important thing. Wait a minute." And I picked up the white telephone: "Mr. President, Bert Marshall, the brother of General Marshall, thinks that thing you and I were talking about — that I was wrong about it. He's not a fellow whose opinion I would push aside. Would you let him come in about ten and state his case?"

Well, the boy's eyes were this big. "You mean you want me to tell the president I think you are wrong?"

I said, "Exactly. Go over and do it."

He did, and the president was very nice to him, but he decided I wasn't wrong. And Bert said, "What a place this is. You can go straight to the top."

Well, he was working seventeen times harder than he ever had before, and he's so loyal to the president and me that it's really wicked. I think it is important that the relations between the president and his secretary of state be quite frank, sometimes frank to the point of being blunt. And you just have to be deferential. He is president of the United States, and you don't say rude things to him — you say blunt things to him. Sometimes he doesn't like it. That's natural, but he comes back, and you argue that thing out. But that's your duty; you don't tell him only what he wants to hear. That would be bad for him and for everyone else. I said you may be thrown out on Pennsylvania Avenue on your behind, but this time it's going to happen one way or another.

This was about Lew Douglas — not the one who got the fishhook in his eye — wanting to resign as his ambassador to Great Britain. I told him to come on home and think about it. This was a big position, so we kept it a secret, and I had discussed the matter with the president. I went over one day, and the president said, "Well, I haven't said anything to you, but I guess it's really settled. I've asked Jim Bruce to be ambassador."

This you can't put in the book because enough trouble has come of it already. I said, "Of all the people in the world, why Jim Bruce? This is a great position. He's a nice fellow, but he hasn't any capacity to handle it."

The president said, "He raised a lot of money, and in '48 we were in a bad fix. He really put his back into this thing. And I think I have given him my word."

Well, if he has given his word, that's the end of the argument. So, I said, "Here it goes." I said, "Mr. President, I heard you give your word to something else, and this is inconsistent."

He said, "Who did I promise this to?"

I said, "You had your right hand up and your left hand on a Bible, and you said, 'I will to the best of my ability perform the duties of the president of the United States . . .' so help you God. You are not doing that." He looked at me, and I said, "Well, what happens?"

After a while, he said, "You are right. You think it over and bring me in a recommendation."

Well, that is what I call blunt. I thought it was essential. I didn't give a damn about one person or another. The man we finally appointed I'd never seen before in my life. It turned out to be Walter Gifford. [Anthony] Eden told me he was the best ambassador we had had in London since he had been alive. He didn't like society much; he was not a social success. But we would tell him what to do, and he would go ahead and do it. After all, he was head of AT&T, and he had had some training in how to get along with people. He got along very well, better with the Labour government than anyone since [John] Winant. Lew Douglas spent a lot of time being social. But the reason I was fighting with the president, Great Britain is our greatest ally. We have to go just like pigeons — when one turns; the others do it, too. We have to fly wing to wing. To have anyone there who would be clumsy, or careless, or dumb, or who would be cabling back, "I don't think we ought to do this, or that," you would be sure to have him coming back once a week to talk policy.

Another thing which is quite impossible to write is a prescription for the relationship between the president and the secretary of state. You have to have an element of affection — which you can't prescribe. We had that even before I became secretary of state. There were a hundred things that built it up — two people of quite different backgrounds became quite devoted to one another. It may be immodest to say, but the president is fond of me, and I am devoted to him. And the sort of thing that happened after I was secretary — you can't get them out of your mind at all. I had a younger daughter whom I have done my best to spoil. She's very close to me. She got TB. For a long time she was at Saranac, and towards the end she had to have a dreadful operation. They took seven ribs out of her back and part of the lung. It was very painful, and dangerous. My wife was there. She had two operations a month apart. She went through hell once, and then she had to do it again. I had to travel to San Francisco to make a speech. I was in San Francisco the day of the second operation. Until she was sailing along, Mr. Harry S. Truman telephoned me every single, solitary day — sometimes to ask me the latest, sometimes to tell me. Mrs. Truman would have gotten the latest from my wife: "The girl is doing fine today." Or, "The 'Boss' gave me hell because I was to call you at nine o'clock, and it's now ten. She wanted to find out how Mary is." You can't write that into a prescription. But that was important, because a lot of things sink into insignificance when you have that kind of relationship.

Another thing, it seemed to me that this role required brains as well as good intentions — the role of being secretary to the president. It isn't enough to say I am devoted and loyal to him. You have to have brains to find out how to do it. I went off in May — I became secretary in January — I went off in May to five or six meetings with the Russians in Paris. I took with me a regular staff. Then I took a small additional staff solely for the purpose of communication. We wrote every day two cables, and every other day I would send a personal cable — or twice a week — to the president. There would be one very long report which I had these special fellows there to do. They attended all the meetings; they sat in the back of the room and took notes, and then they would stay up until 1:00 or 2:00 A.M. — this was the long report, in detail. Then we had a short report, which condensed all that into the main things so that the president could look at it and know what was going on. Then the long report, if the president wanted to go into it in detail, and it was also there for the department. There were a lot of fellows interested in it. The short one was one which the president could look at if he wanted to get a quick drift of the matter. And it was something to show to Senator [Arthur] Vandenberg, something which wouldn't embarrass you if they went out and talked. It was more accurate that way. Then a couple of times a week before going to bed I would get a secretary to come in, and I would dictate a sort of chatty one. I remember I sent one from Lisbon in which I said, "Don't tell anyone, but I think this is going to be a grand slam. It's bad luck even to say it, but I just guess everything is going to come out just the way we wanted it." That is more revealing to him than other things. Or I would say, "The thing is really fouled up now, and I just don't see how we'll ever get it straightened out." He always felt as if he were sitting at the conference with me. Occasionally I would ask him for instructions as to what to do. Rarely he would give instructions. Occasionally I would get messages from him, and I knew he was reading my reports. He would tell me good luck, etc. There wasn't the basis for worry he had with Jimmy. Jimmy never took the trouble — General Marshall did it about halfway between Jimmy and me. The general was always crisp and bit it off in a military way.

But all those things helped the feeling of confidence. I think the president, when he came in, thought of the State Department as a hostile agency which would try to gum up what he wanted them to do. When we got through, he thought of the State Department as a part of the White House office. It was part of his secretariat. I used to tell him: "I am secretary of state. What is that? In England I would be secretary of state for foreign affairs. I am just a high-class secretary to the president — what [Sir William] Cecil was to Queen Elizabeth." The Department of Agriculture is not a secretary to the White House. They are fooling around with corn, chickens, and hogs. We don't produce anything. We are not trying to sell anything or to put out a bond issue. We have only one job. The Constitution says the president is to conduct the foreign affairs of the United States. We are doing that for him, the way he wants it done. . . .

The Woodrow Wilson part I only know from reading about it. I never knew any of those men, and I don't know what happened. I was undersecretary in 1946 when Jim Forrestal got carried off with the British cabinet system. He thought we ought to have a secretary of the cabinet; our cabinet was a mess, and we ought to do something about it. They started having luncheons. There was one with John Snyder in 1946 — I guess it was [Fred] Vinson, in that room of his. The attorney general had a room at his place, and in the Pentagon there was a luncheon place. They were the only shops equipped for luncheons. It started out as a nice friendly business; then they began talking about things. Two things were developing. I remember a long discussion that his meat rationing business was bad and that the president was taking the wrong line. They ought to just all get together and tell him he was making a mistake. An election was coming up and we'd lose it. I thought, "Just a minute; that doesn't look good to me." Then they began this cabinet business. I think Clark showed up — Clark Clifford — and they were talking about why we should have a secretary for the cabinet. Well, we were riding home from one of those things, and I said, "Jim, this is really bad stuff" —

Q: Jim? Jim Forrestal?

Acheson: No, no. The director of the budget, Jim Webb. Webb and I understood what was going on. I said, "A few hundred — three hundred — years ago Queen Elizabeth got disturbed by just such a thing, and a lot of people left their heads around the Tower." I recalled [Robert] Lansing having called a cabinet meeting when Wilson had his stroke, and the president, from his bed, fired Mr. Lansing, and I said, "This is really high politics, and I'd hate to be a fellow telling tales, but I think we better stop by the White House and see HST and tell him there's a conspiracy going on." I told the president that they were playing with matches and that someone was going to get hurt; that he had better tell them it was all right to have their luncheons, but if they were going to talk about matters of state, they had better do it in the presence of the president. Well, he took occasion to make it quite clear in the next cabinet meeting that he was president and that a presidential system was different from a cabinet system. Perhaps we might leave such discussions until we were all together. He did it in a nice way, but he made it plain that it wasn't a good thing.

I remember that from the Wilson period. Wilson was the secretary of state; Mr. [William Jennings] Bryan wasn't; Lansing wasn't; [Bainbridge] Colby wasn't; he was. Perhaps it was all right for him to be. It was rather simpler then than now. With FDR . . . . Mr. Hull was always going to tell everyone where to get off, but he never did — Mr. Hull was a very sweet gentleman — if he had, he would have scared the daylights out of Roosevelt. I think Roosevelt wanted people to do exactly what he told them to do and not waste a lot of time talking about it. The president and I were talking this morning at breakfast about Roosevelt firing me in 1933. I said I thought we were both right. It was just sad. The president was right to do what he did, from his point of view. I was right to stand firm and get fired. He was telling me to sign a paper allowing the RFC [Reconstruction Finance Corporation] to buy gold and increase the price. I said, "I'm sorry, but the law tells me to do exactly the opposite. I must do everything to maintain the price at the statutory figure. If you want to change it, the Congress will do anything you want. Get the law changed."

The president said, "The attorney general says you're wrong."

I said, "I know he says so, but he won't write it. Here I go ahead and do what you say, the attorney general won't put it down — he can't spell it out. Only Stanley Reed is able to do a thing like that."

The president said, "I order you to do it."

I said, "You will have to get someone who will do it. If you want me to resign, I will, but I will not sign that paper."

He got very angry, and I left, which was quite all right with me. But Roosevelt had that kind of temperament. I don't mean he was a dictator, but — he wanted no advice from subordinates . . . Sumner Welles — I think Mr. Roosevelt had been made his guardian; his parents had died when he was young, and Roosevelt looked out for him — that sort of arrangement, of a ward to a guardian. Also, Mr. Hull just plain bored FDR. He was tiresome, never gay, never had a joke, and Sumner was different. Poor Ed Stettinius. After Mr. Hull got ill and left, he put Ed in there — I think he just said, "Let's have someone who will do exactly what I say." Ed wasn't well. There was something wrong with his back; he was always suffering. He would go to the hospital two or three times a day. I had the feeling the thing was too big for him. He didn't know how to handle it, and it made him physically worse.

With Mr. Byrnes the trouble was really quite deep. The president has told you the story about the 1944 convention. Well, Jimmy always had the feeling that he had been euchred out of his rights. If things had happened as they should have, he would have been president of the United States. I don't know how he felt about Mr. Truman's part in it. The president thinks he made it clear to him that he had done this reluctantly, that he had been ordered by FDR, but Byrnes said, "yes, I know, sure . . . , yet you didn't have to be ordered much." It was a hard relationship. I think he always regarded Mr. Truman as a junior senator. Here he had been in the Senate for years, been on the Supreme Court, and director of mobilization, I think, during the war. Mr. Truman was a very promising young man whom he expected someday would go far. That was the attitude he had towards him.

I remember shortly after he came in office — he'd been to Potsdam and back again — people around Ed Stettinius were trying to put over something very bad; they were really trying to set up two secretaries of state, with one in the UN, just like the Dutch have at this time. Byrnes grabbed the telephone: "I want to speak to the president. Harry?" And he went on talking about it.

After he had finished, I said, "Mr. Secretary, you don't want any advice from me, but no one does anything like that. No matter who you are, he is 'Harry' to no one except Mrs. Truman. Not even his twin. Not anymore." Theodore Roosevelt resented it very much; every president must. Not that he thinks — but when a man is president, he is the president.

"Dean," he said, "of course you are right. I shouldn't do it." But the fact is, he did it. It was symptomatic. Then he thought he understood what was necessary, and he would go ahead and run these special things. He had a tendency towards a one-track mind. There was the Moscow conference on the peace treaty — off he went. I think he thought that the idea was that the president thought he was the hottest thing in the world, that the president would say, "Take it over and don't bother me with it." Now the London — no, the Moscow meeting — he went off to that. You will have in your file twenty-seven telegrams, numbered from one to twenty-seven — that is all. I don't know how many hundreds there would be from my conference in Paris, but it would be a file that big. Some of his were purely personal — to Mrs. Byrnes — not more than a half dozen revealing anything. We had some discussion about the control council that was set up in Tokyo. We went back and forth on that, but that was worked out.

The president had come home for Christmas. He was out here in Independence when we began on the ticker over our communications system — the communiqué from Moscow. But before that was completed, it was in the newspapers. It was out on the streets before we had it in the department and sent it to the Map Room to go out here. The message from

Jimmy got to the president after the *Kansas City Star* had it. This, of course, raised his blood pressure a bit. Then he came on back. I got a message from the "Sacred Cow" to arrange for a four-station, all-line network hookup. Mr. Byrnes would arrive home on Saturday, and on Sunday he would address the nation and give them the results of the conference. Well, that wasn't quite the thing to do. The secretary comes home and tells the president what happened, and if the president wants him to, he makes a speech. But I didn't know what to do. I was the ham in the sandwich; I'd be fried ham with the president on one side and Jimmy on the other. I had to be loyal to two men who were not getting along very well. So, I thought, "What is the decent and right thing to do? I guess I will do what I was told to do." I got a four-network hookup, but I was uncertain as to what night I wanted it for. I think it is Sunday or Monday — but don't cancel anything yet. Bill Benton and I did that.

I told the president what I had done. He didn't like it. I said, "What do you want me to do?"

And he said, "Firm it up, but I want to see Jimmy as soon as he gets back."

I met him at the plane. The president had gone down the river on the *Williamsburg* — or was it the *Sequoia*? Jimmy was very tired, and he hadn't shaved. He had had to fly a long time in a nonpressurized plane, and he was as cross as a bear. We had a little chat, and I said, "I think the president would like to see you."

He said, "Oh hell, where is he?" I told him, and he said, "God damn it to hell, I can't do that. I've got to work on this speech."

I said, "You really ought to. As president of the United States, is he going to have to listen to you over the radio to find out what all this is all about?"

We got a plane and flew him down to that marine place. They took him out. He spent the evening there, and he got into a bad fog driving home. What happened I don't know. Jimmy maintains he had a pleasant evening, that the president had a misunderstanding, but that was cleared away. They drank bourbon and told stories. The president's story is that he gave him unshaded hell. Both men have accounted it to me in detail — two things that could not have happened at the same time. There are a lot of tales about Jimmy and his living which I see no point in putting in. Maybe the president is putting it all in his book — I just don't know. But I will tell you — some part of this you can only possibly have found out from me, and I would be embarrassed. I am quite friendly with Mr. Byrnes. I don't want to have a row with him.

Has he told you about Eisenhower and his trip to the Orient and his talk with General Marshall? Let me say this, and then let's talk about whether it's a good thing. Mr. Byrnes was going away in April 1946 to Paris to begin the satellite peace treaties. This was a task which took him until September when he came back—I was reading a book review the other day, a book which has taken the old story of Aphrodite and the young man she fell in love with. She didn't want him to die, so she gave him the gift of immortality, but she forgot to give him the gift of eternal youth. He got older and older and older, and damned if he could die. I think it is quite important that the president rather lean over backwards in dealing with Jimmy Byrnes because—for instance, in the Yalta and Moscow Conferences the president has a perfectly good complaint for not keeping him informed. But he constantly goes on to the way Jimmy appeased the Russians. I just don't find that in the record. I don't see that at all. I don't know if I can spell it out, but anyone who looks at what was done can't find much appeasing the Russians in it. Control arrangements were set up in Tokyo and the Far East—

Q: Nothing was done about the presence of Russian troops in Iran, and Byrnes agreed to their presence in the Balkans. Those are the two points the president specifically turns on which show we [gave] in to them and got nothing in return of any significance at all . . .

Acheson: The latter one is not clear in my mind, but so far as Iran is concerned I should think the record is clear he did not give in to them. I don't think he could have settled it then. What we always did before a conference was to have a complete agenda—what our positions were. We would send it to the president for his approval. If he didn't, we would change it. But he knew what we set out to do, and when you reported back, you reported on items he knew about. Byrnes went off to the conference of foreign ministers in Moscow without telling the president what he was going to do. I think this is fairly important to what I say about this Byrnes period.

Q: Was he miscast?

Acheson: I think he was.

Q: And so was Marshall?

Acheson: No, I don't think Marshall was. I think Marshall made a great contribution. I have somewhat the same feeling towards Marshall that the president has. But Jimmy — didn't we talk about how I became under-secretary of state? When I came back and started in on this thing, I think I told you that there was no organization in the department so that, al-though I was second in command, things didn't flow through me. When he went off, I had to find out what was happening, pick it up, and run it. When he came back, the iron curtain went back down — until I started the 9:30 meeting. In April 1946 he was starting off on a meeting in Paris. I had a strong feeling that this long absence was going to produce a worse state of affairs than his absence in Moscow had. The central point was that there should be no Dean Acheson between the president and Byrnes when the grindstone was grinding. So, I wrote a letter dated, I think, the thirteenth of April 1946, tendering my resignation to take effect the first of July 1946 when Mr. Byrnes returned, or, if it was later than that, I would stay through his absence. I gave this to Mr. Byrnes and told him frankly why I did this. I said I thought I would not survive the row between the president and him which I thought was coming. When I left, I wanted to leave on a resignation which was put in before the trip started, not one that's exacted from you on the ground that your grandmother is about to expire.

Jimmy read this letter, and he said, "Dean, you are smarter than I thought you were."

I said, "Thanks, but I'm smart enough to get out of the way of a loco-motive."

The next day, or two days later, he said, "Look at this," and he showed me his own letter of resignation to take effect when he got through with these meetings. He said, "You didn't copyright this idea. I am going to take it over and leave it with the president. At Bethesda they found a mur-mur in my heart. It's not too serious, but they said, 'You can't keep up the pace you are going at.'"

"That's your business, Mr. Secretary," I said, "but don't forget to give him my letter." Well, he saw the president and came back. I asked, "What happened?"

He said, "I left my letter with the president. I think he understands my situation."

"What happened to my letter?"

And he said, "I thought it was unnecessary to complicate the matter," and off he went.

You know the story of General Eisenhower going out and talking to General Marshall. I didn't know anything about it until quite a good deal later. I suppose that happened in the summer of '46, but I don't know . . . no, it had to be before that. It had to start in May, or June, very close to this letter dated the fourteenth or fifteenth of April. I didn't know about it until autumn when General Marshall started out on his mission. At the last meeting held at the White House, Mr. Byrnes, General Marshall, and myself had a talk with the president. His instructions were clear. General Marshall said he wanted a rear echelon, someone in Washington fairly highly placed who would be responsible for his communications. He didn't want these things to disappear in the great maw of the Pentagon or the State Department where they would never come up again. The president said, "Who do you want?"

The general pointed to me and said, "I want Acheson."

Mr. Byrnes asked if that was satisfactory. It was. It was agreed on by everyone. I hired a colonel in the army, Jim Davis, who is now a member of a law firm in Cleveland. He was a lawyer from Iowa who went into the army during the war. A bright fellow. And he was assigned over to this. There's an amusing story about that — remind me later. Colonel Jim Davis was succeeded by Colonel Marshall Carter. They had access to the military communications system. We didn't use ours because we didn't have any in the Far East; it was under military control. He [Davis or Carter] got these things and took them away. No soldiers fooled around with them at all. He was to come to me at any hour of the day or night. It was my business to see that General Marshall's cables were answered. These cables had to be answered some way or another within twenty-four hours, but you had to say you had it and were working on it and would get an answer off in a couple of days. He couldn't sit in China not knowing if anything was happening. Many were addressed to me and many to the president, but they all came to me. I took them to the president. Along in the autumn there were some odd things in the messages which were not clear to me. I mentioned this to Mr. Truman, and I said, "I suppose you know what this is all about; is it anything I have to do?"

"Oh no, but you may as well know that Marshall is going to be secretary of state. I am accepting Byrnes's resignation."

I said, "Does Mr. Byrnes know this?"

He said no. Well, that was fine. It really put me in a very good position — here was I knowing more than my boss did about what was going to happen to my boss. The president told me to keep my mouth shut, and I did. By the end of 1946 there were more and more rumors that Mr. Byrnes was going to resign and that his resignation had been accepted. Mr. Byrnes asked me and I said, "I don't know anything about it." But there were no rumors about a successor. Byrnes used to talk to me about it. Could it be that the president was going to accept his resignation without any idea who was going to be in there? I said it seemed impossible that he would. That meant I would go on as acting secretary until he picked someone else.

Well, it got hotter and hotter. On the night of January 7 there was a diplomatic reception. We sat around with Mr. Byrnes in his office — Ben Cohen, maybe Doc Matthews, Don Russell probably — and Mr. Byrnes, before he went home, brought out a bottle of bourbon, and we speculated about it until it was time to go home and get dressed for the diplomatic reception. Mr. and Mrs. Byrnes, my wife, and I came to the east door of the White House and were walking up the stairs together when word came bouncing down that the White House had just announced that General Marshall was going to be secretary of state. It hit Mr. Byrnes on the stairs. I suppose he went on up to the president. And that night he acted very well; you would have supposed he'd known about this for months. He was talking to everyone, saying how happy he was to be relieved of all this and that General Marshall was a fine man. He was around just a very few days, and then off he went. I have just told you I think this should not be in the book.

When Marshall became secretary, everything changed. He was sworn in on January 20, or along in there. We went over to the White House, and I saw that he was left with the president. I came back to my office in the State Department Building. Ten minutes later General Marshall walked in. He sat down and said, "There's to be no nonsense about anything. I want you to stay."

I said, "Yes sir, of course I will, if you want me to. But I don't want to stay too long. I came here in February 1941 to stay for a year or two, and I've spent six years. I'm a lawyer. I have a practice, and I had better go back and get in. I will have no means of a livelihood if I don't do that. How long do you want me to stay?"

"Would six months be unfair?"

"Just so long as it's definite." So, we made it July 1947. I said, "What do you expect of me? What do I do?"

He said, "You run the place."

I said, "If that is what you want to happen, it will, if you make it clear."

He asked me about the State Department. Well, that shocked him. He said, "You're the chief of staff. Everything I say to the department will be said through you."

I said, "You can't run the State Department that way, but we will start out that way; it's a good starter." I said, "My relations to you, General, what should they be?"

He said, "I want the most complete and blunt truths from you, particularly about myself."

"Do you really, General?"

He said, "I have no feelings except a few which I reserve for Mrs. Marshall."

I said, "All right, sir. We will operate on that basis."

He said, "Is there anything you want me to do now?"

I said, "I want to get rid of someone. Will you accept his resignation?"

"Has he given his resignation?"

"No, but I'll have it. It's Joe Panuch, Don Russell's assistant."

I said he was completely unreliable, and he said, "All right."

And I said, "I want to get Jack Peurifoy to take that position."

He said, "I am not prepared to do that, but you put it in there as active, and after a while, I will see."

The general got up and left. There was no more need to talk. From then on our relations were just the way he described them. They couldn't have been a bit better. I continually used to press on him the fact that this type of organization was all right for his sketch of the line of command but that he must depart from it in one respect. In the stages of development of a problem, he must [include] the officers working on the problem with me. It is important that they should get an idea of what he and the president are thinking about. He never liked that very much. Conferences seemed to him to be too much talk. But within the department those people whose interests are continuously in one line will have different views in another line — that always happened in Middle East and African and European problems. The people dealing with former colonials wanted us always to take an attitude of friendship at the expense of losing our allies. Well, you have to do both. So, General Marshall would sit there with these debates going back and forth until he couldn't stand it anymore. He would say, "Gentlemen, don't fight the problem; decide it."

He was magnificent when the great turning point of American foreign policy came in the spring of '47. That is when the policy was made which went all through the second administration when the president developed all these things in Europe. It is still what the Eisenhower administration is doing, as I said at the press conference, with less power, less skill. He was magnificent on the Greek-Turkish thing, on the Marshall Plan.

I'll tell you a story about him. You may know it — on the Greek-Turkish business. It came up while he was there, but he was about to leave. He asked me to take charge of the thing in the department. Our conference began on the tenth of March. The president made his speech on the twelfth of March. He probably left on the sixth of March, so he kept in touch with the thing as long as he was there. He told me, "You have to carry the thing through. Therefore, you are the commanding general, and I will be your helper and adviser — but you are the commander." Actually the president took command, but I was his army commander. The general started off; and after he had gone, the final decisions were made to go ahead with this business. I took it up with the president. Here was General Marshall going to Moscow to talk to the Russians. We were going to do something that would be painful to the Russians in Greece and Turkey. It was only fair to tell him that it has been decided and ask him whether this was all right with him; he is going to be in Moscow when the bomb goes off. We sent him a telegram at Paris, and he sent this very abrupt message back. He said to proceed without any thought of him, that we had our job to do. Marshall would have given his eyeteeth to have been our commander in Europe. But he stayed in Washington and ran this thing which he hated — dealing with Congress, the draft case, and so on. All the things that were going on over there — that is what he had been trained for since he was a second lieutenant. But you never heard a squeak out of him. This was his job now, and he did it. On the Marshall Plan arrangement — he did that with great help from the department. The Marshall Plan is a whole lot of things which happened to come together at the same time —

Q: Your speech in Mississippi must have been the beginning of the Marshall Plan —

Acheson: There were a lot of streams which — where were we? The Greek-Turkish thing I guess you have pretty well. When the Greek-Turkish matter came along at the end of February — the twenty-first of February, I think — when we first heard about it, we worked on it in March. The president made his speech on the twelfth of March. It was very fast, coordinated work — the government was working the way a government ought to work. The army, navy, air force, and the State Department within a matter of days were pulled together — everyone got to work on a common memorandum. People were working like the dickens getting up the most complicated data for operation in a surrounded or occupied area. Who do you deal with? What agreements with whom? How to run the supplies; who gets them? What kind of money to use? A coordinating committee was set up to take care of all this. It was a good working instrument to pull out from the three departments what was necessary. We had a lot of work to do in our own department. Both War and Navy had to work. Here was an instrument for getting it done.

Q: What were the circumstances leading to the Greek-Turkish thing that necessitated this?

Acheson: The British had something like one division in Salonika. They had carried the financial and political burden of taking care of Greek-Turkish needs. They were the great influence in the eastern end of the Mediterranean. We had taken over before V-E Day a supply obligation as to Greece through the army, but it wasn't enough to keep the people from starving. Our dealings were with the British. On Friday afternoon the British ambassador called and said he wanted to see General Marshall. It was about four in the afternoon when he called. General Marshall had gone to Southern Pines where Mrs. Marshall had to live all winter on account of her sinus — she got shingles of the eyes later. Being a five-star general, he had a plane waiting at all times, and he would pop into it and spend the weekend with Mrs. Marshall. I asked him if he [the ambassador] would leave it with me. He said no, that it was too big. He had to see the secretary. I said that he had better give me a copy then so we could get to work on it. I couldn't recall General Marshall — he was in the air. We would work on it over the weekend. We did. It was a note saying that no later than the first of April they would have to pull out of Greece and Turkey. Their financial situation was so bad that they couldn't handle it anymore.

I put everyone at work right away. I alerted the War and Navy Departments and the coordinating committee. We started at five Friday afternoon and worked right straight through until nine Monday morning. What was the situation? What would happen if we did nothing? What were the policy considerations? By the time General Marshall got back, we had a memorandum which outlined what the situation was — we had a copy of the note attached to it — and made recommendations as to what ought to be done. This was all done over the weekend; we had started within an hour of getting the note. On Monday the British ambassador came down and gave Marshall the blue-ribbon copy of this thing we had and asked for an appointment with the president. Marshall took him to luncheon with the president. Forrestal was there. When they got through talking about this, they looked at our memo. The president said, "This is the right line." Forrestal agreed, and the president said, "Keep on working this way and give me a further report on Wednesday." We went on with that. Then he had a meeting the next day or so with the leaders on the Hill and outlined the thing to them. They said, generally speaking, that this suggestion was the right thing to do but they didn't have the details. How many dollars would be needed? The president said we would have a second meeting on the tenth of March at which time the whole business would have been worked out, showing everything, exactly what was needed. They met with him and they approved . . . .

At the first meeting General Marshall made a rather crisp statement on this thing and then stopped. The president had asked him to take over. It seemed to me that these people were bewildered about it. Greece and Turkey were a long way off. It was rather cold. I asked the president if I could explain what the general had said. I made a longer speech and pointed out the strategic aspects of this matter. The situation in Greece and Turkey was that if either one crumbled, the other would, too. They were facing one another. Everything to the east would be lost — Iran certainly would be. And this would also have a bad effect on Italy, which was not very far away — and Yugoslavia, as well as Italy, right up to Austria. This is the kind of a thing where, if you let them start, you will have a terrible time. Well, that got through.

[Senator Arthur] Vandenberg said, "I think I am sold on it provided you put this up to the American people in that way so they will know what it is about."

Then we developed the thing. That talk was really the beginning of the Truman Doctrine. We didn't do quite what Van suggested we do. We put it up in almost military terms. What became known as the Truman Doctrine — they panned that as being too military. Then they began to like the Marshall Plan because Mr. Truman had reformed under the influence of the old soldier. That is the way that thing started. The president was given what was necessary for him to have, in a form he could consider and make up his mind on. It was worked out in stages so he could say, "Not so fast, boys, not in that direction." It was an ideal example of the way to do something.

The Cleveland, Mississippi, speech came about in this way. The president was scheduled to go stay with Mr. and Mrs. William Wynne in Cleveland, Mississippi. They are very charming people. And he was to make a speech to the Delta Council — a very important meeting in the South, from Memphis to New Orleans, where the most progressive farmers in the South were turning from cotton to cattle and grass cultures. Anyway, it was a great powwow, and it would be made if the president came there. But the man Bilbo was on his last legs. . . . The president didn't want to get into the state, because he wouldn't escape with his life without being trapped into a political fight. So, he told them he would be unable to come. He told me — whether it was by way of flattery to encourage me, I don't know — that they would forgive him in part if I would come down and make an important speech on foreign policy. I said, "Of course, if you tell me to go, but it's a hell of a comedown from the president to the undersecretary."

We then talked about what I should say. I said that in one way I was glad to have the chance because we had been doing a good deal of work in the department, so, with a catastrophe of major proportions coming along . . . I thought we had underestimated the disintegration of Europe. We thought of it as physical destruction — this was the least of the problems. There were economic, political, and social disintegrations throughout Europe. Hitler did what Napoleon was unable to do. He took an area which had to import from the rest of the world — he took that and made it self-supporting. That disrupted every kind of business connection in Europe. Factories didn't make the same things. Politically, most of the governments were discredited; their countries were occupied. They had their tails between their legs. There was a deep division between the workers and the owning classes who had either collaborated or left — escaped the country. We had underestimated all this. We thought UNRRA [United Nations Relief and Rehabilitation Agency] would do it, but it didn't. The dreadful part of the situation was that almost all of our funds were going to come to an end in July. We were coming to July '47 with no plan. This was April. What I would like to do is merely state the problem. There's no answer at all. Just look at the situation in Europe. You see that it is running on a deficit of six billion a year — which we are making up. If that stops, then what happens to Europe? I said you ought to think this over carefully. This is like kicking a ball. The ball's going to come down. It won't say up forever, and someone had better catch it. The president said he approved, and I worked out that speech and made it.

It had some attention immediately in this country, not a great deal. It was a good story for the fourth or fifth page. There was quite a lot in that part of the South. Its real impact was in Europe. It was printed in full in London, Paris — the impact on the United States came from foreign newspapers reaching here and then the columnists saying, "This is more important than we thought." It was built up and up. Everybody began to consider the problem. I imagine the president, knowing more about politics than I ever dreamed about, had hoped that this thing would happen — pressures from the public to do what he knew he would have to do. It's better than whipping the public into doing it. Ben Cohen made a speech a little afterwards in San Francisco in which he went over the same thing. They had begun to pick up this figure of five or six or seven billion a year. Then Alben Barkley made a speech. Alben was not to be outdone, and he said it was eight billion dollars. This same group of State, War, and Navy — the coordinating committee now came up with the question of whether to ask for money for any other countries than Greece and Turkey. The talk in the message which was being drafted was general although it was directed to Greece and Turkey — you always broaden what you do, to take in a broad perspective. I just made this decision myself to keep the talk general — no money for any other place because we were not going to get into a position of being asked, "What place do you have in mind?" Either you don't know, in which case you make a fool of yourself, or if you begin mentioning places, they are going to be on your doorstep: "Thank you very much. I'll take it in twenties." No country was mentioned. The thing went up that way. This committee went on studying what countries were likely to be needing money. Everybody was in need of it. Without anyone telling them to do this, they did it, because it was sensible and proper to do in such a program.

Will Clayton had gone off to a meeting of the Economic Committee for Europe, and he was scared out of his boots. He was reporting to all of us, and we took him in to General Marshall. He said this is galloping consumption in Europe. There is now a town-country split. The farmers are not producing any more than they need for themselves. The money they might get is not worth anything. So, they plant less — the same with chickens, hogs, cattle. Prices are going up. There's less and less food. This will be a terrible social split.

You will see that kind of thing reflected in General Marshall's Harvard speech. General Marshall was convinced that there was no use fooling around with the Russians, getting agreements, because they were counting on the collapse of Europe. Once it had collapsed, they would not have to have agreements. He was convinced, apart from anything else, that this had to be done. We talked about it a great deal. What he and the president said, I don't know. He was the closest-mouthed person in the world. After a while he told Chip Bohlen to prepare a speech for him. The question was where he was going to make this speech. It was quite clear he could get any floor he wanted. He finally decided on this commencement business at Harvard. I opposed that, but he had made up his mind. Other people said it was a good idea. I don't know quite why he decided on that. No one pays any attention to commencement addresses, you know — "there's no end; this is the beginning," the kind of stuff you say. It is reported by a fellow from the college paper who gets it all mixed up. To me this was really not the thing to do. But maybe Marshall was smarter than I was; let this come out gradually and take hold rather than have a big buildup. One of the things he talked about was that this must be a European plan, not an American plan imposed on them. If all you people can get together and produce something to restore yourselves, we will be willing to hear the matter of financing it, but you have to do it. That was very bright. That was the right idea. In this group there was talk about whether this thing should be limited to Western Europe. There I think General Marshall made absolutely the right decision. We were not to be the people who divided Europe. But against that, if the Russians were smart and came into it, they might be able to frustrate it. But he said, "Play it square. Offer it to everyone."

A couple of days before he spoke, I got three of my good friends together from the English press — Leonard Miall of the BBC, Rene MacColl of the *Express*, and [Malcolm] Muggeridge, who was then on the *Express*, now editor of *Punch*. I used to meet with these fellows and talk to them frankly and with the greatest possible success. They are not interested in the competition you run into when you talk to our people. They weren't writing that kind of stuff. I told them that General Marshall was going to make a speech of the greatest importance and that I hoped they would not fool around with telegraphing the thing. Get London on the telephone and read it — get it over at once. And one other thing, "One of you have your editor send this to Ernie Bevin and say Dean Acheson wanted him to look at it." And that is what happened. An amusing thing was that the ambassador was away; he's a very good friend of mine, still in the foreign service of Great Britain; he had been given hell about telegraph bills. Someone said, "Marshall made a speech." And he said, "Put it in the pouch." He said then that he began to get bombarded from London about this speech. He had never even read it. Well, I was afraid something like that would happen, and I wanted Ernie to get it. Well, he practically jumped out of his chair, called in people in the foreign office. Everybody's excited. Someone says, "Don't you think you ought to telegraph and find out more about this?" and Bevin says, "For God's sake, don't ask him anything. I want to believe him on this basis." So, the thing got off the ground. The only other thing we —

Q: Didn't Bevin telephone to Marshall?

Acheson: No, I think there's no truth in that. I think he got right in tough with Israel, and they began working out this meeting. Mr. Bevin and the general — two men whom I love — just don't like one another. The general thought Ernie had run out on him. I thought he was raising his standard a little too high. Ernie was supposed to do something at a certain time, and he didn't do it at that time. Ernie was always baffled by the general; he felt he couldn't get through this formidable exterior, which isn't formidable at all. He's the most delightful companion in the world. But if you are dealing with him officially, I wouldn't fool with him.

With my speech, other speeches, the general's speech, everybody got quite excited. Van called Secretary Marshall and asked was he going to be confronted with a vast bill on the last days of the Congress? Well, we had a meeting at Blair House. There was a lot of talk about the whole thing. Early in the game the general said we were not going up with any vast bill in the last month of the Congress — perhaps for money to take us over the summer, but not much. The Europeans have to work out their own plans. And there are groups in this country working on it. We won't do anything big until Congress comes back next year. Well, that relieved Van. Van always started out completely negative; he had no creative qualities, but he was one of the greatest advocates alive. He was blessed by being in that "do-nothing" Eightieth Congress, and the administration was throwing out ideas like — it was our creative period, suggestions and proposals were shooting out everywhere, not only in foreign affairs but others. Here was Van in an ideal position in which he could knock down the birds that were not any good. He potted those off and got the credit for it. He always opposed everything. He was against it. But if you worked with him, then he liked it; then he liked it a great deal. He put the Van brand on it, and then off he was like a jet-propelled plane. Once you got him going, you didn't have to worry about it. On this thing he picked up this idea of the secretary's to have groups in this country look into it. He thought we better have something special; we would have to pick some vice president, some president or chairman — a sort of Hoover Commission. Well, that about wraps up the Marshall thing.

One other thing. His [the president's] attempt to make me head of the ECA [Economic Cooperation Administration] — that was in '48, just after the bill had been passed. I suppose it was May or June — the ECA bill. And the president asked me to come over to see him. At that meeting he said he wanted to nominate me to the position Paul Hoffman had. I said, "Do anything you want, but I think it would be a great mistake." Van set great store by this ECA. One reason was there was going to be an election in '48, and Van didn't want this thing he was supporting to turn out in any way to be a feather in the Democrat cap. He wanted credit for it, the same as Mr. Truman. The idea had also gone forward that this money could be used some way to affect the election. I don't see how it could, but it was possible that this could have been pictured as a Democratic thing. I said, "So far we haven't got all the money. We have to go back and gets lots of money from these people. If you put me in, you will be charged with double-crossing them. They have been trying to separate this from the State Department, and you will be putting it right in by making me head of it. If you nominate anyone without talking to Van, you will make an enemy of the best friend you have in this.

The president said, "What do you think Van wants?"

"No doubt he wants Paul Hoffman." I said. "That's all right. If I were you, I would consult with him and tell him what you want to do. He will oppose it and tell you what he wants to do. I would do that. If he says Acheson, you will take it, and I will do it."

Well, their conversation went exactly as I told him it would go. The president was mad as can be and said it was my fault: "Damn you, I think I'll send your nomination up anyway."

Washington, D.C.   June 30, 1971

Interviewed by Theodore A. Wilson and Richard D. McKinzie

Wilson: At the end of the war and the first year thereafter, was the role that the State Department, perhaps, saw itself as playing, one not just in planning but in the administration of programs? There is some suggestion that some people within the department thought that State would take an active role and that others were horrified by this. I wonder if you would have any comments on that question.

Acheson: I think that you have just about said it. I would think that — as I recall the thing, which is only vaguely — there were many people, including the older members of the State Department, who believed that it was not our role to undertake eradication of "hoof and mouth disease" and a few various other things around the world, feeding people, or building factories, or that sort of thing. There was a view which is pretty sound, I think, that this really had to be done by more technically qualified people; and if you got all those damn people at the State Department overcrowding us with a lot of administrative tasks which are alien to what we were trying to do, with this view, why, I had sympathy. The question was in getting things done in a quick way. A whole lot of things are mixed up in foreign aid — a few being Point Four — the Greek-Turkish program, of course, was a crash course, and that had to be treated differently. There we did administer, and we did everything we had to do, which was *not* to be a permanent part of the effort of the department.

I wasn't a fusser about *who* really should do things, but there wasn't anybody who was equipped or able to do this sort of thing; therefore, if we could do it for the time being, we picked up somebody who knew about it and got him over in Greece or Turkey or wherever the hell we had to send somebody.

Wilson: When the big program came, the very large program, the Marshall Plan, and then followed MSA [Mutual Security Agency], the documentation we've seen suggests that because the State Department was not the administering agency for all this aid, it was placed — or at least the tone of relationship between the State Department and ECA, then MSA — the documentation suggests it was a negative one and that State was acting as a brake.

Acheson: I don't really know whether it was acting as a brake or not, but I should think you are right. We were probably saying, "Take it easy; do what you are supposed to do."

McKinzie: These things are all so innovative that came out of these years, the whole idea of massive injections of developmental capital and particularly the business of extending technological assistance. Did it not strain a little bit the traditional idea of what a diplomat was supposed to do? We've been concerned about rigidity versus flexibility in departments, and I gather that it took some little stretching of things to get the idea of technical assistance incorporated.

Acheson: Yes, I think this is true, and, of course, then people didn't realize as clearly as they realize now that we were dealing with something as fundamental as we were. It didn't really strike home to us that the British Empire was gone, the great power of France was gone, that Europe was made out of four or five countries of 50 million people. I still looked at the map and saw that red on the thing, and, by God, that was the British Empire, the French Senegalese troops in East Asia and in Germany — all of this was gone to hell. These were countries hardly much more important than Brazil in the world. If we had known all of that and seen what we were really trying to do — to use this instrument of foreign aid to bring about an integrated Europe — we would have just said, "Sure, this is the very essence of diplomacy"; but I don't think that any of us really saw it that way. Therefore, I think our judgment was colored by a lack of comprehension of the reality. And although you could put it in any kind of way, these were stuffy old diplomats who never wanted to get out of the tea party and pick up the slide rule. We didn't see that this was that important. This was an outgrowth of UNRRA. This was relief work, like taking care of the present Pakistan refugees. They all were together, too. They kind of grouped together under the Red Cross. That was more the attitude of it.

Wilson: In a sense, then, President Truman's inaugural address of 1949 can be thought of as breaking away from the wartime patterns and immediate postwar patterns of thought, as well as going forward in something new (in a number of directions in our mind) — and I think your book has suggested this — and it announced that the United States was going to take a very strong and new, in some ways, position — if necessary, acting alone.

Acheson: Yes, I think probably the most imaginative view of it was my press conference where the Point Four Program was announced, when I talked about using "material means for immaterial purposes." That's reproduced in *Present at the Creation*. I think this was way ahead of the president himself. I don't think he had thought this thing out at all. This was really Clark Clifford's contribution, and it was written out. The State Department didn't think a hell of a lot of it, and the president overruled the State Department and put it in. I don't think General Marshall ever put his mind on it at all; he was sick. We were really making a lot out of nothing, and I tried to blow it up so it had more intellectual content than even I thought it really had.

McKinzie: Now, this may be an unfair question, but do you think that after it *was* created and in operation, that it did what you anticipated it might be able to do?

Acheson: To some extent, yes. It was really not until the Schuman Plan came along that the possibilities of this sort of thing began to be seen. I don't think I really saw it until Jean Monnet talked with me about the Schuman Plan.

Wilson: Another basic problem we have to face in our work is the negative contribution of the United States Congress with regard to foreign aid. It comes up again and again that Senator Kem or the Wherry amendment, etc., etc. If there had been no such institution, how much difference would it have made for the programs that were carried forward? Would the administration have been much more bold than happened on occasion, if it didn't have that check?

Acheson: I think probably so, but this is sort of an unreal question —

Wilson: Yes it is.

Acheson: — because in order to get the money you have to go to a nonexecutive branch.

Wilson: Perhaps putting a real question — it is our impression that so many of the representatives and senators with whom you had to deal were amazingly uneducated about the problem.

Acheson: You see, you all start with the premise that democracy is some good. I don't think it's worth a damn. I think Churchill is right; the only thing to be said for democracy is that there is nothing else that's any better, and therefore he used to say, "Tyranny tempered by assassination, but lots of assassination." People say, "If the Congress were more representative of the people, it would be better." I say the Congress is too damn representative. It's just as stupid as the people are; just as uneducated, just as dumb, just as selfish. You know the Congress is a perfect example, and created to be a perfect example. We are sure to get Rooney out of Brooklyn. He is absolutely perfect. He couldn't represent anything better than he does Brooklyn. He's the perfect type.

Wilson: There have been a few.

Acheson: A damn few.

Wilson: By accident . . .

Acheson: In the old days when liberalism didn't persist and senators were elected by the legislatures, you got some pretty good senators, because they were *not* representative.

Wilson: These people in Congress practiced the representative principle in their view — that is, they did vote, on the basis of what they thought were the prejudices or views of their constituencies, or did they? In that sense, there was very little in the way you could do to educate them.

Acheson: There wasn't very much; you did some. Vandenberg is a typical example of somebody who got educated, and I think, very largely, Cordell Hull did this. He took a fellow from Grand Rapids, who was a perfect editor of the Grand Rapids newspaper. He didn't look any further than furniture, not a bit. And Hull began to tell him about the world. What you had to do to get certain results. And Van was sort of like having Marco Polo come home and talk with you. "I'll be damned; you really mean it's like that?"

"Yes, it really is."

And he said, "Well, God, then we're going to do something about it." Then he became a fellow who had ideas but never strolled far off first base.

McKinzie: Bob Taft, I take it, was uneducable in these matters?

Acheson: Well, Bob was very educated on certain things. Public housing he knew a lot about and was for, and was radical as hell on that; but so far as them foreigners out there are concerned, to hell with them; they didn't vote in Ohio, and they were not good, and shiftless. Get a good army, navy, and air force, and to hell with it.

Wilson: How deep did bipartisanship go? That is something that we have been wrestling with.

Acheson: Well, don't let it bother you too much. Bipartisanship was a magnificent fraud. I had a group of Williams students in here today, and they said that James MacGregor Burns, who teaches there, had come up with the idea that bipartisanship in foreign policy was a grand thing. And I said, "Well, don't take him very seriously either." The question "Who is it bad for, and who is it good for?" is what you ought to put your mind on. If it is only good for the Senate of the United States, this doesn't get you anywhere. Bipartisan foreign policy is *ideal* for the executive because you cannot run this damn country under the Constitution any other way.

Now, the way to do that is to say politics stops at the seaboard, and anybody who denies that postulate is "a son of a bitch and a crook and not a true patriot." Now, if people will swallow that, then you're off to the races. I said Van swallowed it, but every once in a while he *knew* it was a fake. And he would say to me, "What the hell happens on election? Do you go around my state of Michigan and say what a grand man Senator Vandenberg is because he voted for this, that, and the other, and you ought to reelect him?" He said, "Not at all. Say some labor leader runs against me and is an isolationist that isn't worth a damn; he's a fine Democrat and the president gets photographed with his arm around him shaking his hand. Now," he said, "this is fraud."

I said, "Sure it's a fraud, but it's a necessary fraud. You won't get much mileage out of opposing the administration; you get a little going along, perhaps break even, 50–50." I said, "Of course, the biggest fraud of all was President Truman when he said the Eightieth Congress is the do-nothing Congress." I said to President Truman, "You ought to be ashamed of yourself; that is the biggest fraud ever perpetrated on the American people. The Eightieth Congress was the best Congress in foreign policy we ever had. We were damn lucky to have it. And you've come up with this idea and got elected, and I'm glad you did; I think it's fine; that's all right; but it is ridiculous and is not at all true."

He said, "Well, it worked."

No, I wouldn't be too serious about bipartisanship. It's a great myth that ought to be fostered. And don't bring too damn much scholarship to bear on it. You'll prove it out of existence if you're not careful.

McKinzie: This is one thing that we've been most struck by in the work we've done, is that you can raise this stuff to the level where human beings and human emotions are completely absent from it. Particularly in this trip to Washington, as we've talked to people, most people end up telling us: "You know, after all, government is a matter of people and that personal relationships end up being as important as the process and the rest of it."

Acheson: That is right. It isn't the fact that policy is nonpartisan that's important; it's the fact that it's good. Now, the Korean War was perfectly nonpartisan, and it stank just as much when it was nonpartisan as it would if it was partisan. The nonpartisan aspect of it doesn't make it good or bad. It's merely an instrument in making it possible. If you use that to make possible good things, then it's a hell of a good instrument. Take Bob Taft's view that the opposition is supposed to oppose; that we will run on the adversary principle. We have two great parties, and the one out of office ought to be criticizing the hell out of the one in office; and we have a Constitution which makes treaties necessary to have two-thirds of the Senate. We have to have all these legislative impediments. Read my little book which has now been republished, *A Citizen Looks at Congress.* It's a hell of a good book and is now reprinted. You can get it quite easily. You see, the Congress is not two great parties. The Congress is the committees of Congress. That's what really makes the Congress work, and the committees are damn near evenly balanced whatever the election shows. You may have two more majority members than minority members if the election is a landslide; otherwise, you might have one more.

Now, these people live and work together, and you don't have Republicans and Democrats; you have votes all split up; and if you have any important minority on the committee, the damn thing won't work, because when it gets into the Congress, they will not follow the committee report. The Foreign Affairs Committee of the House never amounted to a damn, and doesn't today. Nobody wants to be on that Foreign Affairs Committee. It's a bore; it's a nuisance. It doesn't carry any weight. The great committees are the Ways and Means, and Appropriations, and Armed Services. The Senate Foreign Relations Committee was very important for a long time, and a lot of chairmen of other committees were on it. The real leadership of the Senate was on this committee. I used to go up to the Hill, have lunch in Les Biffle's office with fifteen senators, most of whom would be on this committee, and others. The real leadership of the Senate used to be an extraordinary group, and most of them were on Foreign Affairs. Now they're not; now it's a maverick group. Lyndon Johnson ruined the damn committee by putting people on as a reward for certain votes.

Jim Webb and I went over to see President Truman, who was mad as hell at our friend from Arkansas.

Wilson: [J. William] Fulbright?

Acheson: Mr. Fulbright said that, under the British system, the election of '46 having been lost, President Truman would have resigned and considered him [Fulbright] as president. He said, "This damn Rhodes scholar is educated above his intelligence," which was true; he is and was. So, he was mad as hell.

So, Jim and I said, "Well, now, when these elder statesmen are through, the only young man in there that has got any brains is Fulbright. Now, let's butter him up, take him into camp, and get him on our side."

The president said, "All right, bring him in. But," he said, "it won't work. I'll tell you it won't work; but anyway you are young and hopeful; bring him in here." So, we brought him in. He went back on the Hill and immediately attacked the RFC — the administration was corrupt. Truman was quite right.

But as I say, the committees almost always operate as a unit. They have the same style, the series of them; there is very little minority organization on the committee. Therefore, you stick close to the majority leadership. You've got to.

I used to have a terrible time between Tom Connally and Vandenberg, just like two prima donnas. If the producer would take one out to lunch and not the other one, why, he got in a hell of a row. And if you had conferences, you had to have them both in, and if you didn't have them both in together, they thought you were doing some trickery because you had them separately. It was a hell of a job. This was really like producing an opera, to get this committee to work together.

I sent a telegram to a meeting with the Russians in '49, to the chairman of the committee; and he had the clerk of the committee read it to the committee at an executive meeting. He started to read the telegram, and Tom said, "No, no, no, begin at the beginning."

"I am beginning at the beginning."

He said, "No, you're not; give me the telegram."

So, he gave him the telegram, and he began, "Dear Tom" — he didn't want the "Dear Tom" left out. This was the most important part of the telegram to Tom, but it wasn't the most important part of it to Vandenberg.

I think it's very important in thinking about these things to think about the organization of the body that you're trying to make nonpartisan. And if in fact it really is that, particularly if it's against you, you can get the committee 100 percent against you without any trouble at all. That's the easiest thing in the world to do. If you want them 100 percent for you, you've got to get some kind of a formula. You don't need any formula if they're 100 percent against the president. This is the separation of power; it's what we're here for. Those guys will sell their country down the road; watch them; look out. Skepticism, cynicism, don't believe all you hear, is terribly important to them.

Wilson: And I wonder how much again the contrast between the previous man's administrative efforts had to do with your obvious admiration and ability to work with Truman?

Acheson: You mean FDR?

Wilson: Yes. It was so much better.

Acheson: Truman was straight, aboveboard, straight in line.

Two days ago, Monday, former president Sachar of Brandeis University was here and talked about President Truman. He started off by saying, "Let me read you two or three paragraphs here about Mr. Truman; criticize that."

And I said, "All right."

And he began about how with totally inadequate preparation, education, and everything else, Mr. Truman was turning out to be one of the best presidents, and went on and said, "What do you think of this?"

I said, "I think it's the goddamnedest collection of clichés I ever heard in my life, and none of it is true."

Well, he said, "You agree that he didn't have any education."

I said, "I don't agree to that at all; he had a remarkable education." My younger daughter had TB at nineteen, after she had been in college one month, and just been married and her husband went off to the war, and she spent five years in Saranac and lost her lung; and in the course of that time she spent in bed, she read and read and read and talked to all kinds of people. And she's far better educated than I am. I went to the best school, the best college, the best law school. That isn't the way you get educated. The point is what enters into your innards.

Suppose somebody sits under John Kenneth Galbraith for three years to get an education — a hell of a waste of time. Mr. Truman read every book in the Independence library, which had about thirty-five hundred to five thousand volumes, including three encyclopedias, and he read them all the way through. He took in a hell of a lot more out of that effort, which he took out of farming when he did it, than he would listening to all of this crap that goes on at Yale and Harvard, and perhaps in other places — Harvard Law School education.

I sit here and talk about his preparation. I would think he did more preparation by being on the county court — or whatever it was called in Jackson County — than he would have being a justice of the Supreme Court, a hell of a lot more. See how people work, how the thing runs, what makes it tick, what are the important things, what are the unimportant things. And it's sort of significant comparing to other presidents. Well, I think I said Washington should have been president. Tom Jefferson I would give a very low rating, too; he was a man of words and was a poor governor, a poor ambassador to France. The only thing as president that he really did that was really worth a damn was the Louisiana Purchase. And that was contrary to everything that he was —

McKinzie: That he believed in, yes.

Acheson: Well, he said, "What do you think about Lincoln?"

I said, "The best thing that can be said about Lincoln are the Trumanesque qualities that he had."

He said, "That's the damnedest thing I ever heard; you usually think it's the other way. The thing that is good about Truman is the Lincolnesque."

I said, "That isn't what he had at all; he didn't have Lincolnesque qualities. Lincoln had Trumanesque qualities. He did things that were contrary to the baloney that he talked; he didn't believe his own book. A house divided against itself doesn't fall if you stand up and fight; the house stands up, and he proved it. All these things — it isn't true that a drop of blood drawn by the lash has got to be paid for by one drawn by the sword, or that the judgments of the Lord are true and righteous — poetic talk; that's fool talk. Dr. Johnson said to Boswell, "You can talk foolishly, but don't think foolishly."

3

Konrad Adenauer

Bonn, Germany June 10, 1964

Interviewed by Philip C. Brooks

Konrad Adenauer (1876–1966), first chancellor of the Federal Republic of Germany, was Truman's staunch ally in the cold war. From 1917 to 1933 he was the lord mayor of Cologne. During the Weimar Republic, he declined the chancellorship of Germany. As a critic of the Nazis, he was removed from office and imprisoned on two occasions — once for his involvement in a plot to kill Hitler. After the collapse of the Third Reich, he founded the Christian Democratic Union and took the lead in rebuilding his nation.

Adenauer: Now, first of all, I must make a few remarks about Mr. Truman. I have been interested for a long time in Mr. Truman's personality. He took over his office as Roosevelt's successor only a few months after Roosevelt had started his new term. Although it was known that Roosevelt was ill, Mr. Truman had no opportunity to prepare himself thoroughly for the very difficult office of president of the United States. He changed drastically American policy as it had been pursued by Roosevelt. This change which he brought about gives as much evidence of political farsightedness as of his kind heart.

I have read his *Memoirs* with the greatest interest. His *Memoirs* are the most striking example of how a splendid political truth can be expressed with simple words and simple sentences. Naturally, two things interested me in particular: (1) the part which he played at the Potsdam Conference, the splendid part which he played there, and (2) the Marshall Plan.

In my opinion — which I have held for a long time — Mr. Truman will be judged in subsequent historiography as one of the great American presidents. He was here in Bonn, and I was very much impressed by his personality as such, by the man as such, and by his simplicity. This is the essence of my thoughts on Mr. Truman. I must reiterate: In my opinion he will go down in history as one of the greatest presidents of the United States. I can't say any more. That is already a great deal.

Brooks: Would you say something about the importance of the Marshall Plan to Germany? Was it really a turning point in the life of Germany and her attitude toward other countries?

Adenauer: The extension of the Marshall Plan to Germany was first of all a deed of extremely great political significance. Thereby, in spite of her past, Germany was placed by the president of the United States, by Harry Truman, on an equal footing with other suffering countries. The extension of the Marshall Plan to Germany achieved a twofold success: First, the Germans were given new hope, and second, they were helped by the provisions of the plan itself.

Brooks: Would you say that the statement of General Marshall in the year 1947 represented the first time that the Germans had confidence that the United States wanted to help them?

Adenauer: Yes. Because you must not forget that at that time there existed strong intentions among the victorious powers simply to efface Germany from history as a great country. That is why President Truman's decision had such an extraordinarily good psychological effect on Germany.

Brooks: Would you say anything about whether you expected the Russians to join in the Marshall Plan, and whether it was a good idea of Mr. [British foreign minister Ernest] Bevin's to invite them?

Adenauer: Neither the one, nor the other.

Brooks: How about the Greek-Turkish aid plan of the American government? Did you feel that this was closely related to the Marshall Plan, or did you look on it as something separate? Was it of concern to the Germans?

Adenauer: Indirectly. Through the extension of the Marshall Plan to Greece and Turkey, these nations were readied for their participation in NATO, and Greece was at that time, exclusive of Germany, the poorest European country. By coincidence I read only today that the Greek economy has become extraordinarily strengthened and improved in the last few years — Turkey not to the same extent.

Brooks: I was in Greece about three weeks ago and noticed it. Did you feel that the German interests were fairly considered at the Paris Conference in 1947 when the plans were being made for the Marshall Plan?

Adenauer: That is a very — but how should this be translated? — you know, a "ticklish question." He who receives the gift regards it differently than the one who gives the gift. He who receives it sees only his own poverty; he who gives it sees also the poverty of others. That is why this is such a difficult question to answer, but I do want to tell you that this Marshall help, the Marshall Plan was for us an extraordinarily great help, psychologically and materially.

Brooks: Did you hope that the Marshall Plan would eventually lead to something like the Common Market, toward an economic union of Europe?

Adenauer: Well, . . . I do not believe that one thought that far ahead at that time. No, I see the significance of the Marshall Plan in the fact that probably for the first time in history a victorious country held out its hand so that the vanquished might rise again.

Brooks: What would you say about the comparative importance — since we are looking at this from the point of view of the history of the Truman administration — what would you say is the comparative importance of the Marshall Plan, and the Berlin airlift, the establishment of NATO, and Korean action?

Adenauer: I believe that without the Marshall Plan this development would not have been possible.

Brooks: Very well, thank you. What about the airlift, or NATO?

Adenauer: Well, I feel that the Berlin airlift was a truly visible sign that America recognized her duty to be the leader of free nations and wanted to fulfill it, and NATO was at that time — the founding of NATO — a great accomplishment, and I only hope that the vigor which was then in NATO will be preserved in NATO.

Brooks: Which of these various developments do you think had the most effect in establishing the reputation of Mr. Truman himself in Germany? Which of these developments were the most important from the point of view of the German people?

Adenauer: You have already mentioned them: the Marshall Plan, the airlift, the establishment of NATO. Well, in all of these one saw the determined will preserve freedom here in the face of the Communist threat.

4

George E. Allen

Washington, D.C.   May 15, 1969

Interviewed by Jerry N. Hess

George E. Allen (1896–1973), who became secretary of the Democratic National Committee in 1943, was among a group of party leaders urging President Roosevelt to replace Vice President Henry A. Wallace on the '44 Democratic ticket. After FDR chose Truman, Allen became their strategist for the fall campaign. When Truman moved up to the presidency, the jovial political operative gained public notice as his confidant. He was referred to by *United States News* as a conservative influence on the new administration. Truman later named him to the Reconstruction Finance Corporation. Allen served as the first chairman of the foundation that raised funds for the construction of the Truman Library.

Hess: Mr. Allen, when did you first meet Mr. Truman?

Allen: I first met Mr. Truman, as I remember, when he first came to the Senate. I think that was in —

Hess: It was '35 when he came to the Senate.

Allen: Yes, when he first came to the Senate. I know very well he was in the Senate when the fight for the Senate leadership was up with [Pat] Harrison and [Alben W.] Barkley, and the senator voted for Harrison, who was a great friend, although he was very close to Barkley, and Barkley afterwards became vice president with him. But he voted because he had promised to vote for Harrison, and he stuck to that promise. That's when I first met Mr. Truman.

Hess: Could you tell me about the events that led up to Mr. Truman's nomination on the Democratic ticket in 1944?

Allen: That I could tell you quite a bit about, because that's quite a story. As you know, Senator Truman didn't want the vice presidency, as far as that was concerned. He was perfectly happy in the Senate, as I remember. Now, at that time, Frank Walker was chairman of the Democratic National Committee, and I was secretary of the Democratic National Committee, and Ed Pauley of California was treasurer. Ed Pauley deserves more credit than anyone else for stopping Wallace. We all felt, really, that possibly Roosevelt wouldn't live, and that the man we were nominating would become president.

Hess: Would he deserve more credit in that than Robert Hannegan?

Allen: Oh, much more. Pauley saw this quicker than anyone else, and Pauley had it in for Wallace more than anyone else — at least he thought Wallace would be a bad influence on the country. So, Pauley worked out a deal with "Pa" [General Edwin M.] Watson, who was then the secretary to Roosevelt, that any Democrats that came into Washington would go in and tell the president that under no circumstances should we have Wallace, that the president should run again, but we shouldn't have Wallace. Now, that was Pauley's idea, and he worked with Watson on this, and Roosevelt realized that the political leadership of the Democratic Party was against Wallace. Labor was for Wallace, of course, and the very left-wing people were for Wallace.

Hess: What do you recall about Mr. Truman's campaign in 1944?

Allen: Well, President Roosevelt and [Harry] Hopkins sent for me one day and they said, "We want you to go with Mr. Truman during the whole campaign for vice president," and I was really the campaign manager for Mr. Truman in '44 [when he was running] for vice president. We started out in Los Angeles, and we worked all over the country and we had some very unusual experiences. He used to speak sometimes to as many as five or six people, sometimes ten or fifteen thousand. And I remember very distinctly he was speaking in some little town out west, and somebody said, "Senator, how old are you?"

And he said, "On my next birthday, I'll be sixty."

So, I remember now how old he was because of that. And we had some great experiences during that campaign. Hugh Fulton was his speechwriter, and Hugh wrote some pretty dull speeches, and Truman did better when he just spoke off-the-cuff. And he made a number of these speeches. I remember we got into New York and we were meeting at Madison Square Garden, and Truman and Wallace were both to speak. Well, the CIO [Congress of Industrial Organizations] wanted to show up Truman and show how strong they were for Wallace. So, we got to the old Madison Square Garden, and Wagner, Bob [Robert] Wagner was up for reelection to the Senate, and I remember Truman and Wagner, we were all sitting there, waiting for Wallace. And their strategy was to have Wallace come in after Truman. Well, our strategy was to have Truman and Wallace walk down at the same time so that any ovation they gave, Truman would get just as much of it as Wallace would.

So, first of all, we were about an hour late. Wallace first lost his glasses and had to go back to the hotel. They used every excuse in the world. But, finally, he did show up, and they walked down together, and that's the way that turned out. But Truman was a great campaigner, and one of the sweetest men that ever lived. There's no doubt about that he was a fine, lovable fellow.

Hess: How was the liaison worked out between the Truman campaign and the Roosevelt campaign? Just how was that handled? Mostly through yourself?

Allen: Yes, I worked with Hannegan, who was running the Roosevelt campaign out of New York, and I would report back to Hannegan from California or from wherever we were. But Truman never worried about the little jealousies in politics. He was really too big for that. We would try to think of all those things, but it didn't bother him at all. If a man wasn't a friend of his, that was that; if he was, that was fine. He was really a great *campaigner.*

I was in Las Vegas when Roosevelt died, and Truman's office phoned me and told me about it, and I came back. Ed Reynolds and I worked on the first three speeches that Truman made as president. We did all three. Well, *that* there's no question about. Matt Connelly said, "We've got to make three speeches. . . ." In fact, we had worked on Truman's speeches as vice president. Now, Hugh Fulton sort of dropped out of the picture after that, because we worked on most of the speeches after [Truman] became vice president, during that time. I remember one or two of the speeches we helped prepare — we got a lot of criticism on them; said we weren't much [in the way] of economists — because we said there was going to be no slump after the war was over, and it turned out that we were right. We got a lot of letters — Truman did. So, during those days there was Matt, myself, and Charlie Ross. No, first, we had a press secretary named J. Leonard Reinsch. He didn't last but about two days.

And then the president took Charlie Ross, who was then with the *St. Louis Post-Dispatch,* and Charlie became his secretary. So, there was Matt, Charlie, Harry Vaughan — Harry was in on everything — and Jake Vardaman, who was his naval aide. They attended the morning conferences, which used to start about *seven* o'clock every morning.

Hess: Let's take a few of those men, just one at a time, and tell me about your impressions of those gentlemen when you met them. Now, you had worked with Matthew Connelly probably on the campaign. Is that right?

Allen: I hadn't known any of them. You see, I was a Roosevelt man, and this was a new group that came in. There was a boy named — the druggist that joined us on the train, too — what was his name? — from Kansas City — Evans, Tom L. Evans. And a lot of other fellows came in. But they were nominated. My friends had been the Roosevelt people up until then. I had been in Roosevelt's "subadministration." I had been commissioner of the District, and I had done a lot of things for Roosevelt.

And if anybody belonged to Battery D, he could get right in. There was a great fellow, was his partner, too — what was his name? — that ran the haberdashery.

Hess: Eddie Jacobson.

Allen: Yes, he was in there. If you look over there, you will see some very interesting photographs. That's when we used to go down on the *Williamsburg*, and the president would autograph all our placards after the meeting. [Originally built as a luxury yacht, the *Williamsburg* was a gunboat in World War II and in late 1945 became the presidential yacht.] We used to have a lot of poker games, and the president loved to play poker, and so did Fred Vinson. The president's trouble in poker was that he liked to look at an inside straight. Vinson and Joe [Joseph E.] Davies, Scott Lucas, Stuart Symington, and Clark Clifford were always there. Clark and I were usually in on all the poker games. But we quit at eleven o'clock at night. We played what we called a "poverty" poker game. In other words, you could only lose a certain amount, and then you would go on poverty. So, nobody could get hurt. It was just a social game. There wasn't anybody trying to make any money.

Hess: Were you along at any time when there was business of a substantive nature discussed on the *Williamsburg*?

Allen: Oh, yes, they used to talk business all the time, and you can't be around a president without the world affairs being there all the time.

Hess: Do you recall a particular incident, a particular problem that may have been discussed?

Allen: Oh, I think so many that I wouldn't know what . . .

Hess: In some files that I have run across, I found a memo from you and from John Snyder and from Judge Samuel Rosenman giving some suggestions of things that might come up at Potsdam that I believe you discussed with the president early in July.

Allen: That was his first trip as president you know, his Potsdam trip. That's right.

Hess: Do you recall that episode?

Allen: Well, you'd make suggestions all the time. Some of them would be accepted; some would be thrown out. Now, you mentioned about the Stettinius thing. That was really an interesting thing.

Hess: Tell me about that.

Allen: Well, we were on the *Williamsburg*. You see, the president had three things to do when he got in office: He had to address Congress; he had to address the armed services; and then he had to go out and address the United Nations on its formation, and it was just being formed in San Francisco. No, it hadn't been formed in San Francisco. The war wasn't over when he got in.

Hess: I believe that was when the charter was signed, was it not?

Allen: That was in San Francisco when the charter was signed. That was after the war, but anyway, we were on the *Williamsburg*, and it was decided there that somebody should go out to San Francisco to represent the president. At that time, the "big five" was meeting there: Russia, England, China, United States, and France. And, so, they were setting up the meeting. So, it was decided that someone should go out to represent the president, and I drew the assignment. So, I went out. Our headquarters were at the Fairmont Hotel. So, I was talking to the president over the phone one day, and he said, "Are you where you can talk?"

I said, "Yes."

He said, "I want to make Jimmy Byrnes secretary of state. Would you go see Ed Stettinius and tell him this and see if we can't put him in — isn't there going to be something in this new organization where Ed could fit in?" And it was, as secretary-general.

Well, Ed was furious. He said that he wouldn't resign. So, we had two or three days of real tough . . .

Hess: How did you convince him that he should?

Allen: I finally said, "Ed, who are you close to in this delegation that you trust?"

He said, "Dr. [Isaiah] Bowman." Now, Bowman was the geographer from Johns Hopkins; he was president of Johns Hopkins at one time.

So, I said, "Well, get him in here with me," because I wanted him to hear my argument. Because Ed wouldn't listen.

He said, "You Democrats are just trying to throw me out, and I've done a great job."

So, I convinced him — and Bowman agreed with me — that the president had the right to have his own secretary of state; he didn't have anything against Ed. And Ed said, "No, this job is a terrible job. It doesn't amount to anything."

And then we made possibly one of our biggest faux pas in the Truman administration right at that time, I think, because we intimated we were going to have a big announcement to make in Independence. This was after we had had the meeting out there. The announcement was that Ed Stettinius was going to become secretary-general and that Jimmy Byrnes was going to become secretary of state. Well, everybody knew it anyway. So, we'd built this big press conference up, and the boys thought something was going to happen. And they were very much disappointed when something that had been prophesied all the time did happen. So, I remember Charlie Ross realized that he had made a mistake intimating that there was going to be such an unusual announcement, because it had been prophesied all along.

Hess: What was your opinion of Mr. Truman's choice of James Byrnes to replace Mr. Stettinius?

Allen: Well, I had known Jimmy Byrnes ever since I had been in Washington, and I had great respect for him; of course, they broke afterwards, as you know. But I thought it was a good move. I have a letter from Ed Stettinius thanking me afterwards for the courtesy I had shown him in this matter. Oh, so then, I finally got the letter up [Stettinius's letter of resignation] that he was to write Truman, and the letter that the President would send him, and then Truman came out a day or two in advance and went up to Mon [Monrad C.] Wallgren's in Olympia. So, I flew up there, took him Stettinius's letter and the suggested letter, and the president agreed on it. And then we announced it in Independence later.

Hess: When Mr. Truman first came to the White House, what seemed to be his degree of awareness of his new position, its responsibility, its powers, and his duty?

Allen: Well, he was unbelievably great. He was humble. There was not an ounce of arrogance in him — maybe he might shoot off a little quicker than he should and without thinking something through — but it was an honest fault if he did it. And he was a kindly, very kindly fellow. Oh, Truman will go down as quite a man in history.

Hess: You mentioned a few moments ago about some speeches that you worked on.

Allen: Three, the first three. There was the speech for the joint session of Congress, and the speech to the armed forces, and the speech to the United Nations. There was another one in between there. The United Nations' one was done by Samuel Rosenman, I think — yes, I know it was.

Then Jonathan Daniels was made press secretary. And then Steve Early came back, and, if you remember, when Louis Johnson became secretary of defense, Steve Early became deputy secretary of defense. That was because we couldn't get anybody to be finance chairman except Louis Johnson. That's why he became secretary of defense. And [James] Forrestal had gone nuts then. That's no way to speak of it; he'd slipped.

Hess: What are your recollections about Mr. Truman's campaign in 1948?

Allen: Well, I think Clark Clifford deserves more credit on that than anybody. That was a great campaign. I phoned Mr. Truman the night of the election, and I said, "I want to be the first fellow that says that I didn't think you had a chance." And I didn't.

Hess: Was that the way you felt?

Allen: Oh, sure, I didn't think he had a chance in the world. I thought it was a cinch. I didn't think he had a ghost of a chance.

Hess: President Truman and General Eisenhower tended to draw apart politically and personally. What was the basis of their misunderstanding?

Allen: That was really a telephone call. President Eisenhower was in Kansas City, and President Truman called him and President Truman said he [Eisenhower] never returned the call.

Hess: What time was this?

Allen: The time I don't know. But anyway, Eisenhower felt very badly about it. He looked into it. He checked with the Secret Service. They couldn't find the call that had come in, but they got very friendly towards the end there.

5

Thomas Hart Benton

Kansas City, Missouri   April 21, 1965

Interviewed by Milton Perry

Thomas Hart Benton (1889–1975) gained international renown in the Depression era for his bold wall paintings that revived murals as an art form. He was a major influence in three movements of American art: modernism, regionalism, and abstract expressionism. The former president chose him to paint a mural in the lobby of the Truman Library's museum. Benton completed *Independence and the Opening of the West* in 1961. In the last months of Truman's life, the artist painted a memorable portrait of his friend. "Great individuals are accidents," Benton said in 1970. "Only rarely does an Alexander or Shakespeare or Michelangelo turn up. The only individual who stands out in my lifetime is Harry S. Truman. If there is an ounce of vanity in that man, it has yet to show itself."

Perry: Tom, could you tell us just why you elected to do this mural — the Truman Library mural?

Benton: I didn't just elect myself to do it, Milton. I was nominated, you might say, by David Lloyd and Wayne Grover. Mr. Lloyd was secretary of the Truman Library in Washington, D.C., and Dr. Grover was archivist of the U.S., but I guess I was elected by President Truman. Anyhow, his was the vote that counted most.

Perry: Well, how did Mr. Lloyd and Dr. Grover come to nominate you?

Benton: One day — it was in the late fifties; I've forgotten the exact date — Mr. Lloyd and Dr. Grover came into my Kansas City studio to look at a mural I was completing for the Power Authority of the State of New York. When they saw the painting, they said, "We ought to have something like this for the Truman Library."

I said, "I think you should, too."

A little later they paid me another visit, and Mr. Lloyd asked how much a mural for the Truman Library would cost. I said, "Let's look at the space you want to have painted." After I'd seen the space at the library, I said we ought to talk to the man for whom the library was built and see if he wanted a mural. So, we started a series of discussions with President Truman, who, it turned out, *was* interested. He agreed that a mural would be appropriate for the entrance hall of the library.

Perry: Did you discuss costs with the president?

Benton: Eventually, of course. But that aspect of the business was left almost wholly in the hands of Mr. David Lloyd. I talked ideas with the president — what the mural would represent — what historical meanings it should have. It took several months of discussion for us to get into accord on that — on the theme, I mean.

Perry: Who did finally decide upon the theme for the mural? I mean the subject "independence and the opening of the West."

Benton: I don't think any one of us, the president, Mr. Lloyd, or Dr. Grover, made that decision — not alone anyhow. The theme just grew up out of our discussions. It *was* decided quite early that the mural would include Independence because it was the President's home as well as the site of the library. I thought at first that the president would also want to be included in the mural, but he very emphatically turned that down. He said he didn't want to be memorialized in the mural — that the library itself was enough in that line. He said that in effect — I don't remember his exact words.

Perry: Did President Truman advance many ideas to help decide the theme?

Benton: He sure did. And they were all good ideas, in terms of history. You know the president is a first-class historian. The trouble we had in getting together was not his *ideas* but that they sometimes got too vast for me to be able to paint them.

Perry: What do you mean, "too vast"?

Benton: Well, for instance, at one point in our talks the president wanted to include Thomas Jefferson and the Louisiana Purchase in the mural. There wasn't anything inappropriate in that, only I'd have needed a space ten times as big as the library entrance hall to encompass it. The Louisiana Purchase involves a lot of history.

The president, you see, was thinking history, but I had to paint it. I had to be concerned about images as well as historical meanings, and every single image would need so much space. They couldn't be multiplied indefinitely.

Perry: And, I guess, President Truman wasn't used to thinking of history in terms of images?

Benton: Of course not. Why should he be? But just the same he arrived at accommodating himself to the fact that I had to. After that, the working out of the mural theme came along easier.

Perry: We have in the library files a letter which you wrote President Truman explaining what you had in mind for the mural. Why did you write it when you could have talked it over with him?

Benton: Well, we had already done a lot of talking about the theme, but I wanted to clarify, for the president, what it was possible for me to do about it in painting. Clarify it precisely in that direction. That letter solidified and brought to a point all of our previous discussions. It settled the theme not only in terms of history but in terms of *paintable* history. That letter got the president, David Lloyd, Wayne Grover, and myself completely together. When the president accepted its recommendations, the mural was put completely in my hands. And let me say here that he never went back on his acceptance. In all the time I worked on the mural, he never kibitzed once. Maybe he wanted to now and then, but he never did. I call that a good patron.

Perry: So, it was you after all who decided how the theme would be presented and how it was to be interpreted, too?

Benton: Of course. Who else could do that? I had to do the work, didn't I? You must remember that the theme was worked out *verbally, and with large generalities*, but I had to translate it into the precise images of the mural and relate these images in the mural space. I had to turn the *history* of the theme into the *form* of the mural.

Perry: It was after the letter then that President Truman signed the contract for the mural?

Benton: After the letter, after I had decided how much the mural would cost, and after we knew we could get the money for it, . . . then I set as reasonable a price as I could — I was reasonable because I very much wanted to do the Truman Library mural.

Perry: And you came to $60,000?

Benton: That's right.

Perry: Were you ever previously acquainted with the president or with Mr. Lloyd or Dr. Grover — I mean, before you began considering the mural?

Benton: I had met the president once in Washington, but I had the opportunity for only a few words. It was at the White House when he was actively president, and there were a lot of other people there. Lloyd and Grover I had never known before. However, when we started our mural discussions, I soon felt I had known them all for a long time. President Truman has a way, I'm sure you realize, of putting people at ease.

Perry: But you did have a sort of message to the viewers of the mural, didn't you? Didn't you want the mural to say to them something you had in mind?

Benton: Yes. I did want them to get the sense that America was made, built up into the powerful country it has become, very largely by the actions of the common people spreading out over the frontiers on their own and without any kind of official prompting. The mural was conceived as a *folk* story and, if it has a deliverable message, that would be about the preeminence of the *folk* in the development of our country. But as I said just now about the values of a work of art being finally determined by its spectators, so also will its meanings be finally determined. And that is all right. It's not what's in the artist's mind that is important, but what his art raises in the spectator's mind — that's what counts in the long run.

6

Omar N. Bradley

Kansas City, Missouri   March 29, 1955

Interviewed by William Hillman and Francis Heller

Omar N. Bradley (1893–1981), General of the Army, was awarded his fifth star by Truman in 1950. Bradley, who led American troops in the Normandy invasion, became director of the Veterans Administration after the Allied victory. Like the Democratic president, he grew up on a Missouri farm and never forgot his humble origins. Another quality that the two men had in common was modesty. When Bradley succeeded Dwight D. Eisenhower as army chief of staff in February 1948, Truman said: "Marshall to Eisenhower to Bradley — I think that's one of the finest exchanges I know." Bradley would later become the first permanent chairman of the Joint Chiefs of Staff.

Q: One of the questions on which we have to get a perspective is what was the feeling about the Russians occupying all of their zones when we were so far advanced with our troops?

Bradley: The decision dividing up Germany into occupation zones was made long before we met the Russians. I think about the middle of January 1945. As I remember, . . . I always understood it was made in London. It was discussed at Tehran and Yalta and implicated at Potsdam and was not entirely to our liking at that time. France wasn't in on it originally. I think it was the United States, England, and Russia, and I don't know where you will find the records on that meeting. What I am telling you is pretty much hearsay, but it came to me at the time that the United States wanted the boundary of the occupation zones to pass through the center of Berlin, but that the Russians insisted on something like what we ended up with, and the English went along with them. We were outvoted.

When we advanced into Germany, we knew that every foot we advanced was ground we would have to give up to the Russians because the decision had been made long before. On whether or not we should try to take Berlin — I discussed that with General Eisenhower, and I know that he and I felt the same way, and that was why should we spend [troops] —

there would probably be 100,000 casualties — taking Berlin when we would have to turn around and go back to the zone boundaries the Allies had agreed upon. For example, we crossed the Elbe River to take German troops away from Berlin so that the Russians could take it that much easier. Our instructions were to cross the Elbe in two places and then try to tie them up, which would force the Germans to send a certain number of troops against those two bridgeheads. Actually, one of those bridgeheads wasn't successful, but we did succeed in holding the one, and several divisions of German troops went up there.

Actually, we had no intention of going to Berlin. That can be illustrated by a story. While I was at General [William H.] Simpson's Ninth Army headquarters — it was at the time of the capture of Marburg — well, while I was sitting there, a report came in that it looked like they were going to capture the bridge, as the Germans were falling. What should we do with it? I said, "Well, that presents a problem. Throw in enough troops to hold the other end of it."

Well, we talked for about twenty minutes, and the phone rang and they said, "You don't have to worry about it anymore. They destroyed the bridge."

That is an illustration of the fact that we didn't want to expose our troops to any greater danger than was necessary if we were going to have to pull back. We were uncovering concentration camps all along the way. I proposed that we try to move the Russians and the Poles up into their own zones and put them in a position so that when we withdrew we would leave them in the Russian zone and be rid of them. That was the first time that I realized that these fellows didn't want to go home, although they were Russians. So, we had difficulty. I thought all we had to do was fix places for them, but they wouldn't go. So, we had a deuce of a time; we didn't get many to go up there.

But those boundaries were definitely fixed before we got there; the military didn't have anything to do about it. I understood General [George C.] Marshall was pretty insistent about putting the boundary through the middle of Berlin, but it was never done. After the occupation boundaries had been set, there was the decision to hold at the Elbe River — that was a military decision in order to avoid any extra casualties. And all the commanders fully agreed with that. I know I did.

Q: Did Churchill intervene at that time with messages that you were aware of?

Bradley: There were some intimations that Mr. Churchill suggested, "Let's rearrange these boundaries to comply with the ground we now occupy." That came after we had stopped fighting so far as I remember. It didn't come before. It came just after Berlin was taken. I don't know what General Eisenhower's reaction was. Mine was that this was a hell of a way to keep agreements — this was a funny way to do diplomacy.

Q: It would be a difficult principle to apply elsewhere — in Trieste and in Austria. In other words, if we unilaterally tried to handle agreements like that there, we would have difficulties trying to get the Russians to keep their agreements elsewhere —

Q: You see the whole picture has to be considered, not just one corner of it.

Bradley: That's undoubtedly true.

Q: Some Americans wanted to avoid the possibility of a clash with the Russians. Did you think there was any such possibility?

Bradley: Yes, there was considerable chance of clash with the Russians. A meeting of two forces where there is a chance of mistaken identity is dangerous business. We went to considerable pains to work out schemes to recognize each other when we met. The war was pretty open at that time. There were even cases where we fired on our own troops, and it is a bigger problem if a fellow is coming from the opposite direction and you have no information on it. We mutually agreed — on a high level — that we would make certain markings on our tanks and vehicles so that we would recognize one another. I think there was a fear of a clash coming through accident, not through intention, but because of a lack of identification. When we met and established contact, there was no fear or suspicion on our part that fighting might start; there was on the part of the Russians.

General [J. Lawton] Collins was telling a story of the time he paid a visit on the other side. As he passed a certain place, he noticed that they were digging in facing us. He mentioned this, and the commander asked him the question, "Aren't you digging in, too?"

And Collins said, "No, we are not." So, he stopped the operation.

The Russian troops were very friendly. They were a bunch of peasant-type folks, very friendly and peaceful. As far as the individual soldier was concerned, . . . it was only as you went back to the high commanders did you get more and more suspicion. When I visited [Ivan] Konev — he commanded the Ukraine army, the group opposite mine — I took along a map. We used to do that with our allies. You take a map along to show them your disposition. And I wanted to see just how much information he would give me. It wasn't much — I would even have given it to the Germans at that time — there was no risk. I took it over and explained where our various units were, but he didn't give me any information at all. Then he came to my headquarters, and I took him into my office. I showed him my big war map. But again not a word. He didn't tell anything interesting.

Q: What was your feeling about the Russians first starting off with the Germans and then switching to us?

Bradley: I've thought about that. It's my opinion that it was a far-reaching plan to fight on the German side until they got Poland and then turn against them. I suspect that they knew all the time that they would fight up to a certain time and then switch over against the Germans. With a group of twelve or fourteen people controlling policy, you can do more long-range planning than if you have to depend on the results of an election. We have to educate 168 million people, but all you have to do there is convince these twelve or fourteen people, and you are off on a long-range program.

Q: Was there no feeling that if the Russians were hampered in reaching their zones, they might become violent and attack?

Bradley: Well, there was always . . . I don't think there was any feeling that they would attack us although we were prepared in case it came. It might be illustrated by my remark to General Eisenhower when I came back. He said, "What do you think of their troops?"

I had gone back twenty miles inside their lines, their front lines; and I had noticed their supply columns, maintenance and so on, and I said, "I think we can take them on three to one and lick them — but I'm not sure they don't have five or ten." It was hard to tell what strength they had back of them. But I would think, with our equipment, we could have taken them on three to one. Now, what made me think that was this possibility that we might have a clash.

Q: There was at no time a disposition on the part of the military to accede to Churchill's policy?

Bradley: Not as far as I know. It wasn't up to us. It was something our government would have to go along with. I remember my reaction at the time was that this was a hell of a way to keep a bargain.

Q: That is what the president's idea was? You can't ask for agreements by breaking agreements?

Bradley: I think it would be interesting to get hold of the records of that meeting. I remember at one time the British denied that it had been done, but they calmed down later and admitted it. I think it was about January 15 in London at which time we were represented by our ambassador.

Q: The Berlin airlift — you touch on this question of access to Berlin in your book, and apparently in the military consideration this outpost of ours was just intended to be there in good faith . . .

Bradley: We were assured we had that supply line. The trouble was that they didn't put it down in writing —

Q: Assured by whom? Or in what way? Was it agreed among the military that it was a sure thing?

Bradley: That is the way I remember it. I looked at a little of those things at the time I was writing my book. At the time of the blockade there was the question whether we should have tried to run a few convoys through there or not.

Q: Were you back as chief of staff at the time of the blockade?

Bradley: I became chief of staff on February 7, 1948, and was chief of staff until August 15, 1949. It was about a year and a half.

Q: The question of what to do when the blockade first arose . . . you were right in on the discussions that were carried on at that time?

Bradley: Yes.

Q: You didn't favor a military convoy through there?

Bradley: General [Lucius] Clay recommended a military convoy, but the chiefs never would go along with it. I don't know whether it was right or wrong. Our contention was that they might not oppose it by armed force, which of course would be war, but they could stop you in so many ways short of armed resistance. A bridge could go out or roads closed for repairs — they probably needed it at that time. Then you would look foolish running a train through there. A bridge could go out just ahead of you and then another bridge behind, and you'd be in a hell of a fix. But we decided on an airlift, and we won it. Maybe the other would have been better; I don't know, but I have my doubts. It might have led to considerable embarrassment. We would have been embarrassed if a bridge had accidentally gone out front and back and left us sitting there. Or they could have put nails in the road for our trucks — all sorts of things they could do to you.

Q: I understood that the air force was dubious about undertaking this task. It was only by pressure on them, telling them we would have to use a military convoy where there would be danger of an armed clash — do you recall that?

Bradley: I don't recall the degree of enthusiasm the air force had for the job. It was a terrific task. The Russians could have embarrassed us on the airlift, too, but it would be harder to do, short of war, than with a convoy, we thought.

Q: Would you care to characterize the Berlin episode?

Bradley: I think it had a great effect on the world and on the Germans — the fact that we stood up to that thing and solved it. It wasn't only standing up to it; it was a terrific achievement. It had far-reaching effects on our friends and also on the Russians.

Q: Did it have any noticeable effect on the status of morale in our forces?

Bradley: I think it must have given our people a feeling of satisfaction, particularly the air force. It showed them what could be done in a pinch. They had never run anything such as that before, with planes coming in as fast as they did for twenty-four hours a day, regardless of the weather . . .

Q: During your time as chief of staff, were there any urgent or immediate problems you were confronted with so far as the military picture was concerned?

Bradley: Yes, quite a number of them. It was during that period that the army got to such a low strength — it depended on voluntary enlistments and got down to approximately 500,000. Our authorized strength was 660,000, so we were way under our authorized strength. That was a big problem. During the same time, in figuring out the requirements for our overseas garrisons and our increasing need for antiaircraft artillery, we succeeded in having our authorized strength increased from 660,000 to 820,000 — or something like that — to meet our additional requirements. That was probably the first step towards a comeback in strength after our low point, which was 500,000. From there we started going back up. The president authorized an increase, and the Congress granted some of it in the way of appropriations, but we had started to increase before Korea came along. Those were some of the things that happened during that year and a half.

During that year and a half there was the separation of the air force from the army; it had been the army air force, and it became the air force. In the final stages of that, there was the problem of who transfers and who doesn't. This had to do with the human element of the thing. Along towards the end the air force was taking only the very top cream. So, I said, "This goes two ways." I said, "No one transfers without my personal approval." Well . . . There were five cadets from West Point who had passed their physicals, but they were five more than the quota we were allowing the air force, and they were disapproved. On the evening of July 31 — the last day we could transfer them — I had gone home about 6:30. I was just starting to sit down when the cook came up and said, "There's a second lieutenant in the kitchen who would like to see you."

I said, "In the kitchen?"

She said yes, that he'd been waiting for me. Well, I went down, and there was this young lieutenant, all shiny in his uniform. I invited him into the living room and asked him what I could do for him.

He said, "I am one of the five lieutenants who can't get into the air force. I had just got married and gone to Florida. When I found out about this, I left my bride and came right up here. I was a lieutenant in the paratroopers, and then I came home and went to West Point with the sole ambition of getting into the air force. And now I miss it by four or five files." I guess his grades were not quite high enough; that was the way it was decided. . . . Anyway, he said, "My life's ambition is lost."

Well, I said, "Anyone who leaves his bride in Florida and comes clear up here to see the chief of staff is showing enough initiative that he ought to get in. Tomorrow morning I'll go back down and approve your transfer, but I can't approve you without approving the others. Are you sure they all still want to?"

And he said, "Yes." So, I did. But it didn't have too happy an ending. Korea came along, and he had flown his fifty missions as a fighter pilot and was ready to come home on rotation. But he requested and got permission to stay over and come back with his old paratroop bunch. Well, they were dropping troops north of Seoul, and he got killed. . . . I guess I should have left that out of the story . . .

Q: Did your experience as chief of staff in that first period lead you to some reflections as to what it means to have an army in a democracy after a war? Would you care to talk about that?

Bradley: Of course, I had believed for a long time that we should have some form of universal military service, because I just don't think you can depend upon voluntary enlistments to keep your armed services at the strength you want them or to build up a reserve which is ready when you want it by voluntary methods. I don't think my opinion changed in any way while I was chief of staff—I probably became more convinced than ever.

Q: Do you see any acceptance in the future of UMT [universal military training]?

Bradley: I doubt it. I haven't studied the president's proposal very much, or not enough to be able to comment on it intelligently. I just feel that some time we will have to come up with a program that will provide for a ready force, . . . because when the next war comes, you aren't going to have any time . . . .

Q: How much of a force would you need in atomic warfare?

Bradley: I don't know what the final figures would be. You need increases in antiaircraft. There was only one antiaircraft battalion, and I think today you'll find there are 175 or something like that in the regular forces. Those two articles I wrote about a year and a half ago. I considered them a report to the people. There was much discussion in my office on how to render the report. I felt there were certain things the people ought to know about this. And after some discussion, and after clearing it with the boss, I wrote these two articles for the *Saturday Evening Post*. I discussed them with him [Truman] before he went out, and I also cleared them with President Eisenhower. It was just a vague thing when I talked to him about it, in that I pointed out that some of your best defense would be made by a formal commitment to certain National Guard units — that their assignment in time of war was the defense of their own home city.

For example — well, Kansas City is not on the top of the list of targets, but supposing it were — you have a battalion of antiaircraft, and you get the top people in electronics, trained people out of the factories, to become members so that they'll stay in for ten or twenty years — if they know that they would be defending their own homes right here and not be sent off somewhere else. This antiaircraft stuff is so technical now that it takes about thirty-three months just to learn how to take care of the equipment, and we don't get regulars to stay in that long. So, what do you do? You depend on civilians . . . will they be available to you in time of war? If you could build it up in your city by getting those people who are trained in electronics — it would fit right in with their regular business — and they stay with you for years and years, you wouldn't have a much better defense.

As far as I know, the only favorable reaction to this came from Governor [G. Mennen] Williams of Michigan. About a year ago he came to Washington with some National Guard officers and asked me to elaborate on this. He was interested in that arrangement to defend Detroit. Detroit would undoubtedly be the first target. What he did about it I don't know, but that is one suggestion — to get reserve units to defend their homeland. How much infantry you would need . . .

Q: The president was very interested in getting your description of the relationship between the chiefs of staff and the president — how they functioned together.

Bradley: I know the chiefs felt that they had access to the president at any time they had any opinions which they felt he ought to hear.

Q: Individually, or collectively?

Bradley: Either individually or collectively. After Korea broke out, and for the last year after I became chairman, I used to see the president practically every day for a long time to give him the situation and to keep in touch with what he was saying. I would let him know what the chiefs were thinking. And from time to time I would take all the chiefs over because I [had this] feeling — if I was going to see him every day, I thought the chiefs of the three services should see him once in a while. I explained that to the president, and he fully understood. So, once a month or so, we would go over. And I fixed it so that they had something specific which they could present to him. I would give them fifteen minutes, but you know how closely he had to schedule his time. Frequently we would all come over, and each chief would get a chance to discuss his own problems with the president — we had access to him at all times. He always told me to come over any time I had something I felt he should see. Of course, I would call the White House switchboard beforehand. I saw him as late as 10:30 at night and as early as 6:30 in the morning. We felt very free to present to him anything we thought he should know or on which we wanted a decision.

Q: What decision would you put up to him as commander in chief?

Bradley: He approved all messages going to the Far East, for example, in connection with the fighting of the war. The machinery was that Defense and State would meet together on it. If it was purely military, we probably drafted it and showed it to State. All orders being United Nations orders, and not the United States', had to be coordinated with the State Department. State and Defense worked up these messages. They got approved by the secretary of state and the secretary of defense; then they would go to the president. He put the final OK on it.

Q: Did the president ever express to the chiefs, through you, what policy or what particular plan he wanted to put into operation?

Bradley: No, I don't recall his expressing his opinion ahead of time on any military operations. But sometimes on general overall policy, like the policy of the exchange of prisoners — that was a long, drawn-out one — sometimes he would let us know how he felt before the final message came to him. Normally he didn't tell us what our military operations ought to be until they came to him as approved by the State Department and Defense.

Q: Was he at any time critical, or did he ask questions about any particular military operations?

Bradley: I think he was concerned about some of MacArthur's dispositions in certain phases of the Korean situation. You will remember that after taking Inchon, the Eighth Army went up the left coast, and he had a separate group [X Corps] under [General Edward M.] Almond on the right. Both were answerable all the way back to Tokyo. The one was not under the Eighth Army at all; there was no connection between the two forces. Well, everyone thought that was wrong, and the Joint Chiefs afterwards sent a message to MacArthur questioning the lack of coordination between the two forces. We were faced with the problem of just how much do you try to command from seven thousand miles away? It was theoretically wrong; you could have only general guidance. We questioned him on that. The president saw that message. The answer came back — he [MacArthur] always considered us a bunch of kids. He pooh-poohed the idea and said, "You don't know what you're talking about. You can't tie the two together. I know what I'm doing over here." Actually, when [Matthew] Ridgway got in it, he tied the two together, and we had a continuous line over rough terrain. And it stopped infiltration between the two forces.

The time that he [MacArthur] sent the marine division in — after the Chinese had already hit the Eighth Army on the left — he let Almond's corps go up to the [Chosin] reservoir. The people in Washington didn't like that. They [X Corps] were badly hit and had a deuce of a time getting out. Other than those two things, I can't remember his getting into any discussion of military dispositions.

Q: To what degree did the president interest himself in the organizational and administrative problems within the services? Would he be particularly concerned if the chiefs said, "We are sending this division. Here it is"?

Bradley: He always OK'd those — you mean on the battlefront?

Q: In general terms.

Bradley: Normally we would get the president's approval on the movement of any large unit where there would be a lot of political implications. When it came to sending troops to Korea, he approved the transfer of any large unit to Korea before it was sent. But if it was from one part of the battlefront to another, we did that — that was up to the commander on the front. Anytime you make a movement like that [moving the Tenth Division to Germany from Ft. Riley, Kansas], it must be approved by the president — in peacetime, he has the whole state of Kansas against him.

Q: The President followed closely the Korean matter?

Bradley: During the early days I briefed him every day. Later on when things became a little more general, I usually briefed him once, maybe twice, a week.

Q: Where do you think MacArthur went wrong? What were the accumulative incidents?

Bradley: Well, I mentioned one — the handling of troops, which was bad — and then his attitude when we questioned him about it. He must have known [that the president would see his message], because all messages came to him [the president]. He knew his answer would be sent to the president. If you will remember, the president went to Wake Island to see MacArthur over something he had said beforehand. At that time he assured the president that the Chinese would not come into this action; he just knew they would not — on which he was badly off. It was largely through his recommendation, I think, that the UN took action to proceed north of the 38th parallel — MacArthur's recommendation. He sent back a plan which provided that he would move quickly into North Korea, hold elections, and pull back out, except for South Korean troops. On this he had the solid backing of [Syngman] Rhee, naturally. They felt that now we had a chance to reunite Korea, and since the Chinese weren't coming in, it could be done quickly.

These are the things I think — the accumulations as you call them — that caused the president to relieve him: first, his remarks about Formosa; then his letter to the American Legion — or the Veterans of Foreign Wars — that was the most flagrant thing I think that was contrary to what the president was saying. Then along towards the end, when he was asked for his opinion about an armistice, he went directly to the enemy with his own proposal before we cleared it with the other nations. That was wrong. That was the straw that broke the camel's back. We had to apologize to our United Nations allies over something he had done. So, that was when the president just finally gave up.

Q: Would you say General MacArthur knew he was acting wrongly in the VFW message and other incidents?

Bradley: I think so. General MacArthur has always pretty much gone his own way. I remember a remark made at the time by a general who was senior to MacArthur, on the retired list. He said, "MacArthur said he never failed to obey an order. I never knew him when he did." That was his reputation among his contemporaries.

Q: Do you have any recollections of the Wake Island meeting?

Bradley: It was my understanding that the president went to Wake Island to meet him there — he was bending over backwards. He didn't want to take him out of the battle zone at a crucial time because he could be blamed if anything went wrong. And this way MacArthur was out of his territory less than twenty-four hours. I don't think it would have been right for the president to go all the way to Japan.

Q: Did the president discuss this with you, or did he simply announce it?

Bradley: As I remember, there was some discussion about it. I was one of those who thought he ought to meet him halfway and not keep him out of the theater. A lot of that conference went on with just the two of them present. Then with all of my staff, MacArthur's staff, people from Washington, Dean Rusk from the State Department, Frank Pace, who was secretary of the army, myself, and [Philip C.] Jessup [ambassador to the United Nations], and I don't know who else. The big conference was around a table. . . . We tried to make a summary of that — you undoubtedly have a copy. I don't remember if the president and MacArthur were together again after the conference, but I think perhaps they were. You might say the conference was in three parts, at two of which there were only the two of them present.

Q: Did you feel the atmosphere to be one of mutual cordiality?

Bradley: I thought so. I based that largely on the fact that the president felt that now we had settled the differences, that everything was OK. I am sure he left feeling that way . . .

Certain terms of the [armistice] proposal were sent to [MacArthur] for his comments. We wanted to get his comments as well as those of the other nations involved. But he sprung it over there before we had a chance to get answers back from the other nations. It put the president and the government in a hole.

Q: The president frequently says that he could have settled the Korean thing on the same basis it was, but he didn't want to. He thought the basis on which it was settled wasn't satisfactory, for two reasons: one, the fact that he wasn't satisfied about the prisoner issue; and two, he was afraid it would release the Chinese for activities in Indochina.

Bradley: Well, I went through so long a period of the negotiations in which we changed our views slightly on some point or another that I don't remember when they were changed. This is an interesting point. I don't know how official it is, but along — three or four months after Ike took over, all of us were thoroughly disgusted with the way they hung on. And the chiefs came up with a proposal to clobber them. Well, within a week or two they came around to our terms. For a long time I've felt there was a leak somewhere on the staff — that they let that get out. Recently I heard that that was passed to Nehru by someone in the State Department, and he undoubtedly went to the Chinese. I was worried about some kind of leak because as soon as we came up with that thing, they signed on the dotted line.

Q: That would suggest the line of argument of the witness before Senator Jenner's committee, all of which furnished ammunition for Jenner's conclusion that the Chinese were tipped off that we would attack.

Bradley: I am beginning to suspect now that they might have heard, but that wasn't outside of Korea. There are several things about Korea that people forget. I might just list them: (1) This was a UN action, not the U.S. We were not free to take action as a nation without consulting our allies, and ultimately they didn't go along. It was a question of hot pursuit; we were ready to order it, but our allies were not ready to go along, particularly the British, who were skeptical of our bombing anywhere near the Yalu. We had knocked out those bridges, but all we could do was bomb this end of them because the British were adamant on that question.

Q: Why?

Bradley: They wanted to make sure the war was limited to Korea. There were several reasons why. In the Chinese-Russian treaty, in article 14 or 15, it stated that any attack on China would be considered an attack on Russia and they would come in. And an attack into Manchuria would have been an attack on China. This was not a sole U.S. action.

Now (2), when you talk about strategic bombing, it is only effective if you can go after the source of production. In this case the source of production was in Russia — 90 percent of their supplies came from Russia — and our people were not ready to go to war with Russia. So, strategic bombing in Korea could not be effective. Then you come to the question of tactical bombing with A-bombs. At the time the Korean War was started, our stockpile was not such to permit us to use large numbers of A-bombs and still have enough in case we got into a war with Russia. We had to have reserves in case Russia came in. In 1953 we could have used enough to clobber the hell out of them in certain tactical areas and still have enough to take care of emergencies. But what if they retaliated and used A-bombs against us? If they could have destroyed Inchon and Pusan, just those two, it would have been decisive. So, the question came up: Would it pay to start an atomic war at that time? Those are some of the things that people forget.

Q: Did the president express himself in any way about the use of the A-bomb? It's understood that he was opposed to it and that MacArthur wanted it.

Bradley: He [the president] was opposed to it. What the factor was I didn't know. Either he wanted the stockpile to be saved for a greater emergency, or maybe it was humanitarian — I just don't know.

Q: Did MacArthur advocate the use of the A-bomb at any time?

Bradley: I don't remember. He may have.

Q: Did the chiefs of staff consider it?

Bradley: Oh yes, but they never recommended it.

7

Lucius D. Clay

New York, New York   July 16, 1974

Interviewed by Richard D. McKinzie

Lucius D. Clay (1897–1978), army general and military governor of occupied Germany, led the Berlin airlift when the Soviet Union announced a land blockade of the American, British, and French sectors. In this first battle of the cold war, the general had the total support of his commander in chief. During the airlift, the American general supplied West Berlin with more than two million tons of supplies and food. A descendant of the nineteenth-century politician Henry Clay, the general showed formidable political skills in introducing reforms that led to the creation of a German democratic nation.

McKinzie: General Clay, in December 1944, you joined the organization of James F. Byrnes, the Office of War Mobilization and Reconversion. Do you recall how you happened to get such an assignment?

Clay: I was sent over to France to help General [Dwight D.] Eisenhower break up the blockade — if you want to call it that — at the ports. We were unloading equipment from ships much faster than we could move it forward, and the result was that we had a huge buildup of supplies which couldn't be used by anybody. While I was assigned to Cherbourg, in command of all of the port area, General Eisenhower found out that his supply of heavy ammunition was not enough to meet the new demands that were being placed on our heavy artillery. Our soldiers had found out that by using heavy artillery, we saved lives. With the greater mobility of the heavy artillery of World War II, we were able to move it faster, supply it with ammunition faster, and fire it at a rate that had never been heard of before. He felt that I was, because of my experience in logistics, the one that could convince the War Department of this need. He sent me back home to do it on the basis that I would return to my overseas assignment.

When I got back and made the report, I found that, by what we called "squeezing the pipeline," we could meet his immediate needs, but that we would have to cut back [on] the production. This task fell upon Mr. Byrnes, primarily. It was his responsibility, and he immediately made a condition that I would come over as his deputy to help get that program going. I was to serve as his deputy for the whole program of war mobilization. I had no desire for that job at all; this was not a job for an officer in wartime. I had no choice, though, and General [George C.] Marshall very quickly rejected my plea. I wound up as Mr. Byrnes's deputy.

During the period that I was with OWMR, I became very intimately acquainted with him. We became very close friends. As a matter of fact, I went to Columbia [South Carolina] just not long ago to deliver his funeral eulogy in the state capital. I held him in great respect, and I was always very sorry about the difficulties that came between Mr. Byrnes and President Truman. I had great respect for President Truman, too. I was closer to Justice Byrnes than I was to President Truman, but I'm a great admirer of President Truman and have a tremendous respect for his judgment, particularly in the foreign relations field.

McKinzie: When you were with OWMR, solving this wartime problem, were you aware that there were lots of people in OWMR then who were planning for the peace? They had the idea that the kind of planned and ordered economy that had existed during the war was going to be necessary for some time on into the peacetime period.

Clay: I knew the people that believed that we have to have all of this planning for reconversion. I didn't believe them, and I perhaps persuaded Justice Byrnes that we had enough built-up demand in this country that this reconversion problem was not going to be anywhere nearly the disastrous problem that was being predicted. I think I was proven right on that.

McKinzie: I understand from reading [Robert D.] Murphy's book [Diplomat among Warriors], and some other things, that you weren't too happy at first when you were appointed as deputy director of the office.

Clay: I think that President Truman would have understood that, because he did his very best to get into active military service. Here I was, a man who had spent my entire life in the army. The major war of all times comes along, and instead of being a soldier, I'm on a civilian job the whole time. I would have given my eyeteeth to have commanded a division and had an opportunity in combat. Both my job in production in the army and with Justice Byrnes ruled that out. When I went to Germany, it ruled out any possibility that I could do it in the war against Japan.

McKinzie: You were faced with the problems of denazification, and keeping alive a population that was on the verge of starvation, and numerous other problems.

Clay: We had also a change of administration. The people who had had the greatest influence and developed the occupational powers went out, and Mr. Truman's administration came in with the people that he brought to run the government. I don't think that the so-called destroy Germany policy was ever one that President Truman personally believed in. He had nothing to do with its creation, and I don't think he ever believed in it.

On the food proposition, he sent former president [Herbert] Hoover over to look at the whole European situation. Mr. Hoover came back with the recommendations that we supply food for Western Europe, including West Germany, and Mr. Truman backed him completely. If it hadn't been for this, we would have had mass starvation. Mr. Truman didn't hesitate one minute in backing Hoover, and I think it was a very wise decision on his part to send him. Not only was Hoover a great expert in this field, after his actions following World War I, but he also had the respect of everybody in the country and was a Republican. This got Republican support for it.

McKinzie: General Eisenhower said that he wanted the army to get out of Germany as soon as possible, yet no one in the State Department wanted in evidently [as high commissioner of Germany]. Would you talk on that point?

Clay: I urged General Eisenhower to get out as quickly as he could. I didn't see how he could possibly add to his stature by staying there as military governor. I wanted him to get out, and I'm glad he did — I think that this was fundamental. However, there wasn't anybody of requisite size that volunteered to take the job or would take it, except an army officer whom you could tell to take it. There wasn't anybody in the State Department that wanted the job. Four years later, when there was reasonable order and the economy was back, they found civilian administrators that were perfectly willing to take it. They got one of the finest when they got Jack McCloy to go. He had turned it down when they first wanted him to go over, before I went.

McKinzie: It also makes it difficult, doesn't it, in matters of policy setting, because you had JCS-1067, which was as I understand it, a compromise between the War Department and the Department of State on how —

Clay: JCS-1067 would have been extremely difficult to operate under. [Under this policy directive, the U.S. military government had "supreme legislative, executive, and judicial authority" and could do nothing to improve the German economy.] If you followed it literally, you couldn't have done anything to restore the German economy. If you couldn't restore the German economy, you could never hope to get paid for the food that they had to have. By virtue of these sort of things, it was modified constantly — not officially, but by allowing this deviation and that deviation, etc. We began to slowly wipe out JCS-1067. When we were ordered to put in a currency reform, this was in direct contravention of a provision of JCS-1067 that prohibited us from doing anything to improve the German economy. It was an unworkable policy, and it wasn't changed just without any discussion or anything by those of us who were in Germany. It was done by gradual changes in its provisions and changes of cablegrams, conferences, and so on.

McKinzie: You must have had some backstopping in Washington to be able to do that.

Clay: At that time I happened to have been very close to Mr. Byrnes, having worked for him. I could go to Mr. Byrnes — he was very close to the president — and he would go to the president. We'd get this thing resolved in short order.

McKinzie: Did you discuss with Mr. Byrnes the deteriorating situation with the Soviets before he made his very famous speech, now called the Stuttgart speech, in September 1946?

Clay: I urged him in the first place to come to Stuttgart. I had written him a letter about my own views of the situation and it was that letter which he used as the basis for this speech. He visited me in Berlin, and we went over together. He had that passage in there, "as long as any other foreign country's troops are in Germany we're going to be there," which was the most important part of the speech. He tried all of that morning to get hold of the president by telephone to get his approval and then left word that he was going to put this in if he didn't hear anything to the contrary. I'm sure that whatever he said there he had assurance that President Truman approved. At that time their relationship was very close.

McKinzie: Had you come to the conclusion that the only way to serve U.S. interests was to take a much firmer stand against the Soviets?

Clay: Yes. I learned that from the way they were removing equipment — without any kind of accounting — from East Germany where they were in occupation and still putting in their claims for reparations from West Germany. They were not abiding by the general rules that all of this would be done by the Reparations Commission, representing all of the countries that had suffered damage from Germany. This was the beginning of my concern. I also realized we couldn't possibly work together on the question of currency reform. They wouldn't even consider it unless there were two sets of plates for the same currency, one that they would control, and one that the other Allies would control. We had given them the military currency plates, and they just glutted the country with it.

McKinzie: To what extent did you and your people try to get East-West trade going?

Clay: We tried very hard to get East-West trade going. The initial effort was to get a common utilization of the food supplies, because East Germany was a surplus food production area. When we couldn't get any food out of East Germany, it was quite obvious that there was nothing else to divide. I mean that we would have been foolish to open up trade in the things that they wanted when we couldn't get out of them the food that we had to have. We couldn't get any willingness on their part to share in the food production of East Germany. I think this was by meetings like that, that when you read history there's no orders out, and it looks like this was done without any discussion or reason. But these were all reasonable men, and I had too much respect for the people that I worked for to leave them out on a limb. I think they had enough confidence in me that they were willing to listen to my recommendations, and almost invariably approved them.

McKinzie: Mr. Truman got vitally interested in German affairs at the time of the blockade. How important, do you think, was the evolution of Germany to the president?

Clay: That's very difficult for me to answer. I'm sure though that he recognized the necessity of a revived Western Germany if there was to be a revived Western Europe.

McKinzie: Did you have contact with President Truman prior to the Berlin . . .

Clay: I was with him [Truman] several times at Potsdam in the early stages. I was one of those who wanted Mr. Byrnes to be sure that the president also agreed on the holding of troops in Germany. My actual contacts with him were indirect. I know on several occasions — when my cable authorities would say that this had been talked over at a cabinet meeting and had received approval — they didn't say that the president approved this, but it had been brought up and discussed at a cabinet meeting and was okay. This was like on the bringing of food over [to West Berlin].

McKinzie: Could you talk about your conversations and contact with President Truman at the time of the Berlin blockade?

Clay: My first contacts with him were indirect, primarily through the department and through Bob [Robert] Lovett, who was then the undersecretary of state. My first direct contact with him was when I came back to talk about the airlift and to secure his approval on it — which he gave me. He also told me that he wanted me to know that he wasn't the one that had not approved my armed convoy. All the military chiefs were against it. He said, "I didn't want to go against my military chiefs. If they had been for it, you would have had it," or words to that effect.

On my second trip, I came back because I knew that if we could get some more DC-4s, the airlift would be successful. We'd had some, but not enough. We had about forty DC-4s left, and the chief of their forces did not want to give them to me on the basis that he would have all of his forces committed. If a war came, they would be destroyed, and we'd be without transport. That was all brought up at a meeting of the National Security Council over which the president presided. I made an impassioned plea — at least I thought it was impassioned — supported by Mr. Murphy, but the Joint Chiefs and everybody else were opposed. Without these airplanes I don't think the airlift could have made it, and I was obviously quite depressed.

As the meeting ended and as we were walking out of the door, the president said to me and Ken Royall, the secretary of the army, "Come on into my office." We went into his office, and he said something like this, "You're not feeling very happy about this are you, Clay?"

I said, "No, sir, I'm not. I think that this is going to make our efforts a failure, and I'm afraid what will happen to Europe if it does fail."

He said, "Don't you worry. You're going to get your airplanes."

I said, "Mr. Truman, as I leave here there are going to be reporters out there asking me what's happened. May I tell them that?"

He said, "You may."

I went right out and told the newspapers we were getting these airplanes, and we got them. From then on out there was no longer any problem — to my part — of the airlift being a success. Truman realized that the Berlin crisis was a political war, not a physical military war. I am not being critical of the Joint Chiefs of Staff, because I think they visualized it as a military operation; in that sense of the word they were correct. Truman's a man of great courage, and he didn't hesitate to make his own decisions.

8

Clark M. Clifford

Washington, D.C.   March 23, 1971, April 19, 1971, and May 10, 1971

Interviewed by Jerry N. Hess

Clark M. Clifford (1906–1998), special counsel to the president, joined the White House staff in July 1945 as assistant to the naval aide. From 1946 to 1950, he was a senior adviser and strategist whose efforts helped to shape the Truman Doctrine, the 1947 National Security Act, and the reorganization of the armed services. Among his weaknesses was taking credit for the work of others. He put his own name on a memorandum outlining Truman's reelection strategy that was actually written by the former Roosevelt aide James H. Rowe. Clifford was John F. Kennedy's personal lawyer and, as Lyndon B. Johnson's defense secretary, reduced America's involvement in the Vietnam War. His reputation was tarnished in 1992 when Clifford and a former law partner were indicted on charges of fraud and bribes in connection with an international banking scandal. The charges were based on allegations that Clifford had hidden from federal regulators the foreign ownership of a major bank holding company that he had headed. Because of Clifford's ill health, the charges against him were dropped in 1993.

Hess: Mr. Clifford, when did you first meet Mr. Truman?

Clifford: Well, I grew up in St. Louis and went to college and law school at Washington University. I came to the bar there in 1928 and practiced in St. Louis. I had a friend there, some years later, named James K. Vardaman, and after I was married, my wife and I would see a good deal of the Vardamans.

On one occasion, in the late thirties, we went over to the Vardamans for cocktails, and Senator Harry Truman was there. He and Mr. Vardaman were old friends, and we visited — not for long — with Senator Truman. That's the only time I had seen him or talked to him before I came into the White House in the spring of 1945.

The circumstances surrounding that event briefly are as follows: In addition to being a friend of Mr. Vardaman, I was his lawyer when he had a shoe company in St. Louis. I left to go into the navy toward the end of

1943, and he, also, had gone into the Naval Reserve. When Vice President Truman ascended to the presidency in about April of 1945, one of the first things he did was have Mr. Vardaman, who was serving as a captain in the navy, come in from wherever his duty was, and become naval aide.

And thereafter, when they began to plan the trip to Potsdam, Captain Vardaman had orders issued for me — I was either out on the West Coast or in the Pacific at the time — to come back to Washington to serve in the naval aide's office while he went to Potsdam with President Truman. I was a lieutenant at that time in the Naval Reserve, and Captain Vardaman didn't want to turn his office over to the Regular Navy, and he wanted a friend to look after the office while he was away. So, I was, of course, delighted to do that for him. It was interesting and glamorous to be in the White House.

While they were away in Potsdam, which took some weeks, there wasn't too much to do in the naval aide's office. I had met Judge [Samuel I.] Rosenman, who was serving as counsel to the president, and I was not interested in remaining in the navy. Thus, as the war was drawing to a close, I felt I had satisfied my obligation to the country by serving in the navy. I must say, I had an enormous interest in what Judge Rosenman was doing. And so I volunteered to him that if he needed anybody to run errands or look up the law or do something of that kind, I'd be delighted to do it.

Hess: What sparked your particular interest in what he was doing?

Clifford: I had always had an interest in government, although it had been somewhat academic. I had had a great interest in American history, and here was a man sitting in the White House working on presidential speeches and taking part in the determination of presidential policy. This was exciting and challenging to me, and when I suggested to him that perhaps he needed some help, he was delighted to get some assistance. Thus, during the time they were in Potsdam, I really was working for Judge Rosenman.

And when the president came back, along with Captain Vardaman, a decision was made for me to stay in the White House, in the naval aide's office, where Vardaman said he could use me. I think Judge Rosenman said, "Yes, I'm beginning to use him, so keep him here." And I stayed in the naval aide's office, but I was spending a better part of my time working on matters for Judge Rosenman.

Hess: At the time that you were working as an assistant naval aide, what were your duties?

Clifford: Well, there were some duties attached to the naval aide's office. You served as liaison with the navy, and then at White House receptions and all, you were a "potted palm." You simply stood around, as there wasn't anything particularly serious going on at the time that would require much effort in the naval aide's office. I did, during that period, develop a very real friendship with Secretary [James V.] Forrestal, which was very valuable to me later on. But during that time I was doing quite a lot for Judge Rosenman. I gave maybe 20 percent of my time to naval aide duties and 70 or 80 percent of my time working for Judge Rosenman — there's where the interesting work was going on.

For example, I know that during the first summer I was there, I began work on a memorandum for Judge Rosenman on the question of compulsory military service. Some attention was being given to that. And I have some recollection either that summer or fall starting to work on a memorandum regarding the possible unification of the services. I remember President Truman saying that we had won the war, but we had won the war despite the organization of our armed forces, not because of the organization.

Often, I might say, I thought the army and navy were fighting each other just as hard as they were fighting the enemy.

Hess: Who assigned those tasks to you? President Truman or Judge Rosenman?

Clifford: Well, as time went on I began to know President Truman a little better, and I might get an occasional assignment from him. At first, however, my assignments came from Judge Rosenman.

And then toward the fall of the year, the president appointed Vardaman to a vacancy on the Federal Reserve Board — Vardaman had been a banker before he became a shoe man. I handled the problems of his confirmation. They had quite a little confrontation up there in the Senate, but he was confirmed, finally, and went over to the Federal Reserve Board.

And then President Truman made me naval aide. But in order to be naval aide, I had to have attained the rank of captain. So, in that short period of time I had gone from lieutenant to captain, a period that ordinarily would take twenty or twenty-five years in the navy. When people asked me how I had made such astounding progress, I said, "Well, it reminds me of the young man, who at age thirty, was made head of his company and somebody asked him how it happened. He said, 'Well, it's one, because I'm intelligent; two, because I'm industrious; and three, because I married the owner's daughter.'" And that's the way I explained it. They got the point, you see.

But then after I became naval aide, I continued to work with Judge Rosenman. And then on January 1, 1946, Judge Rosenman left to return to the practice of law, and it was a great loss and created a very real vacuum. And I might say, privately, I did what I could to fill that vacuum, because I had gotten terribly intrigued with that particular job. There's where the real moving and shaking was going on in the White House.

Hess: One question on that: At the time that Judge Rosenman left, President Truman announced that he was not going to fill that spot.

Clifford: He did.

Hess: And then later, a few months later, you took over the spot. What events transpired to change the president's mind to show him that he had to have someone in this position?

Clifford: I can't ever be sure about all the reasoning that went on in the president's mind, but I can cast some light on it. As I suggested, Sam Rosenman's leaving created a very real vacuum. There was work that was not being done that had to be done. Somebody had to work on the speeches; somebody had to serve as liaison with certain cabinet members; somebody had to be in close touch with the Justice Department all the time. And gradually, in the two or three months that passed after his leaving, I began to work into this: (a) because nobody else was doing it; (b) because I wanted to do it; and (c) because by that time I had developed a relationship with President Truman where we understood each other and were getting along well.

Along toward the spring — maybe it was March or April — came the railroad strike, which was maybe the first real crunch that President Truman had to face up to, or certainly one of the early ones. President Truman wanted a speech written for it, and he handed me some notes that he had and we discussed it. Then he said to me, "Now, I want you to take my ideas here that I have put down in longhand, and I want you to write a speech. And I have decided to go up to a joint session and address them on the question of this railroad strike, because it has become a national calamity."

I went to work and wrote early drafts of that speech, and that's really all that you do as a speechwriter. You don't write the president's speeches. You just take his ideas, you try to put them in written form, and then you resubmit them. You and he then work on the speech together. That's the way we did it. The speech was a very tough speech. I think in the president's mind it helped break the strike. You will recall that very dramatic time that he was delivering the speech; the strike was broken. And he thought the speech really came off quite successfully. And I think that was one of the factors that led him to decide, in May, that he needed a special counsel — i.e., to fill the void that Rosenman's departure had left. Since he and I had worked together well, and I had done quite a lot of writing for him, I was appointed special counsel. So, at the end of May, I got out of the navy and became a civilian and became a special counsel to the president on June 1, 1946.

Then, I had been busy before, but then I really got busy on all of the activities that the special counsel performs: speechwriting, messages to Congress, and veto messages. There was a lot of writing connected with the job. At the same time, the operation was still so new you could move into areas of your greatest interest. And I believe my greatest interest, even at the early stage, was in the field of national security and foreign policy.

And so, I began to develop a very close relationship with Forrestal, who was at Navy, with Judge [Robert Porter] Patterson, who was then secretary of war, as it was called then. I think maybe Dean Acheson was at State at the time in the undersecretaryship, or assistant secretaryship of state. And I know later on I developed a very close relationship with Bob [Robert A.] Lovett, who was [George C.] Marshall's undersecretary of state. And gradually there began to develop contact between me and State and War and Navy, and we began working informally with the president's knowledge and consent. That role was something of the forerunner of a national security assistant that was later institutionalized under President [John F.] Kennedy in the person of McGeorge Bundy, and then later under President [Lyndon B.] Johnson in the person of Walt Rostow, and under President [Richard M.] Nixon in the person of Henry Kissinger, although it was not nearly so big a job. But I think it was possibly the genesis. Somebody is needed on the White House staff who serves as liaison with those departments. It was the area of my main interest, and I think grew up gradually and naturally. So, I was giving quite a lot of time to those subjects at that time.

And possibly, to some extent, that accounts for the assignment which

President Truman gave to me in the spring of '46, to prepare that interesting memorandum which you and I discussed earlier, that had the title "The Relationship between the United States and the Soviet Union."

Hess: This is the memo that appears as Appendix A for Arthur Krock's memoirs, *American Relations with the Soviet Union.*

Clifford: That's it. That's it. That's the memorandum that was prepared for the president in the summer of 1946 and submitted to him, my recollection is, on September 24, 1946, together with the letter of transmission which describes my compliance with a directive from President Truman earlier that year to prepare such a memorandum.

Hess: How do you go about preparing a memorandum like this? Just how does something as vital and as important as this get written?

Clifford: In the particular instance, I had been instructed by President Truman to start in and get the thinking of his senior advisers in government: the secretary of state, secretary of war, navy and the Joint Chiefs, the attorney generals, CIA, and so forth. So, during that summer and on into the fall, I made it my business to have lengthy meetings with each of these men. I have lists of questions which I had prepared for them. I would ask for memoranda on certain subjects as source material. And when you are acting on behalf of the president, there aren't any closed doors; they all open. And I had a memo or letter of some kind from the president that I could use in talking with them and quoting from it so they would understand that it was his idea and not mine. As a result, I received complete cooperation from them, and a great volume of material came in. And then I went to work to distill it and prepare the essence of it. A president doesn't have time to read the mountains of material that are sent. What you do is distill it and put it in as readable a form as possible. Now, I do submit that in the process, I became very interested in it, I became engrossed in it, and the memorandum that was submitted, in addition to carrying the views of these people, certainly carried my own, because you can't remain completely objective about the subject.

Hess: And above the fray.

Clifford: You end up down in it. As I recall it, I think the chapter that I worked the most on, and had the greatest interest in, was the last chapter, which contained the conclusions and recommendations to the president. The duties went on substantially as they had been under Judge Rosenman, with the additional factor of my interest in foreign policy and the national security.

Hess: Which department, and which secretaries, were the most helpful when you were working on this? What I am really fishing for was just how helpful was Secretary Forrestal?

Clifford: It would be difficult for me to say; it's too long ago. It's now twenty-five years ago, do you see, since I did that, and I cannot remember the details of it. I know my relationship with Mr. Forrestal developed and was probably the closest relationship I had in government. But I doubt it came quite that early.

I spent a great deal of time in '46 and '47 on the assignment from President Truman to begin the study of the unification of the services. And I spent quite a lot of time working on the legislation itself. The reason that whole story is so fascinating is that as secretary of the navy, Mr. Forrestal opposed violently the whole concept of unification, and so succeeded in watering down the legislation that when we got the bill in 1947, it really was not a very good bill.

Hess: It had to be changed two years later.

Clifford: Right. President Truman, with his rare prescience and perspicacity, appointed Forrestal as the first secretary of defense.

Hess: Why?

Clifford: I believe he felt he had a lot of ability. He had good experience. People had forgotten Secretary Forrestal started in the White House as an assistant to President Franklin Roosevelt, and he had bypassed the office of assistant secretary of the navy and became secretary. He was intelligent, he was industrious, he was knowledgeable and head of the navy, which was the major service to oppose unification. And I believe the president thought the way to get this job done is to put Forrestal in, because if anybody else takes that job, Forrestal is going to sit back and carve him to ribbons. And it was part of that curious erudition that President Truman had, because it worked exactly that way.

And he hadn't been in that job more than a few months, until I remember him phoning — some things stand out in your mind. He said he wanted to talk with me, and he came over and said, "This job cannot be done under the present law. I've changed a lot of my views, and if this job is to be done, we've got to have a stronger law."

And I said, "I'd like for you to set up an appointment, and I'd like you to come along with me, and I want to go and talk about this with President Truman."

And within two or three days thereafter, as I recall it, an appointment was made, and he and I went in together and in effect he did something that's rarely happened. He said, "Mr. President, I've come in" — and these are my words — "Mr. President, I've come in to tell you I was wrong, and now I want to work with you. I believe the concept of unification is sound. I believe it can be perfected without interfering with the assignments and roles of the various military services. I can understand how, if the secretary of defense is given the power, he can do it."

The first act was so watered down that all we created was the defense establishment. All the secretary was really, was a coordinator. Now, it took two years to get the act of '49, which actually created a Department of Defense and gave the secretary of defense responsibility, authority, and control over the services, and that was a great accomplishment, and from then on, why, the Department of Defense began to be effective as a unit.

But that whole story is most interesting and is illustrative of the attitude that President Truman would take from time to time in just getting right to the heart of a problem; knowing that the unification of the services couldn't succeed with continuing naval opposition, he appoints the major opponent to the idea and says, "Okay, now I expect you to do the job."

Hess: Mr. Clifford, you have mentioned that two of your first duties in the White House dealt with universal military training and unification of the armed forces. Would you like to begin today's session by covering what you recall on those two subjects?

Clifford: Yes, sir. The first assignment, which came during the summer or fall of 1945, was to conduct an inquiry into the background of the whole subject of universal military training. President Truman had the feeling at the time that it would be of tremendous aid to this country in facing any other danger, and possible war, to have a backlog of trained men. We had gone through a very difficult time in World War II, training an army quickly after we became involved following Pearl Harbor in 1941.

I recall President Truman stating that we were slow in getting a military force into action because of our lack of trained men. I also recall him commenting on the fact that it was a national scandal, that so many of our young men were unable to pass the minimum army test from the physical standpoint. I do not recall the percentage, but it was inordinately high; something close perhaps to a third of our young men had physical defects of one kind or another. President Truman thought it would be of great benefit to the country to have our young men appear at a certain age and at a certain point in their educational process, go through a rigid physical, and take the rudimentary and elementary basics of military training. Then, after a period of time, they could leave and go back into civilian life. When the call ever came, these men would constitute a solid core around which a military organization could be built and built expeditiously.

I checked into the whole background of it. I found that at one time former senator [James Wolcott] Wadsworth had researched the subject and believed deeply in it. As we got into it more deeply and we checked with leaders in a number of different areas in the country, I believe we all concluded, at that time, that it would be impossible to get the necessary legislation through the Congress. There was such a reaction after the Second World War; people wanted to forget the war and hoped that this time that this was the last war. So many of our leaders and formulators of public opinion were opposed to it that President Truman reluctantly dropped the idea.

I turn now to the second of the early assignments; that is, a study of the possible unification of the services. President Truman stated, at the conclusion of World War II, that we could never fight another war with the organization that we had in World War II. He indicated one time that we had won the war, but it certainly was not *because* of the organization we had; it was *despite* the organization. There was a definite lack of coordination in our entire military effort. At that time we had but two departments; we had the War Department and the Department of the Navy. Each was represented by a cabinet officer; each considered itself an independent executive department that was not subject to any type of control, except that that came from the president.

There were many instances that — we learned during the war — independence of action on the part of the services was costly to the country, both in manpower and in resources. The president thought that there should be a closer cooperation between the services. He felt that there should be an opportunity to effect substantial economies by having a central type of purchasing. We had learned many times during the war that the two services would bid against each other in a number of areas for rare commodities, and so push up the price for both of them.

Well, I started and conducted a study for him of the background of it. It was something that he felt very deeply, because, as chairman of the war-investigating committee, he had a substantial and rich background of experience.

As a result of that study, which I started at his direction in 1945, I interviewed a number of top military men and a number of our top civilians who had been involved in it. By 1946 we were making progress. I kept him fully and closely posted with reference to it. And finally, we turned our attention to the possibility of legislation. Legislation was introduced, and finally, the first law was passed in 1947. I might say at the particular point that the army favored unification, including the air wing of the army, who favored it because they felt that they could get separate identity and a separate air force. It was the navy who opposed the idea so strenuously.

Hess: What was the basis for their reluctance?

Clifford: The navy felt that its independence, and its power to control its own operation, would be adversely affected if it became but a division in the Department of Defense. Also, the navy had traditionally had great strength in the Congress.

At that time, and for a long time prior thereto, the chairman of the House Naval Affairs Committee, Mr. Vinson, had been a great power in maintaining the independence of the navy. The navy felt that to become but a part of a Department of Defense would subordinate the navy's importance and take away some of the power that the navy had exercised from time immemorial to make its own decisions. It didn't *want* to be a part of a military service along with the army and the air force. It particularly opposed the concept of the air force, because that meant that there would then be three services instead of two, and they felt that that would have a tendency to minimize the importance of the services.

Hess: Did they think they might lose their air wing to the new air force also?

Clifford: Yes, they were concerned about that. They were also concerned about the discussion at the time that if you unified the services, there would no longer be any need for a marine force. The marines could become part of the army, which might have some logical basis, because they were ground troops.

Another *major* objection that the navy had was that unification would mean that the navy would no longer have a cabinet representative in the president's cabinet. As it was, with a strong secretary of the navy, they had immediate and continuing access to the president. They could see that with unification, the navy would not have cabinet representation and feared that the navy could very well be downgraded. So, under the then–secretary of the navy, James Forrestal, they fought a bitter, intelligent, artful, and skillful battle, and they won. The first unification act was so watered down that the secretary of defense became really nothing more than a coordinator. That isn't good enough in government. A service, or a department, or an agency, will assert all of its historic and statutory powers under coordination, so that the coordinator does not have sufficient authority to either rule or direct the service.

After the '47 act was passed — and we took it because it was the best that we could get — President Truman, with that rare judgment that he had, appointed James Forrestal as the secretary of defense, and the result was most interesting.

After some number of months, I recall James Forrestal phoning me and saying he wanted to talk about a matter. We both sat down and discussed this subject at great length. The conclusion that Forrestal had reached was that the Defense Act of 1947 was so weak that he was unable to administer the Department of Defense. He was perfectly forthright about it.

I recall later on that after we discussed it at some length, he said he wanted to see the president and suggested that I go in with him. We went in then, and as I've said a number of times, an incident occurred then that rarely occurs. In substance, Mr. Forrestal said, "President Truman, I have come over to confess to you that I've been terribly wrong." And then he explained why. It was *very* gratifying to President Truman, and I had a notion that perhaps President Truman foresaw what might very well happen to Mr. Forrestal's attitude.

After Jim Forrestal stated that we needed a stronger law, we went to work at once lining up support for it, and that time we had army support, air force support, and naval support. Mr. Forrestal just stepped up with complete candor and said, "We have to have a stronger law." Also, I believe that from the experience of '47, those objectors who were so bitterly opposed had tempered their criticism somewhat, because the navy organization had not been affected as adversely as they had assumed that it would.

So, with that support, we then obtained a new law in 1949. And in it, we finally achieved what we had started to work on in 1945, because the '49 law gave to the secretary of defense the power, authority, responsibility, and control that he needed. And the Defense Department was strengthened to the point where it became a true executive department, with all of the rights and privileges inherent in a department. The three services *gave up* those rights that accrued under the law, to a separate department of government. From that time on, it seems to me that we began to realize the benefits that Mr. Truman foresaw in true unification.

Hess: Now, moving on to a very interesting subject, and that is the subject of the memo of November the nineteenth, 1947. And [Cabell] Phillips says on page 197 [of *The Truman Presidency: The History of a Triumphant Succession*]:

> Late in November of 1947, Clifford put in the President's hands a 40-page analysis of the status of Truman and the Democratic Party that should rank as one of the great dissertations on the art of politics. It did not promise Mr. Truman he could win. What it did was to cut down to size some of the mountainous Imponderables of his situation and to suggest that he did not have to lose.

Mr. Phillips had the wrong number of pages, it's a forty-three page instead of a forty-page memo, but this is the memo that you submitted. What do you recall about the writing of his memo? And just what do you recall about the memo?

Clifford: I spent the summer of 1946 in writing the memorandum on the Soviet Union. Even though President Truman was startled and shocked by the conclusions that that memorandum reached, I knew it had had a very real impact on him. Witness all that took place in 1947, starting with the Truman Doctrine, leading on to the Marshall Plan and the North Atlantic Treaty Organization and so forth. These are developments which, to some extent, could be traced back to that analysis of the thinking of our senior officials as presented in the memorandum of September 1946.

So, as we approached the election of 1948, I had the feeling that maybe a similar type of memorandum would be useful to the president. Now, I did not have much of a political background. I had been interested in politics, but not involved in it. And in the White House, the time I came in in the spring of '45, I was not very much involved in politics. I was involved in government, but there's a great distinction between government and politics.

In the summer of 1947 I began to have the opportunity, or I made the opportunity, of talking to persons who had substantial political backgrounds. I'd question them, and I'd get their opinions. I believe that I could see it more clearly now than I could then.

I think that what I was engaged in was an experiment to ascertain if one, by the application of pure reason, could not reduce political imponderables to understandable equations. I found it a very interesting endeavor. I might say in this regard that I had to see a good many people and reach conclusions based upon, in many instances, the opinions of others. Then I would assemble it, digest it, and present it as I thought it should be digested, which after all is one of the major functions that a lawyer performs.

A lawyer is trained — hopefully — first to go out and get the facts, then to assemble them in an orderly manner, then to analyze them, to reach conclusions with reference to facts, and then to present his case in the most effective, attractive, and persuasive manner. And that's about the process that I went through in preparing this memorandum.

Hess: One further thing on that. Patrick Anderson in his book *The President's Men* says on page 119:

> Drawing upon talks with and memos from former FDR aide James Rowe and other liberal friends and political leaders —

Did Mr. Rowe assist in the preparation of the memo?

Clifford: Yes, I drew a good deal on Jim Rowe, for his interest was politics; he had been in the Roosevelt administration and had an excellent political background. I told Jim Rowe, as I told some others, what I was in the process of doing. And so I got as much help from others as I could get.

Hess: All right, on page 3 of the memo is something that we have already mentioned in one of our previous interviews, but you mentioned that

> It is inconceivable that any policy initiated by the Truman Administration no matter how "liberal" could so alienate the South in the next year that it would revolt. As always, the South can be considered safely Democratic. And in formulating national policy, it can be safely ignored.

We have more or less covered this already.

Clifford: That's right, and as I said before, that obviously constituted the one major gaffe in the memorandum.

There is a basis for believing that. The South, historically, had gone Democratic in election, after election, after election. It had gone Democratic four straight times for Roosevelt, and it seemed a safe proposition at that time, but times were changing and changing more rapidly than I was able to foresee.

Hess: And then on page 8, my eye landed on something I thought was interesting. It says, "It is dangerous to assume that labor now had nowhere else to go in 1948. Labor can stay home." Why was one considered safe and the other not? If one could stay home, the other could, too.

Clifford: Just the expression of my personal opinion at the time.

I thought that the South would go along as it had in the past, and I won't go into all those reasons, but there were a number of historic reasons why they should go.

Labor at the time inclined toward the Democratic Party and President Truman, but you will recall we had had some very fierce battles with labor. We had had a battle with the railroad brotherhoods, and we had had a vicious struggle with the United Mine Workers. What I was saying in this portion was that although labor would be inclined to vote for the Democratic Party, and I did not think under any circumstances they could be for the Republican nominee, yet that was not good enough. What we needed was an active, militant support of labor if we were going to have any chance to win.

Hess: I don't know if I can find it in here, but I believe that you did — here it is on page 2 — you said, "Governor Dewey will be the nominee of the Republican Party." So, you did pick Governor Dewey. And on page 4 you say, "Henry Wallace will be the candidate of a third party."

Clifford: That was a long-shot prediction . . .

Hess: That's right. All right, and then on page 29 you say:

So, a President who is also a candidate must resort to subterfuge — for he cannot sit silent. He must be in the limelight. He must do the kind of thing suggested above to stay in the limelight and he must also resort to the kind of trip which Roosevelt made famous in the 1940 campaign — the "inspection tour." No matter how much the opposition and the press pointed out the political overtones of those trips, the people paid little attention because what they saw was the head of state performing his duties.

This gives rise to the so-called nonpolitical trip the following June, that right?

Clifford: I would say so. The use of the words there, obviously could be improved upon as you look at it twenty-five years later, but the thought is there. Under our system, a president must be a political animal. As we neared the time when the electorate was to make its decision, I was searching for means by which, in an appropriate manner, the president could appear before the people. So that *subterfuge*, possibly, might be too strong a word, but after all this was just a private memo between President Truman and me.

And it was conveying the thought, and was not to be circularized or released to the public. I don't know when it finally did come out. I don't know, but by that time it was all over with. It was a great many years before it ever came out.

Hess: What is your opinion of its value towards President Truman's eventual victory that following year?

Clifford: Oh, I think the president read it with interest, and I think it had some value. I might say that I think the president would accept those parts of it which were consistent with his own views.

I believe the president had no *real* regard, or respect, for my political views. I had no particular political background. He'd been through the mill for twenty-five or thirty, forty years by that time. I had never. I think he must have found it interesting, but he made his own political decisions. He certainly didn't depend on me to make political decisions.

Hess: Was he his own principal adviser?

Clifford: I would say so, yes. I would think again that he might look upon this as I did — as an interesting experiment in the exercise of pure reason. And from that standpoint, it may have had some value to it.

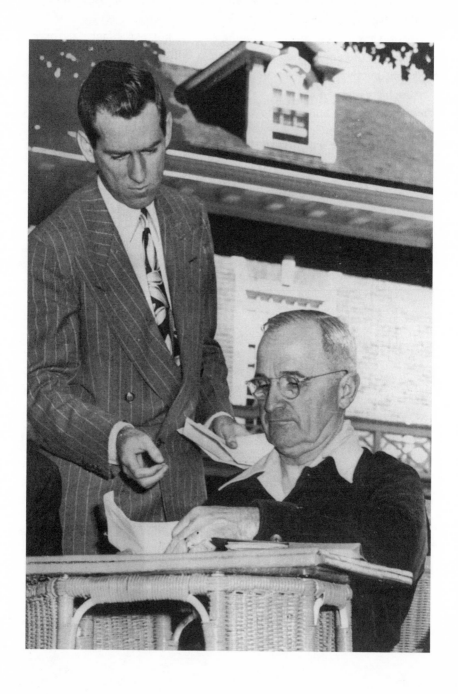

9

Matthew J. Connelly

New York, New York   November 30, 1967, and August 21, 1968

Interviewed by Jerry N. Hess

Matthew J. Connelly (1907–1976), appointments secretary from 1945 through
1953, was Truman's gatekeeper. A janitor's son from Massachusetts, he gradu-
ated from Fordham College in 1930 and moved to Washington, D.C., in 1935 as an
investigator for the Works Progress Administration. The tall, dark-haired Irish
American first worked for Truman as the chief investigator for the Senate Special
Committee to Investigate the National Defense. In December 1955, a federal
grand jury indicted him on a charge of conspiracy to defraud the government. It
was a political prosecution. The cartoonist Herblock portrayed him as the victim
of a miscarriage of justice. But he was later convicted and served six months of
a two-year sentence. Truman fought for his vindication. On November 22, 1962,
President John F. Kennedy granted Connelly a full and unconditional pardon.
"Matthew Connelly is in a class by himself," Truman said. "There never was a
better man in his position."

Hess: How were relations between the members of the White House staff?
     Were there any conflicts that aren't generally known?
Connelly: No, because if any conflicts developed, the president would take
     care of them automatically. He wanted no part of that. He wanted a family.
Hess: On the subject of the president's staff meetings, or the staff meetings
     of the White House staff, how did the president run those meetings?
Connelly: He had a staff meeting every morning. Originally he had them at
     nine and then later he put them off until ten, but at the staff meetings the
     same personnel were there at each meeting.
Hess: Who attended?
Connelly: They were attended by the three secretaries: [Charlie] Ross, [Wil-
     liam D.] Hassett, and myself. They were attended by [John] Steelman, and
     it varied in administrative assistants depending on what subject was com-
     ing up; sometimes there'd be three there or sometimes five, and also

included, of course, was the counsel, but the regular members were the secretaries, counsel, military aide, naval aide, air force aide, and then additional administrative assistants. Sometimes the pattern would vary.

You probably want to know how they were conducted. It was done the same way every morning. Each member of the staff had a location around the desk. It started first with Bill Hassett, who was on Truman's left hand; then it would go around in a semicircle. He would go around, Hassett first; then it would be [Clark] Clifford or [Charles] Murphy, counsel; then it would be one of the administrative assistants; then Dr. Steelman, and then the other administrative assistants would sit on the side. It was done that way, and each one would bring up the problems of his own department, and if there were any discussions, it was discussed openly with the whole group. If there were any differences of opinion, we would bring it up then and settle it. The president made that clear. That's the way he operated.

Hess: Did the president usually like to have a solution presented at the same time that a problem was brought up?

Connelly: You would make recommendations, but he would decide pro or con.

Hess: Was there a time in 1946 when it was thought that perhaps staff meetings ought to be discontinued because of the "kitchen cabinet" objections that were being raised in the press? Do you recall anything about that?

Connelly: I don't recall. It may have happened because the press always has to have something to shoot at.

Hess: In the New York Times I found indications that that may have been discussed.

Connelly: It may have been discussed, but if it was discussed, it was of short tenure. But it wasn't discussed by the president or members of the staff.

Hess: Did you attend the president's pre-press conferences that were held on Thursday before the press conferences?

Connelly: Oh, yes.

Hess: How were those conducted?

Connelly: Charlie Ross or Joe Short, whoever happened to be press secretary at the time, would come in with a list of suggested questions that might be asked at the conference, and then we would hash out what reply should be made to it, and the president would make the final decision on what the answer to that particular question, if it came up, would be.

Hess: Who else would attend those meetings?

Connelly: Well, there would be the press secretary, Steelman, Clifford, my-self, and, I think, maybe once in a while if some particular problem might be coming up, one of the administrative assistants or two, and the naval aide and the military aide and the air force aide.

Hess: The press conferences were held in Mr. Truman's office until April 27, 1950, when they were moved from the president's office over to the Indian Treaty Room.

Connelly: That's correct. In the old State Department Building. It was right across the street.

Hess: Did you stay in Mr. Truman's office when the press would come in when it was held in his Oval Room [Oval Office in the West Wing, built 1909 and rebuilt 1934]?

Connelly: Oh, yes. All the key members of the staff would be there.

Hess: A little while ago we were discussing Mr. Truman's speaking style. How did he develop his extemporaneous speaking style? Some people say that it showed great improvement during the trip that was taken in June of 1948. Would you agree with that?

Connelly: I would say definitely. He was not a natural public speaker and did not like to make speeches. As a matter of fact, I believe that in the Senate, I doubt if he made more than a half a dozen speeches all the time that he was in the Senate. He was not known as a speaker, and, as a matter fact, in my first association with him he was pretty terrible. He was much more effective when he could talk off-the-cuff, in other words, extempo-raneously, but reading from a prepared text, where if he went off-the-cuff and he was sure of his grounds, he could be very effective and also very dramatic.

Hess: Why did the president decide to take that trip in June of 1948?

Connelly: That so-called nonpolitical trip?

Hess: That so-called nonpolitical trip.

Connelly: That was a good name for it, but actually, he had to get well known around the country, and that was a prelude to the campaign.

Hess: Whose idea was it to take that trip?

Connelly: I believe the idea originally came from the National Committee. This I'm not sure of because it was sort of thrown together in those days and everybody had a hand in it.

Hess: Did you go along on that trip?

Connelly: Oh, yes.

Hess: What do you recall about the trip?

Connelly: What I recall mostly is it was a backbreaker. He made so many stops, he covered so much territory, and, as you know, he is an early riser, and he would be up at five o'clock in the morning. If we were at a station somewhere, he would be out on the back platform talking to the railroad workers. He had the advantage of getting to bed early, whereas I would have a little problem of arranging the next day's events. I would be up until two or three in the morning.

Hess: What were your duties on that trip?

Connelly: Coordinating with the advance people on the trip mostly or greeting people that came in, and we shook hands.

Hess: Who were the advance people on the trip?

Connelly: On that early one I'm not sure. I think Oscar Chapman did some advance. He had contacts through the National Committee on who we should expect to see in different states — the National Committee did a lot of it. I believe Don Dawson did some advance work on that trip.

Hess: How does an advance man go about his business? What are the tasks?

Connelly: Well, he goes into a town ahead of the president and sets up the arrangements — where the meeting will be held, how it will be held, who will be there, who will introduce the president, who will be the people on the platform with the president, where the location will be, what time it will be, what broadcast facilities there will be — and coordinates all the activities in advance of the president coming into town. The Secret Service would also have to go ahead and make the security arrangements.

Hess: In Omaha that year they had a rather sparse crowd show up at the meeting. What went wrong that time?

Connelly: Well, the thing that was very bad — we left that pretty much in the hands of Ed McKim, who had just retired to Omaha to the insurance business, but without knowledge or without experience — the thing turned out to be pretty much of a fiasco. We had the biggest hall in town, and it was almost a death knell for the campaign, but fortunately we were able to pull out of it. It was so widely publicized that it was a flop and that there was no public interest, and following on what was happening before the convention, it indicated that the president was not getting anywhere, and the people wanted no part of it, and they wouldn't even turn out to see him. So, that was a great handicap, but that was because of local arrangements.

Hess: When the president passed through Carey, Idaho, and dedicated the airfield to the wrong person, do you recall anything in particular about that?

Connelly: Yes, somebody gave Charlie Ross the wrong information on the thing. The president left the hotel, and we followed him out. I knew where we were supposed to go, but by that time the cavalcade had stopped and the president was greeting, I believe, a private flier or some woman — I don't know. I didn't participate in it because it was just for a few minutes and then it was time to pick up again. I didn't even know that happened until we got to the next stop. It was wrong information given to Charlie Ross.

Hess: Who wrote the speeches on that trip?

Connelly: That was organized by, I believe, Clifford, who was then counsel. I know he was. And Clark had a group picked from the staff — some of the boys we have mentioned earlier, I believe — as speechwriters — David Lloyd, Charlie Murphy. Some of these speeches referred to one phase of an operation — say it was foreign affairs. We would get suggestions from the State Department, which would be forwarded to Clifford or Murphy, who would incorporate the ideas in the speech in the president's own way.

Hess: I believe at a luncheon that was held in Berkeley, the president was introduced by Dr. [Robert G.] Sproul, who was in charge of the University of California. Were you there at that time?

Connelly: Yes, I was.

Hess: As I recall, the introduction that he obtained from Dr. Sproul was none too complimentary. Is that right?

Connelly: That's correct. That was arranged by Ed Pauley, who was on the Board of Regents of the University of California, so that's how that appearance came about.

Hess: Continuing on with information relative to the very eventful year of 1948, what can you tell me about the background and the operations of the Democratic Policy Committee in 1948?

Connelly: Do you recall who was on that so-called Policy Committee?

Hess: I believe Oscar Ewing was on that.

Connelly: I recall the group: Oscar Ewing, Leon Keyserling, and I forget — I think I went to two of their meetings.

Hess: Where were they held?

Connelly: In a suite at the Carlton Hotel. As a matter of fact, they were just thinking and accomplishing nothing, so I didn't return to the third meeting. I would much rather get the opinions of the state chairman or a local committeeman than I would the boys around Washington who were dreaming up policy.

Hess: On February the second of that year was when Mr. Truman sent his ten-points message to Congress on civil rights.

Connelly: Well, that was part of his inauguration speech. That was incorporated in the message to Congress. That was largely drafted by Clark Clifford and the boys in his group.

Hess: And in the October previous to that, the president's Committee on Civil Rights came out with their report "To Secure These Rights," and then the rather strong ten-points message. Did the people in the White House think such a strong stand on civil rights might offend the Southern states and cause a bolt of the Southern states, as actually happened during the convention?

Connelly: Oh, sure, that was a calculated risk. But the major point of the thing was he had to make that statement in the interest of civil rights — that these people should be entitled to franchise which they were being denied, particularly in the South. That was a calculated risk.

Hess: Do you recall the president making any comments along these lines?

Connelly: Oh, he was for the program as he outlined it, and he knew that he would get — having been partially Southern himself — he knew what the reaction would be in the South. It wasn't any secret to him that it came about.

Hess: Well, during the convention itself there were two civil rights planks that came into being. One was the so-called regular civil rights plank, and then the second one was the Humphrey-Biemiller plank that was finally passed and put into the platform.

Connelly: That's correct, and that's what caused the setting up of the Dixiecrat movement.

Hess: Which of those planks did the president support? Didn't he support the regular plank?

Connelly: Initially, because, I believe, the Humphrey proposals didn't come up until it was brought up on the floor of the convention, but after it was resolved by the platform committee, he stuck with the platform.

Hess: Looking back on those days of the Philadelphia convention in 1948, what are your memories. What do you recall? Just start at the beginning.

Connelly: Well, in 1948 I remained, naturally, in Washington, and some of the cabinet officers, some of the people from the administration, were in Philadelphia. John Snyder, I know, was in Philadelphia, and we had the train ready to go, and John Snyder was to contact me when he thought it was a propitious moment for the president to go to Philadelphia. We didn't want to go up there before something was pretty much wrapped up, so I blocked out appointments the afternoon of the last day of the convention.

The president and I watched the "ball game" on television in his office, and we watched the little moves the different people on the platform were making and what you could read behind the scenes that the average fellow wouldn't ordinarily watch. That gave us a little guidance of what was going on up there. We finally got a call from Snyder and set out for Philadelphia, and when we arrived there, the plans had been changed. They were not ready for us. So, Barkley and the president and myself, and I think there were one or two others, sat on the balcony outside to try to get some air. He didn't get on that night — I believe it was pretty near three o'clock in the morning. We did a little staging and brought him in as his introduction was being started, so when he came in, we held him in the wings until his introduction was over. So, of course, there were very mixed emotions in that auditorium, but shortly after he got into his speech, you could see things beginning to change. It was a very forceful speech, and he worked from an outline, not a prepared text, and he really punched those points. He had things pretty well swayed by the time he left there, and he got an ovation, so a couple of seasoned reporters — I remember one very well, Earl Godwin of Washington — came up to me and said, "I never heard a better political speech. This should do it."

And one of the other boys who was there — I forget which one now — came up with similar comments about the speech. But, unfortunately, we were off the air so that three-quarters of the country couldn't hear it anyway, so that part was missed because of the manipulations in the convention, which went awry, but if we had gone on earlier as we planned it, we would have had nationwide coverage, which he never did get, so it was largely lost. But the thing that came out most people remember is that he was going to call Congress back — they called it the "Turnip Congress." [Truman announced in his speech that he was calling Congress into special session on July 26, which the president noted is called "Turnip Day" in Missouri because farmers plant turnips then.]

Hess: Whose idea was that to call the Eightieth Congress back into special session?

Connelly: His own.

Hess: Mr. Truman's own idea?

Connelly: That's right.

Hess: Could you tell me about the developments behind that idea?

Connelly: The details I can't remember now because it's been so long ago. I know it was his own idea; in fact, he was the one that brought up the name "Turnip Congress."

Hess: How important was that, do you believe, to his eventual success in November?

Connelly: It made some people pretty happy that he had the guts enough to do it. It made other people unhappy who had to go back to work, particularly the members of Congress. So, I'd say it was kind of a two-way story, but it accomplished nothing, and he knew it wouldn't; but he just wanted to make the record that he wanted the job to get done. So, that was the reason for that.

Hess: Did you feel before this time, before the convention, that there was a possibility that the party might not renominate Mr. Truman as its standard-bearer?

Connelly: Well, I know it was not only a possibility, but it was a threat. Some of the leading people in the party, as a matter of fact, sent him a telegram suggesting he withdraw, which came to me first and which I gave to him, naturally, signed by some people like James Roosevelt and Jake Arvey, who was the leader of Chicago; Bill O'Dwyer, who was then mayor of New York; Joseph Casey, who was a member of Congress; and there were others who were not enthusiastic about his chances of victory.

Hess: Did they mention in the telegram who they would like to have run?

Connelly: Yes, they suggested he step down and nominate Eisenhower, because they thought Eisenhower would be a winner and Truman wouldn't.

Hess: I believe the Americans for Democratic Action were even backing General Eisenhower.

Connelly: I believe they were, yes. All the so-called liberals were backing Eisenhower. Whatever liberals are — I don't know.

Hess: On the subject of the vice presidential nomination that year, who did Mr. Truman want to run with him on the ticket? Who was his first choice?

Connelly: First choice for vice president? I believe his first choice — I may be wrong on this — was Bill Douglas, but when Barkley started running himself with the aid of Les Biffle — he was his manager; we could see that on the television on the convention we were watching in the office — but as a result of that we decided Barkley would be the best.

Hess: How was Leslie Biffle managing Senator Barkley there that you could see on television?

Connelly: Buttoning and buttonholing the delegates on the stage. And then he pushed Barkley in front of the cameras. There was no question that Biffle wanted Barkley.

Hess: After Senator Barkley was notified that he might be nominated, he referred to himself as a "warmed-over biscuit."

Connelly: That's correct, because he knew he was not the first choice.

Hess: Why do you think he wanted the nomination?

Connelly: For president.

Hess: For president?

Connelly: Oh, yes, Barkley wanted to run for president.

Hess: He did not necessarily want to run for vice president?

Connelly: No, that was not his intent at all. He was running for president.

Hess: Did he think he could take the nomination away from Mr. Truman?

Connelly: Every politician thinks he can win. Mr. Truman at that time was at a pretty low ebb in popular opinion.

Hess: So, his goal wasn't vice president?

Connelly: Oh, definitely not, no. He was running for president. So was Claude Pepper.

Hess: Anyone else?

Connelly: I don't believe there were many at that convention who were not.

Hess: Well, moving through the convention and the nomination of Mr. Truman and Mr. Barkley, anything else come to your mind before we reach the days of the campaign?

Connelly: Well, between the convention and the start of the campaign, which officially began on Labor Day, I was not only kind of busy with my own job but working with members of the National Committee to get the show on the road, work on the itinerary, line up the people who we'd have to meet in different states — who were the important ones and who were not, and labor leaders and that kind of thing — all those things have to be done.

Hess: How is an itinerary worked out?

Connelly: It's worked out — now, we'll say, "Where is the key place to start?" Well, usually Democratic presidents start Labor Day in Detroit — that's the bid for the labor vote because the labor vote was usually Democratic so that was the big thing, the president's big labor event.

Hess: Cadillac Square, usually.

Connelly: Yes. From there it would go on usually out to the Northwest. Other times it would diverge. I would start through the Southwest and move up the West Coast and back east through the Northwest and then the midlands in Chicago, and make special dates for a state like Iowa — they have a big farm festival where they'd have about three hundred thousand people.

Hess: The National Plowing Contest.

Connelly: The National Plowing Contest. So, that was probably the biggest crowd we had in the campaign. I believe we must have had over three hundred thousand at that plowing contest. They came in from all over the Midwest. Planes — a lot of the farmers had their own planes — and, of course, it was pretty tough to figure out how these farmers could be so broke when they could own airplanes, but that's part of the game. But it depends on what were the key spots at the right time, if you can figure it out.

Hess: Do you recall the impression that the president may have made on those farmers in Iowa that year? Was it favorable?

Connelly: It was favorable because he was one of their own. And when they had that boner of the picture taken with Dewey and Warren standing up against the farm gate, which was upside down on the front cover of, I believe, *Newsweek*, they showed the gate upside down, and then every farmer would laugh, of course.

But Truman got to them because he was forthright and down to earth, and they understood his language. They liked the way he looked. "He looks like one of us." Dewey made a big mistake in this campaign.

Hess: What was that?

Connelly: Following Truman. He had practically the same itinerary. He came in a day after Truman or two days after Truman, and the contrast was still in the minds of the farmers particularly. They'd see this city slicker, and they'd still have the memory of how the president looked like them. That made a very definite impression.

Hess: Were there any other mistakes that the Republicans pulled that year?

Connelly: Well, Dewey pulled that famous one on the railroad engineer who backed the train up by mistake, and Dewey on the back platform over the microphone made a few unkind remarks about the engineer, and that took care of the railroad brotherhoods.

Hess: How much of a threat to Mr. Truman's victory did you think Henry Wallace and the Progressive Party would be in 1948?

Connelly: I knew it would hurt in New York particularly because there are so many left-wingers up there. The labor boys in New York — Dubinsky, and Alex Rose, and that crowd — they were all Wallace men because he was farther to the left than Truman, and they were for Wallace, naturally, and he did prevent Truman from carrying New York.

Hess: What could have been done to have prevented Wallace from cutting out such a big block of votes and keeping the state from going Democratic? If it went Republican just because of the Wallace block of votes, what could have been done to prevent that?

Connelly: Well, very little because after Wallace declared — because of the financing, because a lot of these people don't think beyond New York, and they thought they could put him over, and, of course, they had Communists in the act, and Paul Robeson, so that group you couldn't reach anyway. They probably would not have voted for Dewey. They would have voted for Truman because he was the only one left. They do it on that basis. But they still thought that Wallace was a Messiah, so what could be done about it, I don't know, except money. As a matter of fact, the last week in the campaign I arranged to pump some more money in there, but it didn't do any good. Because the contributions were very meager in that campaign. We'd go into a town like Chicago — we wouldn't know how to get the train out. We didn't have the money. We'd call Washington and talk to Louis Johnson, "Come on. Let's get going here." He'd get on the phone and try to talk up enough money to get the train moving. That's how tight it was.

Hess: Did that happen very often?

Connelly: All during the campaign. People didn't think that Truman was going to win, so why back a losing horse? So, that's what happened. That's why he didn't get any money. Nobody thought he was going to win. By nobody I mean the big contributors. And these dollar contributions in a political campaign don't mean a thing. You spend more money servicing those contributions than you do by collecting them because you have to pay for clerical help and acknowledgments, and what have you got left? So, we didn't do that.

Hess: There were times, too, when the money was running a little short when it came time to pay for airtime, is that correct?

Connelly: Oh, surely.

Hess: Radio more than television, at that time.

Connelly: Surely. I'll tell you a story about that. Now, at the start of the campaign our first appearance was to be in Detroit on Labor Day. There was a fellow named Levinson — I believe he was state treasurer or something with the Democratic Party up there — and he had promised to raise money to buy coast-to-coast radio time for that Cadillac Square appearance. So, about two nights before the convention, Roy Turner, who was then governor of Oklahoma, was in Washington at a little cocktail party for some of the people from the Democratic [National] Committee at the Statler Hotel. One of the girls from the committee came in with a telegram in which Mr. Levinson said he had not been able to raise the money and therefore could not arrange the broadcast time. She showed the thing to me, and I showed it to Roy Turner, and he said, "Well, that broadcast is going to be made. How much is it?" I believe we needed twenty-five thousand dollars. So, he takes his checkbook out, and he said, "That broadcast goes on." He handed the check to the girl from the National Committee. So, that's how that broadcast was made; otherwise it wouldn't have been.

That happened repeatedly during the campaign because all during that campaign we operated on a shoestring. But that's a typical example of what we were running into. The fund-raising was done by Louis Johnson at the National Committee, Colonel Louis Johnson — he later became secretary of defense.

Hess: Did he make an effective treasurer for the committee?

Connelly: Well, he was a driver. It required something like that to get the job done. We managed to squeak through it OK, and then the day after the election Johnson got offers of checks from other people he had written to during the campaign. But after Truman won, of course, many of the people who were out to lunch came in with checks. I remember one very particularly. A fellow named Louis Rosenstiel — who was the chairman of the board of Schenley Liquor — he had made a contribution of twenty-five thousand dollars to Dewey, and a day after the election he called Johnson, and Johnson called me. He said, "What do you think I should do? The election is over."

I said, "You have to pay your bills; take it. Just make a little notation."

Hess: Of when it came in?

Connelly: Keep it in mind that he came in the day after the election.

Hess: They had some difficulty getting a treasurer for that campaign, didn't they?

Connelly: Yes, they did, and nobody wanted it, so I sent for some of the leading fund-raising boys of the Democratic Party, and I set up a meeting at the White House with the president one afternoon. I brought William Pawley, who was then ambassador to Brazil; I brought back James Bruce, who was ambassador to the Argentine; Stanton Griffis, I believe, was ambassador to Spain; so we held a meeting, and William Pawley suggested that he would act as a chairman with this group and they would raise the money. I believe Mr. Pawley started reading the Gallup polls, and a few days later he announced he was leaving for Spain on business, and he was gone for four months, but I think he began to think that the chances for him raising the dough were a little slim and he didn't want any part of it. You don't run a national campaign without money, and especially since the advent of television.

Hess: I understand in the campaign that Secretary Krug was rather scarce. Is that right?

Connelly: Well, frankly, all the cabinet members were a little bit scarce. Of course, the secretary of state couldn't get involved, secretary of defense couldn't get involved, so the only two really fighting — or I'd say three fighting — cabinet members in the campaign were Maurice Tobin, who was secretary of labor; Charles Brannan, who was secretary of agriculture; and Oscar Chapman, secretary of the interior. But the rest of them were not very active.

Hess: What about John Snyder?

Connelly: John Snyder was never on the front lines. He was the "Colonel House," he thought, of the Truman administration, so he may have raised some money behind the scenes, but he never appeared out front.

Hess: How much of a threat did you believe that J. Strom Thurmond and his States' Rights Party was going to be?

Connelly: Well, I figured with a combination of Wallace and Thurmond in the act, it would cut pretty deeply into Mr. Truman's bid, but it was very doubtful to me after the civil rights position that the president took that we would carry a solid South. Those "rednecks" down there would never go for anything that even had the smell of civil rights. They'd rather stay home.

Hess: During the campaign did you have anything to do with the Research Division of the Democratic National Committee—William Batt Jr., Johannes Hoeber, Kenneth Birkhead, Frank Kelly?

Connelly: I had contact with all of them. When they formulated something, it was channeled through Bill Boyle or the chairman and then to me.

Hess: I understand that they were set up as an arm of the Democratic National Committee, but their main job was speechwriting for the campaign. Is that correct?

Connelly: That's correct. Not only for the president but for the speakers during the campaign throughout the country. All that speech material was cleared through Clark Clifford.

Hess: In *Out of the Jaws of Victory*, Jules Abels said in telling about the differences between the Dewey and Truman campaign trains, "There was a good deal of obtuseness in dealing with local politicians, who never got the red-carpet treatment from Dewey's aide, Paul Lockwood, that they got from Truman's aide, Matt Connelly."

Connelly: I believe that is correct. You see, I know Paul Lockwood. As a matter of fact, I think he was probably the most affable, friendly fellow that Dewey had around him, but Paul Lockwood never had any experience in national politics. Paul Lockwood was the assistant district attorney when Dewey was a crime buster in New York City, and then he became his secretary when he became governor, but Paul never had the front-line political experience. He was a very able fellow, but he didn't know the dirt farmers — let's put it that way — and they didn't know him. I had the advantage because these people would come to Washington to see the president. If they couldn't see him, they were in a spot when they went home. So, I would have the assignment of seeing national committeemen, state chairmen, sometimes a county chairman — if they were big enough — but make sure they saw somebody, so they could go back and when people said, "Well, did you see the president?" . . .

"No, but I had lunch with Matt Connelly," or dinner with Matt Connelly, or had cocktails with Matt Connelly, so they'd have something to take home with them. As a result, these fellows got to know me better, naturally, than they did the president, because I was the in-between guy.

Hess: Mr. Connelly, I'd like to go over a list of the men who served on the cabinet during the Truman administration and ask a few questions about each man. In most cases we might have specific questions that may apply only in that individual case, but a few general questions would be such items as why were those particular men chosen for the post; how effective were they in carrying out the responsibilities of their positions; what were their relationships with the president; and why were they replaced, if that was the case?

Our first one starting with the Department of State would be a hold-over that Mr. Truman had from the Roosevelt days: Edward Stettinius. What can you tell me about Mr. Stettinius?

Connelly: Mr. Stettinius was secretary of state under Roosevelt, and when Truman took over he had to work with the cabinet that was in office until he could evaluate the performance of each one. Mr. Stettinius did not remain very long after Mr. Truman took over. He resigned from the position of secretary of state to enjoy private business. Mr. Truman did not have complete confidence in Mr. Stettinius because his thinking and Mr. Stettinius's thinking were not in total agreement.

Hess: Could you give me an example of that?

Connelly: There were several matters of policy that Mr. Truman felt he could not go along with, which Mr. Stettinius advocated. In other words, Mr. Stettinius was brought up to represent the thinking of Mr. Roosevelt. Altogether, Mr. Truman did not agree, and as a result his departure was graceful, but not disagreeable to Mr. Truman.

Hess: The next man was James F. Byrnes.

Connelly: James F. Byrnes was sent for by Mr. Truman after he arrived at the White House. He had a great deal of confidence in Mr. Byrnes because of their association in the Senate. Mr. Byrnes came from South Carolina and talked to Mr. Truman and immediately decided that he would take over. Mr. Truman to Mr. Byrnes, I'm afraid, was a nonentity, as Mr. Byrnes thought he had superior intelligence. It later was proved that the opposite was true. So, Mr. Byrnes's appointment was based on the association that they had in the United States Senate, but after being sworn in as secretary of state several disagreements exerted themselves, and Mr. Truman eventually had to request the resignation of Mr. Byrnes over clashes in policy and thinking and in politics.

Hess: Some historians have said that Mr. Truman's appointment of Mr. Byrnes was in the nature of a consolation because Truman had received the 1944 nomination instead of Mr. Byrnes, and had it been the other way around, Byrnes would have been president at that time. What do you think about that?

Connelly: I don't believe that's true. Mr. Byrnes was placed in nomination, or suggested for nomination as vice president, by Mr. Truman. Mr. Byrnes had previously called Mr. Truman and suggested that he introduce him as a nominee for vice president under Roosevelt. Mr. Truman left for Chicago with the intention of nominating Mr. Byrnes. However, things as they developed at the convention ruled out Mr. Byrnes, and Mr. Truman received the nomination. Mr. Truman was completely loyal to Senator Byrnes because of their Senate association, but it was not very long before Mr. Byrnes thought that he had become president and Mr. Truman had not. Conflicts developed, and Mr. Byrnes was later asked to relieve himself of the position of secretary of state.

Hess: The next man is George C. Marshall.

Connelly: George C. Marshall was a great American, highly respected by Mr. Truman, looked upon by Mr. Truman as the chief of staff, and Mr. Truman regarded himself as a colonel. He had great reverence for the chief of staff, and he believed General Marshall could do no wrong. General Marshall was brought into the administration by Mr. Truman, and Mr. Marshall performed with intelligence and integrity and with good faith, all of which were appreciated by Mr. Truman. And George C. Marshall in Mr. Truman's eyes could never do anything wrong.

Hess: We have a couple of questions on the Marshall Plan, but we'll take those up a little later. The next secretary of state was Dean Acheson.

Connelly: Dean Acheson became secretary of state at the departure of General Marshall, who went back to the Defense Department as secretary of defense. Dean Acheson was highly regarded by Mr. Truman. He was an intellectual, he knew foreign policy, he knew the operation of the State Department, but in my own opinion, Dean Acheson, more or less because of his intellect, educational background, and his experience around Washington, impressed Mr. Truman to the end that anything that Mr. Acheson did, as far as Mr. Truman was concerned, was correct. I never quite held that opinion myself. In my book Mr. Acheson was above and beyond the normal realms of government operation. Mr. Acheson, in my vernacular, would be considered an egghead, not a practical administrator, and not a man who represented the opinion of America, or of the people of America. Mr. Acheson, for some reason, was more or less beholden to the operations of the British government. In my opinion, these things conflicted with the viewpoint of Mr. Truman, who was all American.

Hess: In your opinion, why would Mr. Acheson's views be so closely correlated with the British viewpoint?

Connelly: Over a period of many years, the State Department was patterned after the British government. They thought British, they acted British, and they were under a peculiar phobia that the British way was the right way, and the Americans patterned themselves after that.

Hess: Did Mr. Morgenthau wish to continue on as secretary of the treasury for Mr. Truman?

Connelly: After that disappointment of Mr. Morgenthau on his brainchild, he gradually lost interest. And Mr. Truman knowing about that background, and knowing about the discussions that I had with various members of the administration, declined to accept Mr. Morgenthau as a permanent member of his cabinet.

Hess: The next man was Fred Vinson. Why was he chosen to replace Mr. Morgenthau?

Connelly: Fred Vinson was a member of Congress for many years, he had known President Truman for many years, President Truman admired him greatly, and after President Truman found out that Mr. Morgenthau was not the man he wanted, he thought in his own mind that the man that he would put in that position would be a man he could trust and who would be for him; therefore, Mr. Truman offered the post of secretary of treasury to Mr. Vinson.

Hess: In your opinion, did he make an effective secretary of the treasury for the time that he was there?

Connelly: Mr. Vinson made a very effective secretary of the treasury. Mr. Vinson reported regularly to President Truman, explained things, worked things out with him, and as far as I know, they never left in any disagreement.

Hess: What is your opinion of Fred Vinson as a person?

Connelly: Fred Vinson as a person was one of the most decent human beings I've ever known. He was highly regarded by anybody who knew him. He was highly qualified, not only in the science of government, but as a legislator he had achieved a great reputation. Mr. Truman, naturally, having been in the Congress for many years, liked those things about Mr. Vinson. And after Mr. Vinson was appointed secretary of the treasury, he fulfilled his job so well that Mr. Truman had nothing but high regard for him and his performance.

Hess: When the post as chief justice became empty, were there others that were considered for that position besides Mr. Vinson?

Connelly: Mr. Truman made a personal decision on that. As far as I know, he did not discuss it with many people, if any, but due to Fred Vinson's performance, Mr. Truman respected his integrity, his honesty, and decided that Fred Vinson would make an ideal candidate for the Supreme Court of the United States.

Hess: Why was John Snyder chosen to succeed Mr. Vinson?

Connelly: John Snyder was chosen to succeed Mr. Vinson because for many years he had been a personal friend of Mr. Truman's. He was in the banking industry in Missouri, and Mr. Truman had high regard for his financial ability and integrity. And when Mr. Vinson was moved up to the Supreme Court, Mr. Snyder was Mr. Truman's first thought as his successor.

Hess: What was your opinion of Mr. Snyder's effectiveness as secretary of the treasury?

Connelly: Mr. Snyder made an effective secretary of the treasury. As far as I know — and that was not my bracket to evaluate him; he reported directly to the President, and not to me. I know nothing about his activities, except what the president told me he wanted me to do in connection with that department.

Hess: What was your opinion of him as a person?

Connelly: Mr. Snyder, in my book, was a very petty, small-minded, small-town banker, and I never thought he had the stature to carry this job of secretary of the treasury of the United States.

Hess: In your opinion, what was the general opinion of the other cabinet members concerning Mr. Snyder? Do you recall?

Connelly: I believe that Mr. Snyder was so self-involved and secretive, that none of the other members of the cabinet really got to know him.

Hess: All right, he served until the end of the administration. Our next category is secretary of war, and Mr. Henry L. Stimson was also a holdover from the Roosevelt administration.

Connelly: Mr. Stimson was what you might call an international statesman. Mr. Truman had high regard for him because he believed him to be a man of integrity, and his first interest was the United States. He respected his judgment, he respected his sense of fair play, and he had nothing but admiration for him.

Hess: He resigned in September of 1945. Did he wish to stay on or not?

Connelly: No, Mr. Stimson actually initiated the resignation himself.

Hess: He was replaced by Robert Patterson. Why was Mr. Patterson chosen for the position?

Connelly: Mr. Patterson was already in the Defense Department, and Mr. Truman thought that he was the logical successor, because he knew the operation of the Pentagon and the military establishment. He was an outstanding lawyer, and he had in the meantime developed the great respect of Mr. Truman during his performance as secretary of war.

Hess: The next category is secretary of defense. Of course, the first secretary of defense under the unification act was James Forrestal. Why was he chosen as the first secretary of defense?

Connelly: Forrestal was secretary of the navy prior to the merger of the branches of the army, navy, and air force. Mr. Forrestal had been in Washington under the Roosevelt administration, was a highly intellectual fellow, and was a good administrative officer. When the merger was completed to create the Defense Department, Mr. Truman looked on him as the superior of the other members of the military establishment and appointed him as secretary of defense, which office he held very successfully until an illness overtook him.

Hess: Do you recall any instances, any evidences on the job of the mental deterioration that overtook Mr. Forrestal, unfortunately?

Connelly: Yes, I recall Mr. Forrestal called me and told me that his telephones were being bugged, his house was being watched, and he would like me to do something about it. So, I had the chief of the Secret Service detail at the White House make an investigation of Mr. Forrestal's home. I had him observe it; I had him check his phones and found out that he was just misinformed, that he wasn't being watched, and there was no indication that there was any wiretapping in Mr. Forrestal's home. That really upset me, because I realized that the Secret Service would do a thorough job, and I told the president that I was worried that Mr. Forrestal might be a little bit wrong.

Hess: What did the president say at that time? Do you recall?

Connelly: He asked me what I thought, and I said, "I think Mr. Forrestal is cracking up."

So, he said, "Why don't we arrange to have him go down to Key West and take a little vacation?"

So, Mr. Forrestal did go to Key West. There was a repetition down there. Mr. Forrestal had hallucinations about things that were going wrong at

Key West, and he called me from Key West and told me that something was wrong down there. So, I checked very carefully with the navy, who supervises Key West, and Mr. Forrestal later was transferred from Key West to the naval hospital in Bethesda.

Hess: Do you recall what he thought was going wrong at Key West at this time?

Connelly: He thought that the same things were happening, that people were annoying him, and he felt he was under surveillance down there, he felt that he was being watched, and in other words, he was being personally persecuted. So, as a result of that, we had him very quietly removed to Bethesda Hospital in Washington. And history will disclose that is where he jumped out a window.

Hess: The next man to hold that position was Louis Johnson. Why was he chosen for that position?

Connelly: Louis Johnson was chosen for two reasons. Number one, Louis Johnson had been commander of the American Legion. He was a perennial candidate for president. He was a very effective political organizer, and during the campaign of 1948 when things were not very good for Mr. Truman, Louis Johnson accepted the position as treasurer of the Democratic National Committee. He gave up his law practice. He devoted all of his time to raising money for the campaign in '48. He was a highly successful lawyer in Washington, and Mr. Truman turned to him after the death of Mr. Forrestal to take over the Pentagon operation.

Hess: During this time, two important events took place, the cutting back of the armed forces and the invasion of Korea. Some people had blamed Louis Johnson for the reduction in the armed forces. Is that valid?

Connelly: That is valid. He had promised that he would cut to the bone the expenditures of the Defense Department and set out to do so, with the result that when the Korean War developed, we found ourselves very unable to meet our commitments for our appearance in Korea.

Hess: Was this done strictly for reasons of economy? Wasn't it seen that this was a dangerous thing to do in the world situation at that time, or not?

Connelly: Well, World War II was over, and Mr. Johnson thought that the appropriation for the Defense Department could be cut to reduce the overhead we had in maintaining the equipment over here and overseas, and he put on an economy program, and without the Korean war at that time being imminent, he succeeded in his objectives. However, when the Korean thing developed, we were too thin on supplies and matériel.

Hess: In the Korean War the North Koreans invaded South Korea — we'll get to that a little bit later — on June the twenty-fourth, on a Saturday, of 1950. Just when was the decision made to replace Louis Johnson? What can you tell me about the resignation of Louis Johnson?

Connelly: I don't recall.

Hess: Was that offered willingly, do you recall?

Connelly: I don't believe so. I think that the president by this time became dissatisfied with Johnson because of his inability to get along with other members of the armed forces.

Hess: How did he get along with the other members of the cabinet?

Connelly: Louis Johnson was somewhat of an individualist, and Louis Johnson was not what you would call a cooperative member of the cabinet. He was running his own show, and he didn't want any interference from anybody else, and I don't think he asked very often for opinions from anybody else.

Hess: Would he interfere in other departments?

Connelly: No, not that I know of. He was running his own show and was satisfied to do that.

Hess: All right. Now, George Marshall was the next secretary of defense. Why was he chosen to replace Louis Johnson?

Connelly: Marshall had been chief of staff during World War II, and Truman had complete confidence in his ability as a soldier and as an administrator. After Louis Johnson left the cabinet, Truman, knowing Marshall, appointed him as secretary of defense because he realized that Marshall had more knowledge of the Defense Department operations than anybody else he knew of and that he would be a natural to take over the management of the defense establishment.

Hess: He served approximately one year. Did he wish to retire at this time?

Connelly: That I don't know.

Hess: The last man to hold the position was Robert Lovett. Why was he chosen?

Connelly: Robert Lovett had been undersecretary with Marshall. Robert Lovett was a very brilliant administrator. Robert Lovett had pleased Truman with his opinions on things at cabinet meetings when he appeared on behalf of Marshall, and Robert Lovett had become very close to Truman because of his ability and his intelligence. Truman figured him as a logical replacement for Marshall.

Hess: Did he make a fairly effective secretary of defense?

Connelly: He was very effective.

Hess: All right. He served until the end of the administration.

Connelly: Right.

Hess: And the next department is the Commerce Department. Henry Wallace was the first secretary.

Connelly: That's right. Mr. Wallace was secretary of commerce, and Mr. Wallace at one time decided that he was going to make a speech in New York. He brought the speech in to President Truman and told him he would like him to read it, and Mr. Truman could see no point in reading his speech, so Mr. Wallace arrived in New York, made the speech, and the kettle started to boil. So, he was in total opposition to Mr. Truman's theory on how foreign policy should be run, and as a result Mr. Truman decided that he would ask Mr. Wallace to submit his resignation.

Hess: Now at this same time, I believe James Byrnes was at the peace conference in Paris. Is that correct?

Connelly: I don't recall.

Hess: I think that he was. What do you recall about the resignation of Secretary Wallace?

Connelly: Well, he was requested to resign by the president because of this speech he made in New York, and after Mr. Ross indicated it had been approved by Mr. Truman. But Mr. Truman had not approved it, because he had not read it.

Hess: I believe that the president was asked at a press conference — isn't that correct? — if he did approve the speech, and what he later said was that he approved Secretary Wallace's right to make the speech; he did not necessarily approve the content. Do you recall that?

Connelly: That's correct, but he had not read the contents, because he believed that Secretary Wallace would not make a speech in violation of his own thoughts and ideas and what he personally would do himself.

Hess: Which he did.

Connelly: That's right.

Hess: And he was replaced by Averell Harriman. Why was he chosen?

Connelly: Well, Mr. Harriman had had considerable experience in the Roosevelt administration. He was ambassador to Russia, and he held other sensitive spots, and Mr. Harriman being of a section of our economy which was considered to be Wall Street, Mr. Truman placed him in that department because he had knowledge of business, finance, and also that he had many contacts in the business world.

Jonathan W. Daniels

Raleigh, North Carolina   October 4, 1963

Interviewed by J. R. Fuchs

Jonathan Daniels (1902–1981), Franklin D. Roosevelt's last press secretary and Truman's first spokesman, returned to journalism shortly after the new president took office. During the 1948 campaign, he helped as a speechwriter and strategist. Following his reelection, Truman asked him to become secretary of the navy, a position once held by the newspaperman's father. But Daniels, who edited the family-owned *Raleigh News and Observer,* declined the president's offer. In 1950, with the cooperation of his subject, he wrote the first full-scale Truman biography, *The Man of Independence.*

Fuchs: Well, first of all, I'd like to take up a few things concerning your book *The Man of Independence.* One thing you said is that Mr. Truman cautioned you not to trust his memory but to check with his memory, Mr. Daniels, and what did you do to go about finding these facts?

Daniels: Well, I found the facts checked very well with his memory, but I was not willing, when I was first approached by Lippincott to write this book, to merely write the book that was Truman's recollection. So, while the president was good enough to give me a number of hour-long, two-hour-long interviews, in which he told me about his life and various aspects of it, I didn't want to depend on that. So, being particularly interested and also most unfamiliar with his background in Missouri, I went back to Missouri and did — the first thing I did, I went to St. Louis and spent two or three days in the morgue of the *Post-Dispatch* and talked to newspapermen there who had known Truman.

Then I went on out to Kansas City and interviewed friends, enemies, relatives, all kinds of people who had known Truman. I also worked long in the morgue of the *Kansas City Star.* Through a friend of mine in Kansas City, Jerome Walsh, I got in touch with Thomas H. Madden, of the Kansas City Title Insurance Company, who specialized in land-title law. He did

for me a complete record of the purchases, sales, mortgages, and so forth, on the Truman lands.

Then I spent a great deal of time in Independence interviewing a great variety of people who had known Truman, such as friends or political associates, or political opponents, business associates, and got their story of Truman and his background.

I was very much surprised when I went to Kansas City. I knew most of the newspapermen who were covering the president. Many of them had been covering Roosevelt when I was press secretary at the White House. I was surprised to be able to find material which was not even remembered by newspapermen in Kansas City. For instance, while everybody knew that he'd been [Eddie] Jacobson's partner in the haberdashery store, apparently it was completely forgotten that he'd been in the building and loan business, in the oil-stock business, in mine speculation, in the purchase of a bank which almost failed while he was involved. All these things were so little remembered that — I've forgotten the name of the man — I think his name was Shoop — who was Washington correspondent of the *Kansas City Star*, who when the book came out, called me up from Washington, and he said, "My God, you've got this stuff right under our noses that we didn't get."

I was shocked at newspapermen covering a president, going to his press conferences, getting his handouts, the day-to-day news, but while they were waiting around him in his hotel, they didn't do any of the type of research which should be done about any president. I have the feeling that when any man becomes president, the Associated Press, the *New York Times*, such news agencies ought to put trained research men on his story, and as you are doing now for history, they ought to bring up all the raw material of research for current news background material. That had been done about Truman. I doubt that up to that time it had been done on any president, and I am proud that I had enough of the historian and the newspaperman in me to want to go and find out from the source, and that's what I did.

Fuchs: You did this while Mr. Truman was yet president and being a former employee of the White House, both under Franklin D. and Mr. Truman. How did he feel about you writing a biography?

Daniels: I had never known Mr. Truman well at all until the day he came down to the White House to be president. I had met him.

Fuchs: Do you recall where?

Daniels: In Washington around the Senate, and at Chicago. I remember the day or so before he was nominated, he came into the lobby of the Stevens Hotel and seemed to me a little more than just another senator. And he stopped, and we had a long conversation as he was coming in to register, very pleasant. Lucy, my wife, was with me, and we saw him at the convention. But as to my writing the Truman biography: I did a review in the *Saturday Review of Literature* about some book connected with the death of Roosevelt in which I described the people on the funeral train coming back, the movement in of the new politicians into the new president's car, and so forth. And a friend of mine, George Stevens, who was then, and is now, editor at Lippincott, wrote me and asked me if I would do a book about Truman. I had not only stayed with Truman for a brief period after the death of Roosevelt, but he also had asked me to become director of the Rural Electrification Authority at that time. I didn't want to stay in the government; I wanted to get out of it; I'd only come into it for the war, but when the campaign of 1948 began, I had been a delegate from North Carolina to the Democratic national [convention] in Philadelphia, and I had seen Truman there. And then, rather suddenly, he invited me to come to the White House and asked me would I travel with him in the 1948 campaign. I did travel with him on practically all those presidential treks around the country.

Fuchs: Do you remember just when it was he asked you, the month possibly?

Daniels: Well, it was between the convention and the beginning of the first trip. Now I can't fix that, but in the Truman papers you'll probably find that I was set up as a WCO consultant to the president, and so I traveled with him. Then after this, I was asked to write this biography, and I went to see the president about it. He said he would be glad to talk to me and give me such assistance as he could, but I wanted to make it clear to him that I didn't want to write a campaign biography; the campaign was over. I wanted to write a biography of an American president and politician. I went out to do it. He helped me tremendously, and he read my manuscript. The corrections he made were insignificant. One or two were amusing. You'll find most of his comments on the margin of the manuscript at Chapel Hill, and I got a lot of satisfaction out of doing the book.

Fuchs: Did you have any feeling about the validity of one statement as compared to another? For instance, I have in mind Spencer Salisbury's story about Mr. Truman's entrance or nonentrance into the Ku Klux Klan, and there are, as you know, several versions of that. Did you feel that one was more accurate than the other?

Daniels: At this point I can't be sure. I believe now, and as a writer I don't try to remember forever, that there were some good reasons to suppose that the faction that Truman was connected with was in fact anti-Klan, but I wouldn't have any doubt of the possibility that in those days, when the Klan seemed to be just sort of a slightly more militant Junior Order, that Truman as a local politician might have joined it. I haven't investigated this; I put it down in terms of, as I remember it, in terms of the different version — that some said he did; some said he didn't — and I don't think anybody could prove the fact about that, but I would rather depend upon what I said in *The Man of Independence* than what I remember now.

Fuchs: Yes, I can understand that. Well, I don't want to ask you to be a psychiatrist, but I thought that, of course, there would be certain things you couldn't put in *The Man of Independence* . . .

Daniels: I did not really suppress anything, but I have the feeling that Harry Truman as a politician in Jackson County — with my memory of the kind of people who went into the Ku Klux Klan down in this part of the world in its early days when it had not become nearly disreputable — that there was nothing about Harry Truman that made me feel he wouldn't have been willing to join it in the circumstances of the time.

Fuchs: Well, I don't have the thought that you might be suppressing something but that you wouldn't have put in, "Well, I felt Spencer Salisbury was not necessarily telling the truth at this one time." And I just wondered if you did have some thought about Spencer Salisbury, because, as you know, he is a subject of discussion as far as Harry Truman —

Daniels: I have the feeling that Spencer Salisbury's people were more socially prominent than the Trumans were and that Salisbury had that feeling of superiority. He was, as I remember it — and once again I want to say that the best evidence is what I put in my notebooks at the time — is that Spencer Salisbury was a very dashing young man who rode with a black coat on a motorcycle, but that Truman and he were unquestionably very close in business operations in their youth. And by youth, I don't mean childhood; I mean they were people around thirty.

It happened at the time I had a friend who was, at that time, an official of the federal agency which dealt with building and loan, banks, and so forth; and from him I got copies of the correspondence when Truman in anger at Salisbury wired back to slap him down. Salisbury says Truman was just lucky to get out; he persuaded him to get out [of his business dealings]. Truman thinks Salisbury was just a crook. Well, Salisbury became the operator of a drinking club, and Truman became president of the United States. So, it's very easy to say, "Well, we'll take the word of the president of the United States against the word of the president of a drinking club." But there was a time when they were very close and not dissimilar young men.

Obviously, Truman had some characteristics of the gambler in him. If he hadn't, he wouldn't have been in the oil-stock business, the speculation in lead mines. When he ran for the Senate, it was a great, wild speculation that he could be elected to the Senate of the United States. Now, it seems in hindsight to him, very simple. He was a close friend of all the county commissioners in Missouri; he was a big Mason in Missouri; therefore, he had, as he felt, friends in every county seat. But still, it was a great speculation for him to run for the United States Senate from his position as county judge of Jackson County. There is the element of the gambler in the president, as I think there has been and probably always will be in anybody who runs for public office of that sort.

Fuchs: How do you weigh this as a speculation as against his being supported by the Pendergast faction? [Thomas J. Pendergast, the Democratic boss of Kansas City, was the most influential party leader in the state and Truman's political sponsor.]

Daniels: Well, the Pendergast faction didn't control Missouri. There were tremendous factions in St. Louis at that time. I will not try to say to you the details of that political situation, though they are in my book. It's been a number of years — I don't remember — but I tried to set down the imponderables in that thing. The notebooks contain all the material, with the exception of stuff that came out of books of history and so forth; and the things I left out that are in the notebooks were a few vulgar remarks by Spencer Salisbury about Truman. Sometimes I had to assess differences of statement between one man and another, but all that will be clear in the notebooks. When the president read the first draft, there was one little thing I remember. I had said something about the fact that the Trumans were perhaps more prominent than the Wallaces. And his idea was, "Oh God, Jonathan, don't put that in; you'll get me into all kinds of trouble," which was a trivial, personal thing and had no relationship to history, and I was glad to do it.

Fuchs: Did you have anything to do with President Truman's decision to more or less follow President Roosevelt's policies in regard to the press conferences?

Daniels: Well, I wouldn't say that I did, but obviously I was in on the discussions, but Truman took that ball and carried it. The night Roosevelt died, OWI was very eager for a statement to go out to the world that the new president declared that the policies and the fighting of the war and so forth would go forward exactly as they were going. I called up Truman. He'd gone home, and some person — and, as I say, there was quite a group of persons — answered the phone, and I said, "This is Jonathan Daniels at the White House, and I want to speak to the president."

And he said, "Well, I don't know whether you can or not."

"Well," I said, "I insist upon speaking to the president."

And I got Truman on the phone, and he said, "Why, of course, Mr. Daniels, that must go out now, and you have my authority to issue it."

He picked the ball up — nobody else had to. His first press conferences were wonderful. I think they made a tremendous impression. Of course, everybody wanted it that way because the conservatives felt that now they were rid of Roosevelt and that Truman was going to be good old middle-westerner who was not a wild liberal.

Fuchs: What about the policies as to a press conference itself? Did he more or less follow Mr. Roosevelt's ideas about what might be on the record and off the record?

Daniels: There was a little more briefing in the first days, because, naturally, he had to be briefed. He came in like a man on a rocket. He had not been briefed by Roosevelt much, as you know, before he became president.

Fuchs: Your reactions to the president's press conferences then, generally, were that he did a good job.

Daniels: Oh, he came in doing a grand job.

Fuchs: Looking back, did you notice any particular change in his press conferences over the years of his administration?

Daniels: No, I think he always did a very good job. I had a funny experience with him. One day, I went into see him and told him I was writing an article on — I've forgotten what it was — but anyhow, he outlined a plan he had in mind, of something to the effect congressmen should be elected on staggered terms or something — I've forgotten; you'll run into this — and I wrote it in an article for Collier's. Well, Collier's put a hell of a big box rather amplifying what I had said, and Truman had Joe Short say that the article was not the president's views at all, because the article got him into trouble up on the Hill. And so newsmen called me up, and I said, "Well, if the president says that, I stand by my article, and Joe Short can say what he pleases." Then Truman in his book *Mr. President* put exactly the same thing in as I had reported it.

Fuchs: I recall this. He was supposed to have said this to you in a private conversation, and they tried to pass it off as just a banality or something.

Daniels: That was not true. No, no, they denied the truth of it. But when I went up to the White House a week later and went on in to see the president and the newspapermen saw me going in to see the presi on a great basis of friendship, it was clearly a denial for the record.

Fuchs: I see. You don't have anything to offer about various news leaks at the White House, do you, during the Roosevelt administration?

Daniels: Well, I won't say about the White House, but of Washington in general, there are very few leaks in Washington; there are a great many plants.

Fuchs: What did you do at the convention in Chicago in 1944?

Daniels: Oh, Lord, I don't know what you'd say I did. I was around trying to be useful, and I doubt that I was particularly useful, because I had not been informed about the finger being placed on Truman. I remember meeting up with Harold Ickes and [Francis] Biddle, and they were both just astounded, as we all were.

Fuchs: Why did Hannegan push Truman so hard?

Daniels: Hannegan was in there, and they wanted to get rid of Wallace. Now, I quoted Roosevelt as saying — and he said this to me — that he had asked around, that he'd gotten the word from Spellman that while the fact that Byrnes was a renegade Catholic would not necessarily be dangerous, there would be some Catholics who would give the benefit of the doubt against Byrnes because he was. Spellman had denied that he ever said any such thing. But Truman, I'm sure, was sold to Roosevelt as — he was convinced that Wallace was a danger. Truman, I think, was a pretty logical choice.

Fuchs: Were you or your father consulted about the nomination beforehand?

Daniels: I'm sure he was not, and I was not.

Fuchs: Had you come to the conclusion, in regard to Mr. Roosevelt's health, that Truman would be succeeding him shortly, prior to April '45?

Daniels: No, I say I was disturbed by his pictures; I was particularly disturbed by the shape of his signature on my own commission. You have a sense of the immortality of a man like that when you're working with him. His hand shook, but I didn't expect him to die, I know. We were working on his speech at San Francisco — [Robert] Sherwood, [Archibald] MacLeish, myself — and there was a plan that he was going to London that summer, still vague; but the whole world was going forward without interruption. Now, in hindsight, that's perhaps incredible, but that was the feeling then.

Fuchs: You noted in your diary in May '44 that you had a hunch or made an observation that you didn't think Roosevelt would run again, and Hassett observed that he had the same hunch.

Daniels: Well, around the White House there were questions. How close does that come to the visit to Hobcaw [the South Carolina estate of financier Bernard Baruch]?

Fuchs: That was — I think in the same notes you noted the bad state of his health after he returned from Baruch's place.

Daniels: There was a rumor at the White House — which I don't believe was true — there was a rumor that he had had a secret operation. I've heard nothing ever said about it since.

Fuchs: What thoughts did you have about the campaign of '48 before you were brought in as a consultant, and then how did they alter over the course of the campaign, as to prospects?

Daniels: Well, it was pretty rough, but I thought we had a chance and we ought to make a good fight. My friends in Raleigh — I believe one of my brothers — said, "For goodness sake, why are you going down the drain with Truman?" There was a feeling that getting on Truman's train was sort of the flight to oblivion, but I thought it was a good fight, and I enjoyed the work.

Fuchs: Did you feel a change during the campaign at any certain point, when you felt that he might make a strong —

Daniels: I think Harry Truman was the only man on the Truman train who was confident — and I really believe he was — that Harry Truman was going to be reelected. Many of us had moments of high hope, and you began to get more hope as you saw the whistle-stop crowds, but we were so overwhelmed by the reports of the polls and the complete confidence of the Republicans. I remember coming home to vote, and in my office at the paper, I wrote a special piece about Truman and why the South ought to vote for him, and over the wire came the story of the Dewey train coming back into New York on the eve of the election and who was going to be in the cabinet and all this. We have a custom on the *News and Observer* when there is a great Democratic victory — this goes back to my father's time — of printing a red crowing rooster across the front page, and so the night of the election, I asked the managing editor, "Have you got the rooster out?"

And the boys grinned at me and said, "Yeah, we got it out," but the whole implication was that they didn't think they would have need for it.

I went to bed that night. I was not sure at all, but I was encouraged, and I guess it was four o'clock in the morning that Truman called me up from Kansas City and said, "Well, Jonathan, we're in."

And I said, "I'm awful glad to hear it, sir. I want to see it nailed down." He said, "Well, it's going to be."

Ohio, I believe, was the thing that had just hit him — that he was going to get Ohio. And I went to bed about four, and I had to go to New York the next morning on a nine o'clock plane, and I was flying over Richmond when the Dewey statement conceding Truman's election came on. And then that morning when he called me up, of course, he asked me to join him and go with them to Key West. He made a little stop, as you may remember, down at New Bern at a little Baptist or Methodist church — I've forgotten why or what. So, I joined him in Washington, and we went on down to Key West and stayed.

Fuchs: You were serving on a public advisory committee at the time you were asked to come in as a consultant. Do you recall anything about your activities with that?

Daniels: The Public Advisory Committee of the ECA [Economic Cooperation Administration]?

Fuchs: Yes, sir.

Daniels: Yes, he appointed me to that. I don't have the date in my mind, but I served on that throughout his administration. And then he also appointed me to the — whether he appointed me or whether one of the cabinet members — to the National Hospital Council. They were just once-a-month jobs when I'd go up to Washington to attend these meetings.

Fuchs: Is there anything that stands out in your memory?

Daniels: Well, of course, ECA was under Paul Hoffman, and the whole business of foreign aid was just beginning to be developed and worked out, and it was an exciting enterprise. Then I was also appointed as the United States representative on the UN subcommittee with regard to the protection of minorities and the prevention of discrimination. I served on that during the Truman administration.

Fuchs: Were there any particular disputes or problems that arose that stand out?

Daniels: In the United Nations, we were always fussing with the Russians, and they were always trying to use it as a forum to emphasize to the world the mistreatment of minorities in the United States. We tried to get some sort of Bill of Rights — the International Bill of Rights. The Russians were more interested in it as a propaganda device than working out any plans.

Fuchs: What was your principal duty in 1948, in connection with the campaign?

Daniels: I don't suppose I had any particular, special duty. I worked with public relations, some with the press; I made arrangements for this Southern trip, I helped with speech writing, I worked at the White House in connection with speeches, I met people.

At one crucial point once, I was violently opposed to the president's position. We had worked out a plan. We were pretty desperate in that campaign, and we wanted something that would be a dramatic gesture of the president's effort for peace and security in the world. Finally, we came up with a plan that Truman would ask Fred Vinson, then chief justice of the United States Supreme Court, to go to Russia as his personal representative. I don't remember the exact aim, but the purpose was to reach some sort of agreement with the Russians which would assure world peace. Vinson had agreed that he would go. Then we were in a conference in the Cabinet Room at the White House, and the president put in a call to Marshall in Paris. He came back in the room and said no, he wouldn't do it; that, in effect, this would be injection of our foreign policy into politics.

As a statesman he was right, but I said, "Well, Mr. President, if you believe in your foreign policy, it seems to me that you have got to work for its continuance by political means as well as every other; and I think that if you have faith that what you're trying to do is right, it's your duty, not only as a candidate but as a president, to take an act which may bring about your reelection, and therefore the continuance of this foreign policy in which you believe."

I was rather passionate about it. I'm sure that the impeccable patriots would say that I was the politician trying to press the president into what they might regard as improper political activity, but I felt very strongly that his election was the thing necessary to the continuance of the Roosevelt-Truman type of foreign policy; but he said no. I must say that I believe that most of the political advisers there were on my side, but we all respected and, of course, had no other choice than to agree to the president's decision.

Fuchs: Did he make a direct response to you, or did he just listen to the general overall views?

Daniels: We were at the cabinet table, and he did not make any elaborate justification of his position. He didn't have to. He said, "No, Marshall has said this would not be right."

Fuchs: How did you look on Matt Connelly when you worked with him early in Mr. Truman's administration?

Daniels: Well, I want to be perfectly frank about this. I thought he was very attractive. He was always a slick, Irish boy from Boston, well dressed — inclined to give the impression, at least, that he was out for the gals. I wouldn't have put much confidence in his moral fiber, and as the time went on I had less and less. He was a sad sort of boy. Truman gave a dinner at the end of his administration for all those people who had been on his personal staff one way or another, and I was there, and Matt got drunk at the dinner. He was apt to like to talk a bit in dirty language. He was a pretty foulmouthed sort of fellow, but attractive, and I would suspect pretty efficient. I wasn't particularly shocked at what happened to him.

Fuchs: How would you contrast the attitudes of FDR and HST in regard to civil rights?

Daniels: Well, I think Truman was probably more forthright about it. You see, I think sometimes Mrs. Roosevelt irritated FDR. I remember one day in the White House she was practically going to make a cause célèbre of the fact that somebody was complaining that they had white and colored toilets in the post office in Atlanta. Well, today that might seem much more of a dramatic situation than it did then, but the whole attitude around the White House was, "For god's sake, we got so many things to do; please don't have us handling the privies in the post office in Atlanta."

And Roosevelt would not have pushed anybody to that sort of thing. I remember once Roosevelt said to me, "If they immediately ordered the end of segregation in the navy, the navy would deliberately start it in

Charleston, South Carolina," meaning that they'd get him into trouble as fast as they could.

I would say that Truman was the more direct man on the subject, although I remember his sister — Truman's sister, Mary Jane — she said to me while I was out in Kansas City, "Why, you know Harry feels that same way about these colored folks as I do," meaning the conventional Missouri attitude.

Fuchs: Did she say "colored folks"?

Daniels: I wouldn't like to say what she said, but I suspect it was a harder word, unless I've got that written down in my notes made immediately after the interview with her.

Fuchs: In your opinion, was the bolt in '48 and the formation of the States' Rights Democratic Party based solely on civil rights, or do you think there were other factors?

Daniels: Well, there was, of course, a sense that Truman could not be reelected, which gave some strength to some Democrats who opposed him and who were opposed to civil rights. Then there was that Democratic movement, you know, to replace him with Eisenhower; but the bolt as it formed under Thurmond was strictly on the basis of civil rights. I remember coming back from that convention where I was a delegate and about eleven of us from North Carolina who voted for Truman's nomination — some of the politicians in the state here tried to label us as "nigger lovers" because we voted for Truman.

Fuchs: Do you think tidelands oil came into the picture to any great extent?

Daniels: I don't know where Ed Pauley was in that — he was for Truman. Well, I would say if you found out where Ed Pauley was, you would pretty well know where tidelands oil was.

Fuchs: Why do you think Barkley wanted to be vice president in '48?

Daniels: He never had been vice president. It's a great thing to be vice president. Truman had tried to get Douglas, as I remember it, and Douglas declined, so definitely that Truman rather resented it. Well, Barkley was getting along; it was an opportunity. I don't know whether he was coming up for reelection in Kentucky or not. He was a pretty good choice, but he was definitely a second choice.

Fuchs: Who do you credit with the idea of Truman's calling the Eightieth Congress back for the "Turnip Day" session?

Daniels: It sounds like him to me. I'm sure a lot of people will claim the credit for it, but that "Turnip Day" thing seemed to me a pretty good Trumanesque gesture.

Fuchs: How was the relationship between President Truman and the press on the train?

Daniels: Everybody was fond of Truman. I don't think the press thought he was going to be elected.

Fuchs: Did you have much contact with the press on the train?

Daniels: Oh, a great deal, because you see, I knew them all, and it was a matter of — well, I tried to — I don't know whether you call it persuasion or public relations with the press — not merely giving them information. Well, you wanted everybody to write as nice stories as you could get on the train.

Fuchs: How did you view the press coverage of that campaign on behalf of Mr. Truman?

Daniels: I thought it was fair. After the campaign was over, I wrote to a friend of mine on the *New York Herald Tribune*, which was, of course, very strong for Dewey, and I thought they gave — except in their interpretive articles as to who was going to be elected, and I don't think that they were distorted — I think they represented an accepted view of the outcome.

Fuchs: Any particular speeches in that campaign that you worked on that stand out in your memory for any particular reason?

Daniels: No, these two down here were the main ones; others I helped with and read over and edited and things of that sort.

Fuchs: Mr. Truman made a decision to speak more from outlines or off-the-cuff, as you will, and he's remarked about this in his *Memoirs*. Were you involved in that decision, or how did this come about?

Daniels: He was the most remarkable man in the world in that he could speak in Podunk at two o'clock and say a few strong words, go back to his drawing room, lie down and sleep ten minutes, and get up at Bingville and be as fresh as a daisy and make another little speech, and then go back and take another nap. [He was the] most remarkable man about the ability to sleep in the midst of strain that I've ever seen. He's always had that gift. He told me that as a young man in Missouri, he'd be politicking all over the state, and he could drive his car up a side road, lie down on the seat and take a nap, and then go on.

Fuchs: That's interesting. I'm thinking of his speaking more from outlines of a speech or off-the-cuff rather than reading a prepared speech or statement. Do you remember anything about that in particular?

Daniels: I don't think that he reached that decision in the '48 campaign. He was always more effective in my opinion and got his personality across better when he was just letting go than when he was reading words prepared for him. As to reading, he has a certain problem with his eyesight.

Fuchs: Oh, you think that was a definite factor?

Daniels: Well, he never said so to me, but I think so, yes. I don't know. I'm sure he must have bifocals, but you notice how thick his lenses are.

Fuchs: Do you have other thoughts about him as a political speaker?

Daniels: Well, he manages to put across his personality in such a way as to make people have confidence in him. He projects his image, Madison Avenue might say.

Fuchs: Anything that stands out in your memory about the vacation at Key West after the '48 election?

Daniels: No, that was a purely social business. I mean, we swam and played poker, and the president had a pretty good system, you know. You could lose — think you could lose two hundred dollars. Then if you lose two hundred dollars, you automatically get ten dollars back from the pot. So, nobody could lose more than a hundred and ninety dollars. He plays what I'm sure serious poker players would regard as a weird game — all kinds of strange poker hands — "baseball," I know, is one of them — and we played poker and swam and drank a little whiskey and ate and had just a good time.

Fuchs: Is there anything that stands out in your memory about the farewell dinner for the president in December in 1952?

Daniels: It was a very pleasant occasion marred by just one incident, about which I believe I've spoken. There must have been fifty of us there. Almost everybody who had served in any capacity during his two administrations on his personal staff.

Fuchs: What do you know about the inception of the Hillman book project?[1]

Daniels: Very little indeed. I knew Hillman, but I don't think I was consulted. As a matter of fact, yes. A friend of mine, John Farrar — he's a publisher in New York — told me about the arrangements for that book, and I believe he told me something about the disappointment about the book. They had expected a very much larger sale, but as to when it was decided on and when Hillman became the president's writing aide, I don't know.

1. Harry S. Truman and William Hillman, Mr. President (New York: Farrar, Straus and Young, 1952).

I did review that book for *Saturday Review of Literature*, and I pointed out that the book was the definite announcement that the president would *not* run again and showed why and quoted from the book. And I remember I got a great many letters from people like Arthur Krock . . . and then a week later Truman did announce that he wasn't going to run.

Fuchs: Didn't you at one point write or say that Mr. Truman *was* going to run?

Daniels: No, this was a full-page review in the *Saturday Review* in which I pointed out where he said in the book — although it looked like a Technicolor campaign document — in this book he says, "I am not going to run." He quoted some kind of old Latin fable in the book, which I don't recall now, about a man, in effect, going too often to bat.

Fuchs: Well, I was thinking earlier in 1951, which, of course, would have been prior to the publication of the book. There was considerable discussion of an article that you had written and —

Daniels: It's perfectly possible that in '51 I thought he was going to run again.

Fuchs: There was a discussion in the press conference in April 1951 about your article and whether you were still welcome at the White House, and I believe this had to do with an article concerning arrangement of the election of congressmen. Do you recall that?

Daniels: Oh, yes, I remember that that was the time when Joe Short denied a statement, which I attributed to the president, in an article in *Collier's*, but the president himself — I said the president has a perfect right to say what he pleases, and I don't question anything he says. But a week later the president said I was perfectly welcome at the White House, and in his own book, *Mr. President*, he embodied this idea which I had printed in the *Collier's* article; but at the earlier time he had to take the heat off of himself from opposition on the Hill to those who didn't like his idea.

Fuchs: Did President Truman ever discuss a potential candidate for '52 with you?

Daniels: Yes. Once he asked me to go see Adlai Stevenson, and I called Stevenson up — I was in Washington on some occasion — and Stevenson came out to see me at Jim Barnes's house, and I told him that the president thought it was time that he stopped being coy. This was some weeks or maybe months before the convention. Of course, Stevenson made no declaration to me that he was going to be a candidate. In fact, for months afterwards he said he didn't want to be.

Thomas L. Evans

Kansas City, Missouri   June 13, 1963, and December 10, 1963

Interviewed by J. R. Fuchs

Thomas L. Evans (1896–1970), Truman's best friend, rose from a modest background to wealth as the owner of television and radio stations and a drugstore chain. For more than a half century he was Truman's confidant. The two men had much in common. Both were hard working, plainspoken, good humored, and unassuming. During the Truman presidency, he could have had any position in the federal government. But he did not care about official titles or public recognition. It is doubtful whether any American president ever had a better friend.

Fuchs: I believe you went to the formal notification ceremonies at Lamar in August. Do you have any recollections of that event?

Evans: Yes, I was right there. About the outstanding thing of that event in Lamar that sticks in my mind was that Mother Truman was quite old, and she was there. And her eyes were bad and they had her in a car pulled up close to the speaker's stand and they had all these lights and everything shining down, and I came up and I said, "Mother Truman, it's Tom Evans," and shook hands with her.

She said, "I wish you'd get those people to take those damn lights out of my eyes; I can't see anything."

I got the biggest kick out of that.

Fuchs: You related a story one time about Mr. Truman on the campaign — coming out and having a drink one evening in his bathrobe.

Evans: Oh, that was in Boston. There were thousands of incidents on that [1944] campaign, but I think what you're thinking about. We were in Boston staying all night at the hotel, and of course, he had made seven or eight or ten speeches that day and a gigantic, big speech that night in a packed auditorium where former Mayor Curley spoke. You've heard of him — one of the greatest orators I've ever heard. I'd defy anybody to listen to him without tears coming to their eyes. Remember, he was the man who served a term in the penitentiary. He was the guest speaker that

night — I know that, but that's beside the point. We came back — all of us — just worn out completely because we'd traveled all over New England in the caravan making speeches. Of course, Mr. Truman made speeches, not me, but I was doing most all the worrying. But he always said I was his official worrier and did a good job.

Anyway, we came back to the hotel and wanted him to get to bed and get some rest. As you know, Mrs. Evans was traveling with us — the only woman — just Mrs. Evans, myself, Ed McKim and Matt Connelly, and the president. That's all that was there. So, we got him off to his room to bed, and we had a living room, and off of the living room was Mrs. Evans's and my room, and off across the hall was Matt Connelly and Ed McKim's room. So, Ed McKim, Matt Connelly, and Mrs. Evans and I were just having a sociable drink and talking over the events, and there was always a lot to talk about, you know; and we were having a good time. I expect we had two or three drinks, and we heard a door open and a little bit of a tiny knock and looked up and there was Mr. Truman. He had on his pajamas and an old faded bathrobe, and he said, "Oh, please let me come in and join the party."

And we told him that he was supposed to rest. But he did; he came in and had a drink and sat around for a few minutes and then went back to bed. We found out we were disturbing him so we went to bed, too. I think I told you this before and you may have it recorded, but Mrs. Evans now gets quite a kick out of the fact that she finally got up and took him by the arm and led him back and said, "Well, we'll all go to bed; you must get your rest; we've been disturbing you." And she found his socks hanging up drying and he'd washed them, and she just gave him the dickens. She said, "After this, I'll wash your socks." And she did from then on. Every night she'd wash out his hose for him, and he'd been doing it himself all the time on the trip.

Fuchs: On the trip, did you sleep on the train, or was it always in a hotel?

Evans: No, we slept on the train a good deal of the time, depending — oh, I suppose — this is a rough guess — but about half the time we slept on the train. When there were long trips, we slept on the train. When we came down from Boston to New York, there's where we had the big rally — where I think I have told you — that is, a big rally in Madison Square Garden. That's where Mr. Wallace, who was then vice president, was supposed to walk into the hall with Mr. Truman and — I lost another three or four pounds that night worrying — it got time for the rally to start, and the place was packed full of people and thousands jamming outside and loudspeakers out on the walk, and no Wallace. And Mr. Truman said, "Well, let's go on without him." And there was all kinds of members of the National Committee and they couldn't understand it, and they couldn't go without him and, finally, about five minutes after he was supposed to be on, why, in he came. And we, of course, got him, and he marched in with Mr. Truman and up on the platform; and his excuse was that he needed a little air, and he had plenty of time and he walked, and he got into this big traffic jam and couldn't get in. That's why he was late. What was the question you asked? I got off.

Fuchs: About whether you had slept on the train or not?

Evans: Yes, then we had this big rally in New York, and it was midnight when it was over; and we went down and got on — we had been there for two nights at the Waldorf Astoria — but after this we went down and got on the train and then went over to Washington. We got there early in the morning — I think about 4:30 — and, I know, I woke up and here was Mr. Truman all dressed and waiting. I had breakfast with him at five o'clock, and Mrs. Truman and Margaret were there to meet us, and then, they joined us there and they come back to Missouri on the train with us.

Fuchs: Are there any other incidents you recall about the campaign trip that stand out in your mind?

Evans: There's so many of them, Jim, that it's hard — and I tell them to people; I tell them to you; I tell them to Dr. [Philip C.] Brooks, and then I forget whether you've got them recorded or not. Like the main job I had on the campaign trip was a very important one. You know we had this special car on the back of a regular scheduled train, and you'd be amazed in traveling over the country, these little small towns where the whole town would be there to see the candidate for vice president as he went through, and he was supposed to be on the back platform and wave — and that was a pretty dirty place to be with a train going through sixty to seventy miles an hour, and the cinders and the dirt flying — and being gray-headed like Mr. Truman and wearing glasses like Mr. Truman, well, it was my job to go out — and they couldn't tell whether it was him or who standing on the back platform of that car — and wave at them. So, that was my big job on the trip. Mr. Truman admits that I saved him a lot of cinders and a lot of dirt anyway. I've been that much help to him.

Fuchs: Mr. Truman wrote you in July after the convention: "That was quite a night in Philadelphia. I don't suppose we will ever have another like it."

And then he added in his own handwriting, "Thanks a million for what you did up there." Does that have reference to a particular task you performed or just —

Evans: Oh, I think it was the general task by going there and reporting. Oh, I talked to him fifteen or twenty times. I'm sure there will never be another night like it. That was the night it was so hot and rainy and everybody was down in the dumps. Boy, he raised them out of it, though.

Fuchs: Well, apparently you were one of the many who thought prior to the convention that it would be difficult for him to be reelected, and then you felt after the acceptance speech that he had a good chance. Then, did you sort of have a retrogression in that you felt later on during the campaign that he would not be able to, or were you always confident that he would come through?

Evans: Well Jim, to be perfectly frank, I got a tremendous buildup at the convention, but I *never* had the feeling that he was going to lose; he just couldn't win. I mean that's the truth. When he came back from his long campaign all over the country — and if I remember right, he closed his campaign in '48 in St. Louis on a Saturday night before the election was on Tuesday — he came over to Independence Sunday. Monday he was over where the staff was in the penthouse. He came over there and I saw him, of course, and I said to him, "What do you actually and honestly believe? Do you think you can win?"

And he said, "Yes, I'm going to win."

And I said, "I've always said you ought to be the international president of the Optimist Club because you've always been an optimist, but what do you base it upon?"

He said, "Come in here and I'll show you."

And I went into the bedroom with him — of the penthouse — and he threw out a chart that actually didn't mean too much to me, involving the number of people that put down on this chart and how it had gone Democratic in '44 and that they lost so much how it would still go Democratic. [Truman's chart showed him holding together the New Deal coalition.] And when he got all through, he said, "Now you see; I'm going to fool everybody." What he was going by: "These crowds that have come to the train to see me just can't mean anything but victory."

And it turned out he was right. I was a little bit more optimistic but to be perfectly honest, I was worrying about — I knew that I would be at the penthouse the night the returns would come in. I did not know at that time — well, let's say on Saturday or Sunday, where President Truman would be — but I knew I would be at the penthouse because we had a lot of equipment set up and telephones back to New York and Republican headquarters for the Secret Service men. I knew I was going to be there, and we got a lot of reports coming in from there that Connelly had arranged, but I didn't know where the president was going to be. I remember this distinctly: "How bad is the president going to feel when he's defeated?" And, "What's it going to do to Mrs. Evans? How upset is she going to be?" In other words, I'm planning for the ultimate catastrophe and then, of course, the story of the election eve —

Fuchs: Before we go on to that, I would just like to ask a couple of more questions about the convention. When you were talking to Farley and Hague from New Jersey, who was so garrulous about Mr. Truman's lack of chances, did Farley seem to share his opinion? What did Farley say?

Evans: He was not — what shall I say? — mean about it like Hague, but he wasn't at all enthusiastic, and he was more interested in trying to get the boss to quit talking about it in front of me by saying, "You remember Tom Evans, who is a close friend of President Truman?"

That didn't stop him: "I don't care if he is President Truman himself, he hasn't got a chance. My people can't eat snow."

Well, I, of course, did have ulcers in those days. You know, I got rid of them, but boy those ulcers of mine and that day in '48 were turning over and upside down and everything, because that was just terrible. But, I'm sure that Mr. Farley — answering your question — certainly was not outspoken about it.

Fuchs: Did you travel on the train any during the '48 campaign?

Evans: I made only two trips. One from Omaha — I met him in Omaha, I think it was — and came down to Kansas City when they came down. And one when we went from Boston into New York, I think it was. Anyway, I was with him on the train in New York because the reason I remember the New York trip so well, the Secret Service men said, "Now the minute this is over, don't hesitate a minute or you'll miss us because we're going to get right out of here, so you come right in right back of us."

And I got up the minute it was over and was about ten feet back of the Secret Service group, and I turned around to shake hands with somebody and they were up and gone, and I did miss them. I had a heck of a time. They were on a private train. I had to take a taxicab, and I had an awful time getting through to them, but they didn't leave me at the station.

They laughed at me after that quite a lot. I had a lesson to learn not to be back ten feet but to get ahead ten feet of the Secret Service men. They travel fast.

Fuchs: Who did you talk with on the train, and what was the general atmosphere on the train?

Evans: Very optimistic and, actually, most of my contact was with Matt Connelly, who made the trip with him, and Charlie Ross. Matt Connelly was quite optimistic; I don't think Charlie Ross — I think he was about in the same category that I was.

Fuchs: How did Matt Connelly seem to be spending most of his time on that campaign train?

Evans: Oh, he was well acquainted with all the political leaders in all the cities, and he did a tremendous amount of work on his speeches, having them typed, and having the proper people see him. He was the busiest man I ever saw.

Fuchs: Then, in relation to Crosby and Jim Kemper again, was Mr. Truman a particularly good friend of Crosby Kemper?

Evans: Oh yes, Jim and Crosby are brothers; he was a great friend of all of them.

Fuchs: And he suggested that you talk to James first?

Evans: Right, and he turned us down and then suggested Crosby, and he turned us down.

Fuchs: Were there any other normally strong supporters of the Democratic Party in this area who refused to contribute or support Truman in '48?

Evans: Oh, yes, there were a number of people who would make contributions and say they were wasting it because Truman didn't have a chance, but, invariably, they said they were going to vote for him. That was always a peculiar thing; they were sold on him but the people weren't. That seemed to be the trouble. I don't recall — oh, I think there were some probably, but I don't recall who they were. I'm sure Jim Kemper, who used to make a rather substantial contribution, did not contribute to that campaign; Crosby did, but not very much.

Fuchs: Coming down to election day, then, you saw Mr. Truman?

Evans: Yes, yes, he was over at the penthouse visiting, happy as he could be, optimistic as usual, and I asked him where he was going to be — was he going to be there with us or what? — and he said no, he was going to be at home. He had this dinner that he had promised to attend — I've forgotten what dinner — and so he was going to leave fairly early. Incidentally, in the afternoon of election day in the state of Kansas, they start counting the votes. I don't know the hours, but let's say all the votes cast in a precinct up to ten o'clock are taken out and counted at ten o'clock and then again at two o'clock—I'm not sure of the hours. And along late in the afternoon out in Kansas they were—I remember in particular, Pittsburg, Kansas—we got a report that Truman was in the lead, which was normally a Republican stronghold, and Truman was leading by the second count, which I'll say is two o'clock. I may be wrong on the time. A number of precincts out in Sedgwick County around Wichita, and in various places, and invariably Truman was in the lead. It came to my old home county, Pawnee, which is normally Republican, rather substantially Republican; it was almost a breakeven for him. I remember speaking to the president about it. And he said, "Well, I've been telling you I was going to win all the time. It's nothing new."

Well, I just really got quite enthusiastic about it at that time. We had teletype machines in here from the news services; we had direct telephone lines, Secret Service lines, as I say, to the Republican headquarters because if his opponent had been elected, you know, they had to take charge. I remember that the chief of the White House detail was in New York at Republican headquarters to take charge of Mr. Dewey, and Nick, I think—that I spoke about—was here in Kansas City, because, of course, they had to still guard Mr. Truman. So, we were pretty well set up to know what was going on, and a number of headquarters were to call. Bill Boyle was there that evening with Matt Connelly and—I'm not sure Bill Boyle was there; no, I don't think he was—anyway, the phone rang and it was the Secret Service man. I answered the phone and he told me who it was, and he said he wanted to talk to Connelly. I could tell by the conversation that the president was on the line. Then I talked to him, and he said, "Well, I sneaked out of this dinner and I'm over in Excelsior Springs and nobody knows where I am, but this is where you can get me." It's the first time that I knew he was there, and so he was going to be there and spend the night.

Fuchs: Did the reporters suspect that he was missing?

Evans: No. Up to that time they wanted to know where he was; that he had left this dinner—it was out here in Independence some place; I've forgotten where—and I said, "Why, I presume he's home." Well, then, after he let us know where they were, I would go back into another room where the recorders were, and pull it off, then rush out and in, and call him at the hotel in Excelsior and give him the results of various states. And it was amazing how well he was doing and was way in the lead in the early stages, which was surprising for a candidate that was supposed to be defeated, but not surprising for a Democrat because the early returns — they're always in the lead; you know what I mean. I kept on giving those reports.

Then Connelly was busy talking to the various leaders in various states, like in New York and Boston and Philadelphia and down south and out west where the polls had not been closed very long. I was busy conveying this information. Well, he said not to call him until he called me. I don't know what time it was. I imagine it was somewhere around 10:30 or eleven o'clock that I talked to him. He had carried a couple of states that I didn't expect him to, and he laughed, "Well, we're going to win." Then it got fairly late, and, Jim, the election had gotten in this position: that for him to win, he either had to carry the state of Ohio, Illinois, or California. He'd be assured a victory if he carried either one of those three states, and California would be some time before it would come in. Ohio would be in ahead of Illinois because of the difference in time zones.

I remember talking to him. I said: "Well, Mr. President, you're just about in this position that you've got to carry either Ohio, Illinois, or California."

He said, "That's good. Don't bother me anymore; I'm going to bed; don't call me anymore."

And I said, "What the hell do you mean you're going to bed; you can't go to bed until you carry one of those states." Oh, you know, just screaming — I was worn out and excited naturally.

"Why," he said, "I'm going to carry all three."

I said, "Oh, boy, I'll settle for one."

Sure enough, he did; he carried Ohio, Illinois, and California. Then apparently when it was final that he had carried Ohio and Illinois, the Secret Service men woke him and he called up.

Fuchs: Is this the first time he put a call through?

Evans: Oh, no, no, no. He put many calls through.

Fuchs: One time you said he said, "Don't call me anymore; I'll call you."

Evans: That's the first time he put a call through after that, after he had said, "Don't call anymore; I'm going to bed." So, then he called up and he talked to Connelly and he talked to me, and he wanted to know who all was there, and it was final. We were waiting or had been told that Dewey would concede.

Fuchs: Who was there at that time?

Evans: Oh, my, there were a lot of people. The staff in itself was quite large with the Secret Service men, and I remember Jerome Walsh was there with Matt Connelly and I—we were the three principal ones. You remember Jerome Walsh?

Fuchs: Did you stay all night?

Evans: Oh, yes! So, in talking to him, which must have been along about— it was definite he was in—I would say it must have been about 2:30, he said, "Well, I'll see you in the morning."

And I said, "What time are you going to be here because that's what everybody wants to know?" Up until then we wouldn't say where he was.

Fuchs: You knew where he was prior to 2:30?

Evans: Oh, yes, I knew where he was.

Fuchs: But you told people you didn't know?

Evans: That's right, because everybody would clamor—it was just a madhouse. There were 150 or 200 reporters up and down that hall and twenty-five or thirty Secret Service men, and every time they'd see me they'd just clamor to get me to tell them where he was. Well, I didn't know where he was. That's what I kept saying: "I don't know."

"Has he called in yet?"

"Yes, I think Connelly's talked to him, but I haven't talked to him. I'm busy; I haven't talked to him."

Anyway, I said, "What time are you going to be here?" It would be awful if you got over here at six o'clock knowing how early you get up."

"What time do you think I ought to be over?"

And I said, "Eight o'clock."

And he said, "OK. You tell Charlie to tell them that I'll be there at eight o'clock."

Fuchs: Tom, in the last interview [September 18, 1963] we got to the point where you had talked to Mr. Truman on election night in 1948 and suggested that he come back from his retreat at Excelsior Springs to the Muehlebach Hotel around eight o'clock. Could you take up the story from there now, please?

Evans: Yes. He said that that was fine; he'd be there about eight o'clock. So, as near as I remember, I decided to take Mrs. Evans home about four o'clock that morning and I did. I lay down to get an hour or two nap, and about six o'clock someone called — I think it was Matt Connelly — and said the president had arrived. Being the early riser that he was, he was over at the penthouse in the Muehlebach at six o'clock. So, I hadn't undressed and I hadn't shaved or I hadn't cleaned up, but I immediately went down to the Muehlebach and went up to the penthouse. I think it was probably, then, about a quarter till seven, and it was a madhouse. The halls going into the penthouse were full, and I walked in the penthouse and it was packed full. I remember walking in, and sitting on the arm of the chair with the president was a man that was in Dewey headquarters the night before. That made me mad. That man was Vic Messall, who we've talked about before. He'd taken a plane when it looked like Mr. Truman was winning.

Fuchs: How did you know he'd been in Dewey headquarters the night before?

Evans: Because our Secret Service had been talking to their Secret Service men at Dewey headquarters and asked who all was there, and among them they said Vic Messall was there. Here he was sitting on the arm of the chair where the president was that early morning. You, of course, will recall the episode whereby he was not permitted on the campaign?

Fuchs: Yes, we have recorded that.

Evans: You have that in '44. So, knowing that he had been in Mr. Dewey's headquarters the night before and I not having much sleep, I was a little upset, and I guess I used some pretty bad language and said, "What the hell are you doing here?"

And, actually, I was pretty much upset about it, and the president looked up and smiling and he said, "Now, Tom, don't get mad. We're not mad at anybody you know. We won." And he was all joyous and everything.

So, I thought, "Well, that's fine, if it's all right with him." But it was quite a party, and the Secret Service men certainly did not have much control of who came in or out that particular morning. At that time, they were all friends — no enemies!

I think that just about covers that situation then, and, of course, the president said, "Well, I told you all along what was going to happen, but you wouldn't believe me." He was there quite awhile, and as near as I remember, Jim, he went to Independence about ten o'clock that morning. He took a number of personal telephone calls from people, but, of course, there were thousands of them that he couldn't take and wouldn't take. He went home about ten o'clock, and as near as I remember — I sometimes get confused between the '44 and the '48 campaign — but I think he left by special train that afternoon the day after the election and went back to Washington.

12

W. Averell Harriman

Washington, D.C. 1971

Interviewed by Richard D. McKinzie and Theodore A. Wilson

W. Averell Harriman (1891–1986), one of the richest men in America, was Truman's global troubleshooter. As the wartime ambassador to the Soviet Union, he was the first to warn the new president of the direction that Joseph Stalin would move after the Allied victory. Because of his extensive dealings with the Soviet dictator, the U.S. diplomat predicted a long and bitter struggle between the East and West. In 1946 he was named ambassador to Great Britain and then returned home as secretary of commerce. As the chairman of the Committee on Foreign Aid, he recommended a massive aid program to rebuild Europe and thwart Soviet ambitions. When Truman adopted this idea and named it the Marshall Plan, he sent Harriman to Europe as its chief administrator. He later served as special assistant to the president and as director of foreign aid. Elected governor of New York in 1954, he twice made unsuccessful bids for the Democratic presidential nomination. Though Truman endorsed him in 1956, he ran a weak second to Adlai E. Stevenson. The former president knew that his friend had little chance for the nomination. But he valued his loyalty. "I'm just a little fellow, lucky in politics, from Missouri," Truman once said, "but there is one great man in this town. He comes in, after all he has done for the Roosevelt administration, and says, 'I'd like a desk somewhere if you have room. In any way I can, I'd like to try to help the United States.'"

Wilson: One of the most voluminous subject files of information about wartime planning for the postwar world and the immediate postwar period deals with this question of the State Department's efforts, and the effort of the Treasury Department, to create an economic open world — Cordell Hull's idea. We'd like to have you react to that — describe how that might have come to you.

Harriman: I think there are telegrams that may or may not be available, which indicated that I very much had in mind the need to give Europe substantial aid after the war, after lend-lease was over. As a matter of fact, I

felt it should also include countries not involved in lend-lease — whose economies would be completely disorganized. UNRRA [United Nations Relief and Rehabilitation Agency] was not enough. Europe would need not just food but also raw materials and working capital to get the wheels of commerce going again. It wasn't just rebuilding factories; it was getting all the machinery of trade and commerce going again. Since they were without any foreign exchange, I felt it necessary for us to do something. I was particularly conscious of it, because I knew the condition Britain would be in, converting from wartime to peacetime economy.

I was very much concerned over our failure to come to an agreement with the British on continuing lend-lease assistance after the war was over. In fact, when Oliver Littleton was in the United States — I think it was around 1943 — I urged him to consider the needs of the postwar period, but apparently he was under instructions from [Sir Winston] Churchill not to do it, or didn't want to do it. He had immediate wartime emergency needs. This was the period when I used all the influence I had to get the British to abandon their export trade, and as much as possible convert all of their manufacturing facilities to the immediate needs of the war, including civilian as well as military requirements.

I felt a certain responsibility to help the British, as I had urged the British to abandon their export trade and convert to war production. You will remember, the British got most of their raw materials and half their food from abroad. Their ability to buy necessities from abroad was essential. We did give the British a three billion, seven or eight hundred–million-dollar loan. But I was very much upset that we didn't extend the principle of lend-lease into the postwar period.

As far as the Russians were concerned, I felt the reverse; they had adequate gold, if they wanted to buy, and they weren't dependent upon international trade. I felt they were more self-sufficient. The Russians obtained a number of plants under lend-lease which had been authorized by Washington, that I thought were not justified for their war effort. They wanted them for postwar use. I had a friendly feeling towards the Russians, but I felt they didn't need these plants. The Russians often took advantage of lend-lease. On one occasion — I think it was the time [Henry] Wallace came to the Soviet Union when we went to the Kolyma gold-fields — Wallace discovered a dredge which we were supposed to have given the Russians to deepen one of the harbors in the Pacific. But, we found the Russians using it to dredge for gold. Well, they received this dredge under lend-lease.

It didn't rest well with me that they had deceived us in that way. We never knew fully what they were doing. The British we knew; and it was very clear that the whole of Europe would be weakened, and that Communism — without help — would take over. I'm sure that was one of the reasons why Stalin broke his agreements, because the situation looked too good in Western Europe for a Communist takeover. I think Stalin was convinced he could move into Western Europe. He was undoubtedly told by leaders in the Communist Parties in Italy and France that their organizations were very strong; that with some help they would be able to take over Italy and France; and I think they would have done so if it hadn't been for the Marshall Plan.

So, my reports to Washington started in the autumn of '44 and '45 with some telegrams in which my general point of view was directed toward the above. It never occurred to me that we would have as grandiose a program as the Marshall Plan, but I felt that we had to do something to save Europe from economic disaster, which would encourage the Communist takeover.

McKinzie: You did not then get a great deal of Cordell Hull's view that after the war there would be a remarkable amount of commerce — normal commerce?

Harriman: No, My views were just the reverse. I was not at all in sympathy with this idea. You know, I ran the Marshall Plan in Paris. I and a small staff had control of the operations in Europe. We were pressing for EPU, European Payments Union. We had a lot of opposition from the Treasury Department on this and not much cooperation from State. I think their economic approach was just the reverse of ours. We were talking about really getting Europe on its feet. It was our hope that there would be a breakdown of trade barriers in Europe first, and then eventually a breakdown internationally, which would help increase trade with Europe.

I knew this would mean a temporary sacrifice for the United States to some extent. We had a lot of trouble with the Department of Treasury; they were not particularly keen on the European Payments Union. Our whole concept of the unification of Europe was that it would first contribute to economic unification. Then, we hoped to secure an economic-military unity and finally a political unity. In the first instance, it was obvious that, theoretically at least, there would be some sacrifice in trade to the United States, but in the long run the buying power of Europe would increase so greatly that we would gain.

Wilson: How are we to explain the continuation of this universalist philosophy in places like the Treasury? Was it because they were idealists or unrealistic, or was it because —

Harriman: Well, they were working on GATT [General Agreement on Tariffs and Trade]. Everybody seemed concerned about GATT. That's one trouble with bureaucracy. Bureaucrats are like hunting dogs. They are down a certain scent, and they stick to that scent, even though there may be some better scents in one direction or another. I use the word *scents* in a double meaning.

Wilson: Yes.

Harriman: I was all for the ideals, but I knew we were not in a position to get the ideal in the European Recovery Program. I was quite ready to accept certain restrictions on the United States. After all, there was a great dollar shortage. It was quite clear that the more prosperous Europe became, the more business there would be in the United States. My whole experience in banking showed me that. The biggest trade that Germany and Britain had was with each other, in the prewar period; I think I'm right in that. Two highly industrialized nations had the most trade with each other, and it wasn't tariff policies alone that made trade relations better for both of them. So, I had a different view than his idealistic theory of simply breaking down barriers. I was much more involved in the practical problem of getting Europe back on its feet and giving it an opportunity to move ahead — move forward — and everything we did was in that direction. EPU was an example; we had a lot of trouble with the Treasury in putting EPU through, the European Payments Union —

McKinzie: Yes.

Harriman: — and yet the European Payments Union, I'm satisfied, was a thing which made the Marshall Plan a success and made it possible for Europe to move rapidly after the Marshall Plan was finished. And I think in a sense it was one of the things that made it possible for Europe to become viable more rapidly. I was fighting for EPU; it had a good deal of support from the French, the Italians, and the Belgians.

The British were very much opposed to it; they had a great deal of difficulty. Sir Stafford Cripps was adamantly against it. They thought it would interfere with their sterling area; there were a lot of complications. It was hard to fully understand why they were opposed to it. One thing about Cripps was that after he made an agreement, he always did a little better than he said he would. It was very tough to get him to agree to something, but after he came to an agreement, he was very cooperative.

I look upon these theories, which were held in the Treasury and to some extent in the Department of State, as irritants against doing the job which we were trying to do and which we did in spite of their positions. I think the record shows that EPU was the most specific case. Yet, the whole preamble of the second authorization act for the Marshall Plan showed the direction Congress was ready to take about breaking down barriers within Europe. I was anxious that it shouldn't be just a customs union — a customs union which would exclude the United States. I wanted to see more fundamental understandings about greater integration than simply a customs union. That I think is happening, although some people call European integration more of a customs union than I do. I think it's more fundamental. The military aspects are also very important.

Actually, I'd had a certain amount of experience in Europe in the interwar period, as a banker, and I was also a member of the board of directors of the International Chamber of Commerce. I remember meeting in one of the executive committee meetings in Paris. I went there because I happened to be there; I was the only American of any prominence there — of any of the directors. They had a staff. One evening I remember that I met with the leading bankers and industrialists of the principal countries. I remember the British and German, the French — I can't remember who else was there. It was quite a small dinner — it was a private dinner. Yet, they took the International Chamber of Commerce more seriously than we did, and there were very important men present. I asked them why they thought that the United States was moving ahead as we were in the mid-twenties — you remember — whereas Europe was stagnant with built-in unemployment. They said it was because we had a continent of free trade.

And I said, "Well, if that's the case, why don't you with all your influence in different countries make the changes that are necessary to get freer trade in Europe?"

The answer was that unless there was a military understanding, freedom of trade could not exist. Because there wasn't a military understanding of some kind, every country, for its own security, demanded to be as autarkic as possible. And I think one man said, "From casting to forged big guns, to buttons on the uniform." I remember some of the details.

So, I went in to the Marshall Plan with the idea that both economic and military considerations had to be taken into account. This is one of the differences I had with [Paul] Hoffman. He wanted to limit it to economic goals alone, and I was very keen to see the NATO treaty become more of a reality, remembering this experience in the interwar period. Now that isn't an answer directly to your question, but it does show that we looked upon military integration and economic integration as supporting each other.

We did everything we could, of course, to develop the OEEC [Organization for European Economic Cooperation] as a vital organization. We were — I think I can use the word I — was determined that we would get the Europeans to divide aid. I had a horror of fourteen countries coming to the United States with their front feet in the trough. I thought the net result of that would be that we would have fourteen enemies of the United States and fourteen enemies among each other, because of the jealousy that would come.

How could you justify giving Holland twice the amount of money that you gave Belgium? Well, finally, I put it up to them. They said that they couldn't do it; it would destroy them. I said they had to do it. And I finally got support from Hoffman on it. We did get them to divide the aid, and that was one of the things that made the organization successful. We were dealing with the practical realities of the ghastly situation that existed in Europe when we took over. I don't know if you've ever had a full picture of what Europe was in the winter of 1947.

McKinzie: We have done some considerable work on it.

Harriman: Well, you know how desperate the situations were. I don't get into it until April. I went over there the first part of May, and I discovered the British had been very successful in laying down the organization of the OEEC. A young, brilliant economist, Robert Marjolin, headed OEEC, but he had little political prestige in the beginning. It took me a year to get an agreement on a permanent chairman of the ministerial committee of OEEC. We wanted to get [Paul-Henri] Spaak, but we got [Dirk U.] Stikker, who was a fine fellow and a very able fellow. Spaak was a little too active. The British opposition to him was mostly because he was a Socialist. Everything we did was to strengthen European unity. The European Payments Union was an effective move. It was very much in the direction of the integration of Europe.

On the sidelines we had Jean Monnet, who worked on the specifics of the coal and steel community. I kept in touch with him. Any agreement between [Robert] Schuman and [Dr. Konrad] Adenauer was of major significance. I was never directly involved in what they were doing, but these were related to what we were trying to do. So, these were the things that interested us, and not the ideological trade concepts advanced by Mr. Hull. I'm very much in favor of as much free trade as you can get in the world, but I've never looked upon it as an ideological concept. You've got to move in that direction, but also deal with realities.

Wilson: We have the impression from the documentation that a tinge of this ideological idealism may have crept into the Washington office of the ECA [Economic Cooperation Administration] — about how to proceed with European integration. That is, there was pressure for rather large-scale commitments on the part of the European nations to work together, and that perhaps you were rather more interested in going a step at a time again. Is that correct?

Harriman: Well, I think it was true. ECA was separate from State. We didn't clash so much with State as we did with Treasury.

Wilson: What were the circumstances of you taking on the Harriman Committee [president's Committee on Foreign Aid] assignment?

Harriman: I know that the president wanted to have a thorough analysis. He knew how to deal with Congress. Everybody gives General Marshall credit for the Marshall Plan. I don't want to take one iota of credit for the Marshall Plan, but there is one man who is responsible for the Marshall Plan and that was Harry S. Truman, because he developed the plan and got it through Congress. Anyway, I have no idea exactly how these three committees were developed.

There was the [Edwin] Nourse committee, which was the Committee of Economic Advisers. Then there was the Committee on Resources, which was headed by —

McKinzie: Julius Krug.

Harriman: — who was then secretary of the interior.

This [the Harriman committee] was a very strangely organized committee, because you had a secretary of commerce as chairman of it, with all the other members being private citizens drawn from industry, commerce, banking, finance, the intellectual world, labor, Congress. It was a group with very wide opinions. Who got the idea of putting me in an as chairman, I don't know; you'll have to find that out from somebody else. I think at the time — you see this was 1947 — I was still considered more of a businessman than a politician. I don't know why. I don't know who was the man that made the decision — maybe Dean Acheson. I don't know. Have you seen anything?

Wilson: We've seen some early memoranda on the development of the idea. One, there is a Policy Planning Staff memorandum, apparently responding to a speech by [Senator Arthur H.] Vandenberg on or about the fourteenth of June, in which he says the Marshall speech was a fine idea and now we need a bipartisan group — a blue-ribbon group — to see whether it's feasible or not.

Harriman: I know Vandenberg was called in on the composition of this group. I got along very well with Vandenberg. We were very good friends. I had respect for him. I think it really was mutual. He was responsible for the addition of two men. One was Owen D. Young and the other was Bob [Senator Robert M.] La Follette [Jr.]. He felt that selection was not sufficiently wide or popular. He knew the people; he didn't question their ability or anything.

Wilson: Yes, yes.

Harriman: He was looking for people whose names would carry with them a stamp of public approval — the stamp that would gain public approval. So, I remember he added those two names, Young and La Follette. He told me he thought it wasn't quite representative enough. They were very capable men, all of them. He always told me that it was that rapport that made it possible for him to get the legislation through Congress.

13

Paul G. Hoffman

New York, New York   October 25, 1964

Interviewed by Philip C. Brooks

Paul G. Hoffman (1891–1974), administrator of the Marshall Plan, was the proto-
type of the public-spirited industrialist. During the 1930s he gained recognition
as the dynamic young president of Studebaker. After leading the automobile
company's turnaround, he was touted as a potential contender for the White
House. In April 1948 Truman named the progressive Republican to run the Marshall Plan as the chief of the Economic Cooperation Administration. Hoffman,
who had lived the American dream, viewed foreign aid as a national obligation.
"Paul Hoffman came closer to being a saint, in the secular sense, than any man
I have ever met in politics," the journalist Theodore H. White wrote three decades
after the Marshall Plan. Under Hoffman's direction, the Marshall Plan provided
the equivalent of about $200 billion in current dollars to seventeen European na-
tions. Western Europe recovered more quickly than Hoffman had anticipated.
"What we didn't really give importance to, and should have," he recalled, "was
a factor called hope."

Brooks: Perhaps you can tell me how you happened to get into the European
   Recovery Program in the first place. I would be much interested to know.
Hoffman: That story never has been told. Early in March 1948, I heard rumors that I might be considered for the post of administrator of the Marshall Plan. At about the same time General William Draper asked me
   to serve as a member of a commission to study the economic situation
   in Japan and Korea. I accepted at once, thinking I would be in Korea and
   out of reach when the legislation setting up the Marshall program was
   passed. My scheming didn't work. The passage of the ECA legislation was
   delayed, and I was en route home at the time. When I reached Honolulu,
   I found a telephone call waiting for me from John Steelman saying that
   President Truman wanted to have a talk with me as soon as possible. I
   said to John, "Would you mind telling me what it is about?"
      He told me that after some delay the ECA act had been passed and the

president wanted to talk to me about serving as administrator of the Marshall program.

I said, "That is very flattering, but how soon will the president have to have his answer?"

He said, "Immediately."

I said, "In that case, much as I regret it, my answer has to be no, because I have family and business associates with whom I would have to discuss so far-reaching a change."

His answer was, "How soon can you be in Washington?"

I told him approximately five days.

I did arrive in Washington in five days, and before I went to see President Truman, I called my good friend Senator Arthur Vandenberg and told him that I had been informed that President Truman was going to ask me to take on this assignment. I told him that for many reasons it would be impossible for me to do so.

The senator's reply was, "You don't dare refuse if the president offers this opportunity to you."

I said, "Yes, I dare." And that ended our conversation.

I met with President Truman by appointment. He formally asked me to accept the post of administrator. I replied, "Mr. President, I am deeply appreciative of your offer, but it would be a mistake for me to accept it because I don't really want to leave Studebaker at this time. I have been working for the last thirteen years trying to help get the Studebaker Corporation to a point where it was making real money. It is there today, and I want to be around for the next five years. May I add that it would be a mistake for you to appoint me because I have employed a good many thousand people in my day and I never knew anyone who didn't want the job that was offered to perform satisfactorily."

The president's reply was, "Well, Mr. Hoffman, some of the best people we have in government have to be drafted. We hope you'll prove to be one of them, and I am expecting you to say yes."

I said, "Mr. President, I certainly will give it the most serious consideration. I'll telephone Mrs. Hoffman; I'll telephone my business associates and see what can be worked out."

We left on that note.

Much to my surprise, at 4:30 that afternoon when I was involved in a press conference at the Pentagon on the Japanese and Korean economies, one of the reporters asked me, "Have you been offered the post as ECA administrator?"

Because I felt that this was a confidential matter between the president and myself, I replied, with my tongue in my cheek, "What does the job pay?" His answer was twenty thousand dollars a year.

I said, "It must be a good job."

At that moment a loudspeaker came on stating that the president had just announced that Paul G. Hoffman just accepted the post as Marshall Plan administrator. So, I found myself in a job that I had never accepted.

Brooks: Did that bother you at the time?

Hoffman: At the time it seriously troubled me, but in drafting me as Marshall Plan administrator, President Truman did as great a favor for me as one man can do for another. It opened my eyes to many things of which I was totally unaware, and it was the beginning of my real education.

Brooks: Mr. Hoffman, I am curious to know how much you knew about the Marshall Plan before that, if anything.

Hoffman: I had been a member of the committee under Averell Harriman, which studied the report of the committee headed by Sir Oliver Franks, which had been appointed to ascertain the amount of United States goods that would be required to restore Europe to its prewar level of agricultural and industrial production. Their estimate was $25 billion worth of goods and services and a period of four years to complete the program. The Harriman committee's report concluded that a job could be done for $17 billion, but concurred in the estimate that it would take four years to do it.

It might be interesting for me to break in here and tell you that at the end of two and a half years, agricultural production in the Marshall Plan countries was 20 percent ahead of the 1938 level, and industrial production was 40 percent ahead, and the total cost of the program up to that time had been under $10 billion.

Brooks: Were there people who predicted that recovery could not take place in the four-year time period, that it might take even a decade?

Hoffman: That is correct. However, from the very beginning of the program, we made it perfectly clear that we would be out of Europe in four years; that whatever was to be accomplished had to be accomplished in that period of time. We also made it clear that primary responsibility for the recovery program rested with the Europeans themselves. The first line of the Harriman report, a line which I am proud to say I wrote, was "Only the

Europeans can save Europe." And major credit for recovery belongs to the Europeans.

Brooks: This high degree of cooperation among Europeans is what interests me most. Did you know before the Marshall speech of June 1947 about the content of that speech?

Hoffman: No.

Brooks: One of the most significant things that he said was that the European countries should get together and express their needs collectively. This really seems to have been the beginning of European cooperation.

Hoffman: That was the beginning. We were very insistent that there be cooperation, and we wanted that cooperation expressed with something other than words. The Europeans had made two promises to the United States if Marshall Plan help was forthcoming. The first promise was maximum self-help on the part of every country; and second, maximum mutual aid.

In December of 1948, an historic meeting took place between Sir Stafford Cripps and the other ministers who were members of the Organization for European Economic Cooperation, which we helped organize, and my associates and myself. We told them — very pleasantly, I hope, but very firmly — that whereas they had made good on their first promise, that is, maximum self-help, that little or nothing had been done to make good on their second promise, which was maximum mutual aid. I said that it would be our responsibility to tell the Congress of the United States in February of 1949 precisely what had happened unless they took some steps and quickly to make good on their promise of mutual aid. The situation was really intolerable because all the Marshall Plan countries were maintaining not only prohibitive tariffs but also exchange controls and import quotas, which almost completely blocked intra-European trade. We insisted that all devices for blocking trade be sharply reduced.

Brooks: What happened at that historic conference?

Hoffman: Most of the ministers for the Marshall Plan countries were present with Sir Stafford Cripps acting as their spokesman. Along about midnight, Sir Stafford Cripps asked if I would meet with him alone. I said certainly. As our conversation started, he seemed to be somewhat exasperated by my insistence that something must be done to reduce trade barriers and fast. He said, "Well, what will satisfy you?"

I said, "If in February we can report to the Congress that 50 percent of the barriers to trade among the European countries have been removed, Congress would, I believe, be satisfied." I further stated that by a 50 percent reduction, we meant a reduction in the total volume of trade among the countries, not 50 percent of the items that make up trade, in some of which there was little or no volume.

At 3 A.M. he said, "We'll have that 50 percent reduction in effect by February 1, 1949." It was done.

Brooks: You were expecting a great deal of cooperation from the European countries so soon after the war, and many of them had been at each other's throats. It was a rather remarkable accomplishment.

Hoffman: The reduction which took place in January of 1949 was, of course, only one step toward the great expansion in intra-European trade that was needed. Of all the moves that were made, the most important was the organization of the European Payments Union. This followed late in 1949 and made possible the use of nonconvertible currencies on the part of Marshall Plan countries for payment of goods exchanged among them. Once the services of the Payments Union became available, the upturn in trade was spectacular. It was a major factor in the success of the Marshall Program.

Brooks: Another thing I was told in many countries was that much of the credit for accomplishments of the Marshall program went to the Americans who headed the missions in the Marshall Plan countries. Now, these people, I assume, were chosen by you. Did you have any magic device in choosing these officials?

Hoffman: The magic was in the Marshall Plan itself. It provided an opportunity for appealing and constructive work. In a sense, the mission chiefs were given the opportunity to help act as architects for the new Europe that was envisioned.

Brooks: There was a certain amount of idealism involved?

Hoffman: Oh, yes. But the idealists employed as mission chiefs were also realists. This is true of every one of them, but as examples, I'll give you David Bruce in France, John McCloy in Germany, David Zellerbach in Italy, and Thomas Finletter in Great Britain.

Brooks: They were all specifically mentioned to me by the people in Europe. By the way, I gathered you had a fairly free hand in selecting them, did you not?

Hoffman: Completely. I would like to say that no man ever was given finer cooperation than that given me by President Truman. If he had listened to some of his advisers and had tried to make the Marshall Plan a political dumping ground for unqualified politicians, it couldn't have been a success. We had to have good people. And we weren't interested in whether they were Republicans or Democrats. What we wanted to know was their record, what they had accomplished. There were, of course, complaints about our failure to employ certain individuals recommended by highly placed party officials. A complaint would be made to the president and he would ask me why it was that we had not acted favorably on the suggestion of Mr. So-and-So that his friend be employed as a mission chief. I would answer because we had found a better man, and that would be the end of the conversation.

Brooks: Mr. Bruce was much impressed because you had a free hand selecting people and thought that that was among the most important elements in the success of the program. Would you want to comment briefly on . . . well, one of the most important things it seems to me, Mr. Hoffman, about which there was uncertainty at the time — or at least a difference in the understanding and opinion — was how much integration of the European countries Americans wanted or expected. Did you see as one of the aims the achievement of a high degree of economic cooperation, perhaps going as far as the common market, or were you thinking in terms of political union?

Hoffman: Those of us involved in the actual administration of the Marshall program had very much in our minds the building of a new Europe. We had been persuaded by Jean Monnet and others that there was no hope for progress of a compartmentalized Europe and that in a postwar world, Europe's future would be dim unless there was close cooperation among the Marshall Plan countries. Speaking personally, I thought that union would first come along economic lines and that some degree of political union was certain to follow. The reasons for economic union were compelling. In its best prewar year, Europe with almost 300 million people had a gross national product of $150 billion. In that same year, the United States with 150 million people had a gross national product of $300 billion. If Europe's gross national production for individuals had been what it was in the United States, Europe's gross national product would have been approximately $600 billion. Among the reasons for this was the fact that the USA is one mass market. It is only when you have a mass market that large-scale manufacturing which involves very substantial expenditures can be justified.

Brooks: Were you also concerned about the fact that in prewar Europe, workers from one country were barred from going to another country?

Hoffman: Certainly, because some postwar European countries had a surplus of labor and in others there was an insufficient supply. The full potential of labor can be utilized only if there is mobility in labor. If there was to be a new Europe, there not only had to be a common market but also great mobility in labor.

Brooks: I judge you think that the Monnet Plan was a significant factor in the concept of a united Europe.

Hoffman: Yes, Jean Monnet was the father of the concept of a United States of Europe, and his efforts more than those of any other single man helped change the thinking of European leaders.

Brooks: Was there any one aspect of the relations between the USA and the European countries that seemed particularly important?

Hoffman: Yes. I have already mentioned the fact that we helped organize the OEEC. This was quite an undertaking because certain of the European countries felt that they should have the right to deal directly with the USA. We were confident that if this were done, many misunderstandings would result. As a consequence, we insisted that every one of the sixteen recovery programs should be screened by the OEEC and further, that the OEEC should have the responsibility of recommending to us the amount of assistance that should be given to each country.

Brooks: Did you regard the Marshall program as closely related to or quite different from the Greek-Turkish aid program?

Hoffman: Quite different because economic and military aid were combined in the Greek-Turkish program, whereas during the time I was administrator, the Marshall Plan was restricted to economic aid only. This was in keeping with the concept set forth by General Marshall in his address at Harvard University in June 1947, when he said, "Our policy is directed not against any country or doctrine, but against hunger, poverty, desperation, and chaos. Its purpose should be the revival of a working economy in the world so as to permit the emergence of political and social conditions in which free institutions can exist."

Brooks: Some of the people I have talked to in Europe felt that it was a mistake for the Marshall Plan to concentrate totally on speeding recovery.

Hoffman: I am well aware of this. We were in fact under continuing attack because we did not devote our energies to directly fighting against Communism. It was our feeling that such an effort would be divisive and would slow down recovery. Contrariwise, we felt that if speeding recovery did take place as a result of our concentrating solely on that goal, the peoples of Europe would realize that they did not have to give up their freedoms to assure lives of decency and dignity. We were correct in this assumption because the countries of Western Europe are today strong and free.

Brooks: Some of the people in Greece told me that the Marshall Plan was really an outgrowth of the Truman Greek-Turkey doctrine. They said this with great pride.

Hoffman: That is fine.

Brooks: Well, I would like to ask you about a number of people individually. Did you see President Truman a good deal; did you work with him pretty closely?

Hoffman: Oh, yes; I didn't bother him any more than I had to, but I saw him quite frequently, and, as I said, I learned to have not only great regard but deep affection for him. He went far beyond merely keeping his word about no political interference with the program, but went beyond this. He gave active help and offered many constructive suggestions. History will, I am sure, accord him a great place because of many qualities, but among them, courage and never-failing common sense.

14

Robert A. Lovett

New York, New York   July 7, 1971

Interviewed by Richard D. McKinzie and Theodore A. Wilson

Robert A. Lovett (1895–1986), secretary of defense and undersecretary of state, was General George C. Marshall's alter ego. When Truman named Marshall as secretary of state, the general accepted on the condition that the Wall Street banker would be his undersecretary. Three years later, when Truman asked Marshall to become defense secretary, it was on the same terms, with the additional commitment that Lovett would be the general's successor. "He was the very embodiment of the establishment, a man who had a sense of country rather than party," the journalist David Halberstam wrote of Marshall's heir.

Lovett: I went then to the Department of State. I was ripped out of a pleasant day-to-day life to go down as his undersecretary. The most *extraordinary* accomplishments were made in a period — during the period in which the government had a biparty system in operation with the Republicans in charge of the Congress and the Democrats in charge of the executive offices, administration — and it worked beautifully. We had Greek-Turkish aid, we had the Berlin airlift, we had the Marshall plan, and we had the NATO organization.

McKinzie: An exciting period.

Lovett: It was an exciting period and a fruitful period of extraordinary goodwill, thanks largely to the president's amazing leadership and very largely to Senator [Arthur] Vandenberg's chairmanship of the Senate Foreign Relations Committee, with whom I was always completely frank, under the instructions of the president. I would stop by Senator Vandenberg's apartment on the way home with a sheaf of telegrams in my hand and go over what had happened during the day with him, if it was a thing in which he was interested. Some things he'd never talk with me about at all — China.

   "No," he said, "that's not up to you; that's Secretary [George C.] Marshall, the China problem. But everything else," he said, "you're in charge here, and I'd just like to know what's going on."

I've forgotten a detail — don't hold me to the statistics — but I thought there were forty-nine major pieces of legislation produced by that mixed Senate Foreign Relations Committee unanimously, too. An amazing performance; it's worth looking up; it's a fantastic thing.

Wilson: Do you recall the circumstances of your being asked to come back to Washington in July of 1947? Was it for a specific assignment, or did you expect to be there for a long time when you went back into government service?

Lovett: No, no, I didn't expect to go. No, he asked me. We were living then in the old superintendent's cottage on my father's place out at Locust Valley waiting to sell his place. And a superintendent's cottage was a garage underneath, and it had a couple of bedrooms and bath upstairs, and then there was a dining room and a little sitting room and a kitchen downstairs — to get breakfast in my bathrobe and then dressed after breakfast. And the telephone was in Mrs. Lovett's room, not in my room upstairs, with an extension downstairs. And the phone rang while I was having breakfast, and I heard it stop ringing because she picked it up, and she said, "Bob, Washington is calling."

And I said, "Washington? Who is it?"

She said, "I don't know, but you'd better take the call; it's Washington calling."

So, I picked up the phone; I was on the extension, and this voice that I did not recognize said, "Bob?"

And I said, "Yes."

He said, "This is the president."

And I said, "Now listen, this isn't at all funny. It's 6:45 in the morning. I'm right in the middle of breakfast, I'm trying to get the early commuter train to New York, and for god's sake this is no time for jokes!"

He said, "No, this is really the president."

So, I said, "Well, I beg your pardon, sir; I didn't realize that."

And then he said in effect, "I've got to get a new secretary of state, and I've signed up General Marshall on the condition which he made that you'd come down and be his undersecretary. So," he said, "I want you to do that tonight."

And I said, "All right, sir. I've got to go and check with my partners; I've got to get permission to get out of the firm, and the New York State Bank Department has to approve. But I don't anticipate too much trouble; I'll call you back as soon as I've gotten hold of my partners."

And I came into town. I was reasonably sure that they wouldn't make any trouble about it, but getting out of a general copartnership of unlimited liability in a bank is a very difficult process. Particularly since I'd gotten out once before and was out for five or five and a half years or six years. I had to then sell anything that had anything to do with the thousands of companies with which the military was dealing with; of course, we were a very large element in the foreign thing, and I knew the foreign business like the inside of my hat because I'd been in charge of it for some time now. So, I got hold of [Roland] Harriman and I telephoned Averell; saw the other partners and they said, "Well, you're a darned fool, but if you feel you have to do it, go ahead." Then I think I saw Davis and Polk, our lawyers, and they had to draw all these papers and I had to go up and see the superintendent of banks, and the State Banking Department, and he had to call a special session and finally got it wound up over a period of time.

And I called the president the next day. Miss — I've forgotten the name of . . . she cooperated on it — Hackmeister or something like that, called her back and said, "Find out from the president — from Rose Conway — what time the president would be available and I'll call him back."

She did and I said, "All right, I'll be down as soon as I can, but I've got to get unhooked up here first"; because I can't have any interests in anything that has to do with foreign affairs, so I had to get out of the firm completely again, pull everything that had anything to do with it. And that was a very painful process, you know.

Wilson: Your response, though, was automatic; that is, you viewed this in a sense as another tour of duty.

Lovett: I think because of my very deep affection for General Marshall and the president both — the two of them — and I said later when they took me down to Washington, a lot of old-time newspapermen that I knew well said, "Lovett, you're out of your head coming down here; they almost killed you the last time."

I said, "The three people in the world I can't say no to — one of them is my wife, one of them is Henry L. Stimson, and the other is George Marshall. And now we've got to add to that list the president that I think has done an absolutely superb job, and I think we're in one hell of a mess. So, if he thinks I can do anything — I don't think I can — if he thinks I can do anything, why there isn't anything to do but go down there."

Wilson: You came in at probably one of the most *difficult* and *delicate* times, perhaps, in the whole period when the United States had just pushed the European nations to get together to negotiate a package —

Lovett: We hadn't really gotten to that, yet, you see. I mean, here was Europe, a potentially very powerful influence in the world. In particular, we were interested in having some reasonable form of government, some stability, and some economic resurgence, but Europe was down on her knees, and Europe was in a vacuum. Well, not only nature had caused the vacuum, but the Soviets love one. So, the best defense, it became clear — and we felt that way for some time — was to move in and get those people going on the basis of self-help. That's why the Marshall Plan was such a brilliant conception. Incidentally, it's one of the few big programs that this government ever undertook where the estimates were reasonably accurate and where we got out of it and wound it up. Of course, the great principle there was self-help. Let the Europeans make the allocation of funds. Don't rush in between the upper and nether millstones and get ground to bits; let them do it, and make sure that you put in controls all the way through. Well, it worked out; I must say it was the most amazing performance I ever saw.

Wilson: When you came down, was it understood that you would be responsible certainly for economic matters? That is, with your background, I assume —

Lovett: It was General Marshall's instructions to me. You see, the State Department then had, really, two undersecretaries. There was *the* undersecretary; that was me. Then there was the undersecretary for economic affairs; that was Will Clayton. Well, that was an abortive move, trying to give recognition to some of the serious economic questions around the world; but General Marshall always worked on the theory that to have a good military operation, if the captain is hot, the lieutenant has got to know enough to take over. He always said, "Frankly, I don't understand half of this business going on." And he said, "I've just got to have you down here."

Well, of course, I was absolutely devoted to him; he was the most wonderful man, and we got along beautifully, and with the president setting — I think — the tone. The president said, "General Marshall, I never want you to have anything whatsoever to do with politics. You leave that to me; I'll take care of that."

And, of course, this was in a very rough campaign. Everybody was madder than hell at everybody else, and the president said the same thing:

"I want you and Lovett to have no part at all in the political campaign; don't make any speeches; don't do anything." That is the only basis on which the general would take it anyway. Here I am a registered Republican voting independent, which, in my case, meant I was voting the Democratic ticket always — not because I was a Democrat but because I thought they had either better men or a better idea of what was going on.

McKinzie: Were you a little bit agonized — troubled I should say — when later on the China business came up and that did become a little partisan, I think?

Lovett: Oh, that was definitely partisan. It was made partisan in part by a senator from California, [William F.] Knowland, yes, and a representative from Minnesota, [Walter] Judd, who'd been a Chinese missionary. But that was kept embalmed; we never made any speeches, we never attacked them, we never attacked the pro-China party. We would not infiltrate — government was not infiltrated by the pro-Chinese, in the way the government has now been infiltrated by the "doves," and the antiwar and the "peace now" people, and people who I think would walk a very narrow line on treason. I don't know what else you could call it, regardless of what you feel about it now. I think it was one of the stupidest things we ever did to go into Vietnam. We went through Korea, and the understanding was then — and proof of this lies with what was called a "never again club," which I think was started by General Walton Walker II and General Matt Ridgway. They, and even Max Taylor, always said, "Never again get into combat on the mainland of Asia in an infantry sense, ground troops. Don't use ground troops."

So, that's the reason for my yelling about the infiltrators and the "fifth columnists" operation here. Now, you have actually seen — in my opinion — actually seen the peace movement start from a very small group of real peace-loving people. You've seen that taken over by a very well-organized movement which has been able, even though small, to generate a very large following, partly because of the length of time, partly because of disgust, partly because of the stupidity of the whole affair, lack of success in the enterprise; all these things contributed, I'm sure. Nevertheless, there was none of that type of thing in our dealings with the China lobby in Washington. As I recall — it may have existed, but I never saw it.

Wilson: Let me ask one more question about politics. How much did the concern or feeling that probably President Truman would not win reelection in 1948 — how much did this affect the situation that you were going through in 1947, '48? Was that sort of a constant factor, or did you just work on the basis of, well, he's president now and we'll —

Lovett: I never paid any attention to it.

Wilson: Did people around you — did you feel they weren't — they were not?

Lovett: No, never. I believe — and I can't be sure about this obviously — but I believe that Jim Forrestal was affected by the doubts as to how you would turn over the helm of government to a different party with so many critical problems. So that he was for discussing various policies with the *potential* successor government, and I believe that is what caused his breakdown. I think Arthur Krock points that out rather well in his last book; if you're interested in it, you'll find a detailed statement on it.

Wilson: One of the things that's been so intriguing to us is something that you alluded to before we turned on the tape recorder. You were stressing the sense of security that you had and the sense of trust that the president placed in you and that you could count on him. This is a time when there's this man from Missouri, who is not sophisticated in any normal sense, and he has around him a group of very strong people. Very strong — General Marshall and Harriman and Dean Acheson and people who are in a sense very different in background — and yet everyone says basically the same thing that you said.

Lovett: There's no question about it in my mind. I had served, of course, initially under [Franklin] Roosevelt, who had quite a different type of approach, and Roosevelt wanted to play every instrument in the band, really, and that's a good way to get a split lip. President Truman was *practically* ideally equipped for this job. He was blunt in his statements when he had to be; he was courageous, he was thoughtful, he was hardworking, he knew the way the government works as nobody I ever saw before, and he had personal qualities which were extremely attractive. He was modest almost to the point of a fault, but there wasn't any question of who was boss. And, of course, he was helped almost immeasurably by his wife, Bess Truman, who is one of the finest women I ever saw in my life. My wife and I absolutely loved her; she was simply superb, and there was, we felt, a sense of unity in that family, which God knows was lacking in many of the previous ones. I think of the comment that was made by Professor Isaiah Berlin — of Oxford or Cambridge, I believe it was — who said,

"When the history of this century is written, Truman will be one of the five greatest presidents."

Not being a historian, I would gladly accept that. If I were a historian, I would probably cut it down in total number a little bit, because Mr. Truman and Mrs. Truman, as presences in the White House, were absolutely superb.

15

Samuel I. Rosenman

New York, New York   October 15, 1968, and April 23, 1969

Interviewed by Jerry N. Hess

Samuel I. Rosenman (1896–1973), Truman's first presidential counsel, worked with Franklin D. Roosevelt for two decades. Appointed to the New York Supreme Court while FDR was governor, he remained a political adviser and speechwriter. When some of Roosevelt's associates questioned the new president's leadership, the judge stood with Truman. That meant a lot to the subject of this book. HST observed in his diary that Rosenman was "absolutely loyal and trustworthy."

Hess: Judge, in the light of the fact that you held the most important position on the White House staff to be carried over from the Roosevelt administration, could you tell me why Mr. Roosevelt chose you for that position in the first place?

Rosenman: I had acted as counsel to the governor in New York State, during both of his periods as governor. In that position I had the function not only of being a legal counselor, but also doing a great many things that are peripheral to the counselorship, such as helping in speeches, helping in drafting statements, general policy advice. I also helped during his campaign for Governor.

Hess: President Truman states in his *Memoirs*, volume 1, page 192, that he believed that James Byrnes knew that President Roosevelt had his name under consideration at the time that Mr. Byrnes phoned Mr. Truman in Independence and asked him to place his name in nomination. What's your opinion on that matter?

Rosenman: Well, the question is well worded since it refers to opinion, because I have tried to ascertain the facts, without success. I know that among the group that were around the president talking about a substitute for Wallace, Jimmy Byrnes was frequently mentioned. There were two objections to Byrnes: One was that the Negroes wouldn't vote for him; and the second was that the rank and file of labor wouldn't vote for him.

I believe — and it's only a belief — that Byrnes knew about this discussion. He also knew that Harry Truman was being considered, and I believe with President Truman that that's one of the reasons that he called Truman up. I think Truman believes that it was to get him out of the running. I don't think it was that as much as to be able finally to convince the president that he was a good, liberal Democrat; otherwise, Senator Truman wouldn't have anything to do with his nomination. I agree with Truman's opinion. I don't think that it will ever be proved or disproved — except by Byrnes himself. If anybody could get into Frank Walker's skull, I think he probably did tell Jimmy Byrnes.

Hess: What had been the nature of the relationship between Mr. Byrnes and Mr. Truman up until that point in time?

Rosenman: I think up until Mr. Byrnes left the White House and became secretary of state. He thought that Byrnes was carrying out his own policies rather than Truman's, and I'm sure he [Truman] thought of him [Byrnes] in terms of insubordination and as one who wanted to perpetuate his own policy. Byrnes, I'm sure, thought all the time that he should have been sitting in that chair in which Mr. Truman was sitting. I don't think he disguised that belief very much. Personally, I had become quite cynical about Byrnes. Although we started out as friends, I thought that Byrnes was quite selfish and interested only in Byrnes himself.

When I heard from President Truman that he expected to appoint Byrnes right after the United Nations was organized and Stettinius expected to resign — I had had some rather bad experiences with Byrnes in the White House under President Roosevelt. Being a kind of a "no" man, I said to President Truman, "I don't think you know Jimmy Byrnes, Mr. President. You think you do. In the bonhomie of the Senate, he's one kind of a fellow; but I think you will regret this, and if I were you, I wouldn't do it." Well, he'd been a longtime friend of Byrnes, and he appointed him. Later on, he told me that I was right in warning him, but he had nothing to go on. I said, "I've had plenty in the White House with Jimmy Byrnes and so have other people." At any rate, everything was fine until he became secretary of state, and then gradually Truman's opinion of Byrnes began to go down very rapidly.

Hess: What were a few of those unfortunate experiences you had with Byrnes in the White House?

Rosenman: Anytime that we had a conference around the president in which everybody would speak frankly around the table, Byrnes would sneak in, and in the absence of the rest of us, advance arguments which obviously we couldn't hear and refute. Then he was very petty with the president, always threatening to resign if the president didn't do what he wanted him to. I think President Roosevelt was getting fed up with Jimmy, too. There was nothing he could do; Jimmy held a very important war job. And then Jimmy became very much like Louis Howe. He became very jealous of people around the president. He thought he ought to be the only one, and he developed great hostility to me because of that.

Hess: What seemed to be President Roosevelt's attitude towards Senator Truman during Mr. Truman's first term in the Senate?

Rosenman: I never saw anything which would permit me to gauge his attitude. I know that he got reports on how the various senators voted, particularly whether they were voting with the liberal side or the conservative side. So, I assume he must have been very pleased by Truman's votes, because the fact is he had a 100 percent voting record, from Roosevelt's point of view, so far as I recall. I don't think he meant any more to Roosevelt during the first term than any other of the many senators.

Hess: In your opinion, did President Roosevelt's attitude undergo a change after Mr. Truman became chairman of the Special Committee to Investigate the National Defense Program?

Rosenman: No, as I say, I never saw anything to indicate the president's attitude until he actually came down to the time when he chose a vice president. I know that he was impressed by the fact that the special committee of Truman's didn't interfere in the war the way the similar Civil War committee used to interfere. You know, they used to go down and hold their meetings on the battlefield. And Truman was very careful.

Hess: In your opinion, how instrumental was Mr. Truman's handling of that committee to his receiving the vice presidential nomination?

Rosenman: I should say, only auxiliary. I think the chief thing which convinced the president was the fact that he had a voting record in consonance with Roosevelt's principles, on the theory that he would carry on. That doesn't mean that I thought that he thought he was going to die, but he wanted to have a liberal to succeed him, if he did. He had an awful fight, you know, with the conservatives in the convention, and while he must have admired the way Truman handled that committee, I think that that was purely an added reason. The chief reason was the voting record. I don't recall any statement that President Roosevelt made about Truman until June of 1944 when it came to picking an alternative for Wallace.

Hess: In your opinion, why did President Roosevelt think that Mr. Truman would do well in the position?

Rosenman: Well, that's very hard to say. I know that it was very hard to think of anybody who could have done worse than Wallace, who had no means of cooperating with the Congress, with the most idealistic, almost exotic, views. You know, the other man under consideration at the time that Truman was, was Justice [William O.] Douglas —very seriously under consideration. Neither of these men had had any executive experience, either as governor or even as head of a business. I think that Roosevelt thought that anybody whose heart is in the right place as he thought Truman's was, would do all right in the presidency. Roosevelt had had some experience running the state of New York, but there are a great many presidents there who came from the Senate who had never had any executive experience.

Hess: Mr. Truman was labeled by some as being the "senator from Pendergast." Did you ever hear Mr. Roosevelt refer to any connection between Tom Pendergast and Senator Truman?

Rosenman: The answer to that is no. I don't think in the first place that would have bothered Roosevelt any more than the fact that I was a graduate of the Tammany Hall District Club, whose leader eventually went to jail, Jimmy Hines. Had anything ever entered Roosevelt's mind that I would do things, or that Truman would do things for Pendergast that shouldn't be done, he might have felt differently. I never heard him refer to any connection between Truman and Pendergast.

Hess: Mr. Truman states in the first volume of his *Memoirs* on page 28 that before he moved into the White House on April 14, 1945, he did some work on an outline of a speech he was preparing for his appearance before Congress the following Monday and states: "With the help of Steve Early and Judge Rosenman, Roosevelt's personal Counsel, I had already begun this outline." Does that speech square with your recollection of those troubled times?

Rosenman: Yes. You see, I had already sent in my resignation as had Steve Early and all the key men in the White House, in order to give him a chance to get his own staff in. As I said to you, I had difficulty in getting mine accepted, but it was before him on April 14. He said he would like me to help on the congressional speech, which I did. My difficulty was that this was very different from helping Roosevelt because I found that I was trying to write a speech in the presence of a convention! There must have been fourteen people around that table, all of Truman's old friends: Matt Connelly, John Snyder, [James K.] Vardaman, and a great many of his friends; and it was very difficult. That was one of the reasons I went in very shortly to press my resignation. It takes five times as long to write a sentence with fourteen people around as it does to be alone with him or one or two others. But his is right; I did help on this speech. And the next big thing I helped on was a speech to the United Nations organization.

Hess: Which president gave the most help toward the final product: President Roosevelt or President Truman?

Rosenman: I think President Roosevelt did. He gave more help. We knew his style, and the president wrote and dictated a great deal more than President Truman.

Hess: Could you tell me of a few of the major differences in the way that the two men handled the job of the presidency, since you worked with both of them?

Rosenman: I think there were differences in personality — that were very apparent — between Roosevelt and Truman. Their mannerisms, their general approach, were obviously different, and those differences, of course, became very noticeable during Truman's first couple of months in the White House. President Roosevelt was more equipped toward leadership into new fields than President Truman was. So far as the difference between the way they handled the job, I think they were very similar with one major exception, and that is that President Truman paid much less attention to what his actions were doing towards his chances for reelection than Roosevelt did. President Truman did a great many things that Roosevelt, because he knew the effect if would have, never would have done. For example, seizing the steel works. Seizing the railroads was a different thing, but seizing all the steel plants, which led, as you know, to a fight in the courts, was something that Truman thought was necessary, thought it ought to be done, and once he had made up his mind, he had no thoughts about the political effect or about his reelection. Roosevelt always was conscious of the fact that it wouldn't be any use for him to be sitting under a tree in Hyde Park if he wanted to continue to do anything about all the pressing problems, that the only place he could do anything about them was in the White House; and he was willing to make many compromises so that he would last to fight another day, as they say. I don't think Truman ever had that in mind. That to me would be the chief difference.

Hess: In the early days of his administration, what seemed to be Mr. Truman's degree of awareness of his new position, its responsibility, its authority, and his duty?

Rosenman: During Truman's first term, he was overawed, particularly at the beginning, about the responsibility, the authority, and most of all, the lonesomeness of the job. In addition to that, he was committed to the proposition that he was president only by virtue of Roosevelt's death, and that he never would be an acting president or president if it weren't for the fact that Roosevelt had selected him, and that Roosevelt's policies were the things which gained overwhelming approval at the polls. He was very conscious of those facts; and every time he took a step he would say to himself: "I wonder what Roosevelt would have done? Would he think this is the right thing?" You know, he had a picture on the wall of Roosevelt that he could see just by turning, and he frequently said to me, "I'm trying to do what he would like." And he'd look to me because he knew that I knew what Roosevelt would have liked. This lasted until his reelection in 1948. After that, I never heard him say that again. He was then president on his own, after a very bitter and uphill fight; and while I'm sure he often thought of President Roosevelt, it was never in terms of saying, "What would he have done?"

Hess: Judge, Mr. Truman had quite bit to say about your part in the writing of the twenty-one-point message of September 6, 1945, in his *Memoirs*, and I know that you tell this in your Columbia [University] oral history interview, but I have a few questions about the message that I would like to bring up. Perhaps we might begin with the following general question: What do you recall about the writing of the twenty-one-point message?

Rosenman: It has come to be known as the twenty-one-point message, but it didn't start out with that name, and there was nothing magical about the figure twenty-one. The president, coming home from Potsdam, pointed out that practically all of his time had been taken up with foreign affairs in which one crisis after another had come his way; and now that he was coming home from the Potsdam Conference, he had to give some attention to domestic affairs. So, he and I had a talk about it on the ship coming home. It was considered as a sort of a state-of-the-union message on domestic affairs. He told me in general what he wanted to say, and it turned out that he had a very liberal point of view. This surprised me considerably, because I had had many conversations with some of his staff and with his friends whom he had brought into the White House; and I had concluded that President Truman was going to be quite a conservative in domestic affairs. I was agreeably surprised to hear what he said he wanted to stress.

As soon as we got back to Washington, I began to consult with a great many people as to what their views were on the most pressing things that had to be done. I consulted a great many official people in Washington, and I received written memoranda from most of them, in addition to our oral conversations. You have shown me the file which came from the Truman Library, which has a great many of these memoranda, and they are self-explanatory. While I can't say exactly, I know that a great many points in addition to the twenty-one were discussed; but we had to hold the message to reasonable proportions. I think that when we got through with the twenty-one, the message was long enough. It contained not only the general spirit of what he wanted to do but also some very specific recommendations.

The first draft of the message took considerable time. You will notice in the file that you showed me a great many handwritten insertions; they are all in my handwriting. It took quite some time to get this into a well-reasoned message to the Congress.

When I gave him my first draft, he said he would like to circulate it among the people with whom he usually worked. He mentioned them by name. Of course, I had no objection, and could have no objection. There were several meetings held in the Cabinet Room, discussing the various points in the draft. My present recollection is that these meetings were attended by the president himself, Mr. [John] Snyder, Mr. [Fred] Vinson, who later became chief justice, Charles Ross, George Allen, Leonard Reinsch, Jack Vardaman, Matt Connelly — I'm trying to remember whether Clark Clifford attended these conferences, but I cannot remember. He, at that time, was the assistant naval aide, but I used him a great deal to help me. He may have been there, but I have no clear recollection.

Of those around the table, Charlie Ross and George Allen and I were the only ones who were in favor of all the provisions. Charlie Ross was accurately described by you as a member of the "liberal bloc" among the president's advisers. I think the only other two members of that bloc were George Allen and I. Later on, I would certainly include Clark Clifford as a member of that bloc, and Charlie Murphy, Dave Lloyd, and some of the others that came in after I had left the White House — Dave Bell, and some of the younger men.

But when President Truman started off in April 1945, he was surrounded by a group of men who did not believe in the New Deal and who wanted to get away from it as soon as possible. The leader of that group was John Snyder. John Snyder was a fine human being, who was very close to President Truman; they were very intimate friends, and he always wanted to be helpful. He really believed, sincerely believed, that the continuation of the New Deal program would be disastrous to the country and that President Truman ought to resume a middle-of-the-road policy.

Charlie Ross was very helpful to me in writing that message, as he was in a great many other similar enterprises where we worked together. He was also a very old friend of President Truman — a close friend — but he was quite liberal. I don't think there was ever any argument or difference between us as to the merits or demerits of any point in that message. On the other hand, I had several arguments with John Snyder — sometimes rather heated ones — also with Matt Connelly and Jack Vardaman, all of whom sincerely believed that this kind of a message was ruinous for the country as well as for the president. None of those arguments was unfriendly, for I think they did realize that I was trying to help the president according to my own conviction; and, in turn, I realized that they were trying to help the president according to their convictions. It was evident that the two objectives just could not mix or be compromised. This was indeed the showdown for the president — the point of no return — and it is evident that there had to be a long and frank airing of the conflicting views. That is the real significance of the message — it set President Truman on the path of the future which he was to follow.

To the extent I have indicated, I believe that the president in his *Memoirs*, volume 1, page 483, which you have shown me, in which he says, "Most of my advisers agreed with the message," is not accurate. I think that the majority disagreed. The statement is accurate when he says that one of those who advised him against it was John Snyder. In fact, that is quite an understatement by the president. Snyder was not only opposed to it, but he became quite emotional about it. I'm sure that it is not my imagination which causes my recollection that at the time the president put an end to the discussion and signed the instrument, John Snyder had tears in his eyes. At any rate, he was convinced that this was quite a disastrous thing for the president as well as the country.

Mr. Snyder had a great deal of influence on the president. He used to come over and have lunch frequently. He was also a close friend of

Mrs. Truman; and I think that throughout the whole administration he had a great deal of influence. However, that twenty-one-point message was decisive. There was no way that Mr. Snyder, with all of his influence and power, could turn the president back to a conservative policy, or even to a middle-of-the-road policy, after that message went up to the Congress.

Personally, I think that the most important thing that I did for President Truman, and perhaps through him for the country itself, was to fight without letup for that twenty-one-point message. Although I believe that it really conformed with the president's general policy and was wholly consistent with his prior senatorial voting record, it committed him publicly to the philosophy of the Fair Deal or its synonym, the New Deal. Carrying out that message to the extent he did was a great thing for him as well as for the United States.

Mr. Snyder had great influence with President Truman in fields other than that of the secretary of the treasury. So far as I know he made a capable secretary of the treasury, although there is very little information that I can give you either pro or con. I never heard anyone, even among the banking fraternity, criticize Mr. Snyder's policies as secretary of the treasury very much, and I had been used to hearing a great deal of criticism from these sources about one of his predecessors as secretary of the treasury; and I suppose that that's what a secretary of the treasury should be. However, the twenty-one-point message committed President Truman towards a liberal policy completely. Even had he wanted to turn to conservative policies later — which I am sure he never would — the commitments in that message were so firm that he could not return. That commitment remained firmly during the years that Truman was president; in fact, at very many points, it even went beyond the message itself.

To sum it up, I would say that I would call President Truman unequivocally a liberal. If you examine his votes as senator, you will find that they were 100 percent New Deal; and in my opinion that's the chief reason that President Roosevelt chose him for vice president.

16

James H. Rowe Jr.

Washington, D.C. September 30, 1969

Interviewed by Jerry N. Hess (Harry S. Truman Library)

James H. Rowe Jr. (1909–1984), a Harvard-trained lawyer from Butte, Montana, was among the New Deal's bright young men. The tall, scholarly Rowe began his public career as secretary to Supreme Court Justice Oliver Wendell Holmes. He then worked for the Reconstruction Finance Corporation, the Securities and Exchange Commission, and the Public Works Administration. Rowe drafted the Public Utilities Holding Company Act of 1935. From 1937 to 1941, he held the dual role of FDR's assistant and appointments secretary. He moved on to the Justice Department as assistant attorney general. During World War II, he served in the navy. After the Allied victory, he was an official in the Nuremberg war crimes tribunals. On his return to Washington, D.C., he went into private law practice. A brilliant strategist, he drafted the memorandum that outlined how Truman could win the 1948 presidential election by using his incumbency to consolidate the Democratic base.

Hess: Mr. Rowe, when did you join President Roosevelt's staff as an administrative assistant?

Rowe: I was on the White House staff before I was an administrative assistant. I went over early in 1938 as an assistant to Jimmy Roosevelt, who was then the president's secretary. I had been a lawyer in various government agencies, and the last one, I was in the SEC, and I was writing occasional speeches for Jimmy because he was very busy, but he was still trying to run for governor of Massachusetts; and when he started to write a speech, he tied up large segments of the government for two or three days, so I started writing them. He then asked me to come over as assistant, and I took a title that happened to be vacant over there, the executive assistant to the president. I don't know who had been in it before, and I don't know whatever happened to it afterwards. The administrative assistants were created in what was the Reorganization Act of '37 or '38.

Hess: '39.

Rowe: '39. There was an act in '37. And I was appointed the first one, the first administrative assistant, in July 1939. The president appointed three, and I happened to take my oath first, so I was number one, in terms of time.

Hess: Just what were your duties?

Rowe: Well, the president once described my duties as that of a bird dog, which was to do, in effect, whatever he told me to do, and occasionally I would do things on my own without being told. I did a variety of things. It was a relatively small staff in those days. This was before the war, when there were the three secretaries. I used to kid some of my friends on the Truman staff after the war when I came back and said I found nine men doing what I used to do. But I did what I would call the political personnel job that John Macy did. I was one of the Hill men, one of the White House lobbyists. I did a large part of the work with the regulatory agencies because I was, at that time, the only lawyer in the place. I also did a great deal of digesting large reports to the president, summarizing them, giving them summaries. I handled the enrolled bills coming back, the vetoed bills. That was in very close connection with the Budget Bureau. I handled, for instance, the Civil Aeronautics Board route cases, the foreign route cases that the president had to pass on, that kind of thing. It was an across-the-board job. I used to get, oh, say, two or three memos a day from the president saying find out about this or find out about that. That kind of thing. My feeling is that, I suppose, President Truman was probably the best budget man they've ever had. Some people say that Johnson was better. Roosevelt was quite good on all the figures in the presentation of the budget.

Hess: Why would you rate Mr. Truman so high on that?

Rowe: Only because all the budget people told me he was so good. Knew his budget very well, and knew all the details, and this I've heard from several generations of younger budget people, the older ones, and so forth; all of these said that Truman was tremendously good at this. Now, just why he was as distinguished from, let's say, Eisenhower or someone like that, I just don't know. Maybe it was the training he got out of the committee up on the Hill. It might have been something that he picked up in Kansas City. He was known to be excellent on every item in the budget.

Hess: As you know, Mr. Truman ran for reelection to the United States Senate in 1940, during the time that you were at the White House, and I would like to read a short passage from the *Memoirs* regarding the event. It appears in the *Memoirs*, volume 1, page 159:

The President had offered, in a roundabout way, to put me on the Interstate Commerce Commission. I sent him word, however, that if I received only one vote I intended to make the fight for vindication and reelection to the Senate. The President really was encouraging Stark, my opponent.

Were you aware of that offer?

Rowe: I was not aware of the offer, and I'm not now aware of the offer. I might have been. I have a very vague memory, that for reasons I cannot now remember, that we were in favor of Stark as against Truman. This may have been just as simple as the fact that we didn't think Truman could win. We might have thought Stark could win. I can't remember what the reasons were, but I do remember that there was a tendency to favor Stark. I have no memory of why.

Hess: Do you recall what President Roosevelt's attitude toward Mr. Truman was at this particular time?

Rowe: No. You've got to remember that right at this time Truman was pretty much of a junior senator. I think — let me see — about this period he was working with Burt [Burton K.] Wheeler on the railroad investigation, and I think that whatever interest we had was what Wheeler and Truman were doing about railroads. I may be a little off on my timing, but Truman until the preparedness committee — what did they call that?

Hess: The Committee to Investigate the National Defense Program.

Rowe: Yes. Until then he had been regarded as a quiet junior senator, maybe too much a part of the Pendergast machine.

Hess: Did you ever hear President Roosevelt mention Mr. Truman's connection with Pendergast?

Rowe: No, but that doesn't mean he didn't. I cannot now remember anything. Roosevelt was a realist about the bosses. He played with [Frank] Hague, he played with Pendergast, and the New York crowd. He came up, as you know, through that New York machinery, and he was not a man to kick the bosses in the face more than once. He might do it publicly, but he didn't do it privately. I wouldn't think — I just never did hear. I knew Roosevelt had some kind of relationship with Pendergast. You had to if you wanted to carry Missouri.

Hess: What do you recall about Mr. Truman's selection as a vice presidential candidate in 1944?

Rowe: I don't recall anything as I was in the navy and in the Pacific at the time, but I can tell you of the conversation I had with the president in either December '44 or January '45. I was home on leave, and my own opinion as I had sat out on a carrier in the Pacific had been that he would pick Sam Rayburn for vice president, and I had not thought of Mr. Truman. I had been out of the country for, oh, at least a year, and I was a little surprised about where did Truman come from and all that business. Why Truman? So, I went in to visit the president on leave and he had some time, and I, in effect, said, "Mr. President, why did you pick Truman?" And he gave me a very interesting account. He said that he had decided nobody could help him. No vice presidential candidate could help him, and the problem was who would hurt him least.

Then he went through the various candidates. On Bill Douglas he said, "Well, you know Bill said he didn't want to play second fiddle to anybody, and he said maybe he was too much of a New Dealer." I think Senator [John H.] Bankhead — I'm not sure of my names now; maybe it was Speaker Bankhead — one of the Bankheads was talked about as a candidate. He said he was too Southern.

Jimmy Byrnes had been talked about and there had been a Catholic problem there. Jimmy had begun life as a Catholic, but I think when quite young had switched to Episcopalian. The president told me he had sent Frank Walker and Leo Crowley around to see the leaders of the Church, in effect, to see how much a bar this was, and he told me that they came back and reported that it was not a bar. At least the cardinals, or whoever would speak for the Church, understood that this happened to Jimmy when he was a young boy and therefore it would not be too much of a problem. That was not the general approach. Most people thought he was ruled out on this. But the president said labor came in very strongly against Byrnes, and he said when you got all through with the various people — he said that the one fellow that the Southerners liked, and the one fellow that labor could accept, was Truman.

Hess: What did he say about Henry Wallace at this time?

Rowe: Well, now, he said that the bosses had been in — Ed Flynn and all the rest. I've forgotten; he told me who they were. They came down and waited on him, in effect, and said they just couldn't take Wallace; he would just have to, in effect, get rid of him.

Hess: Did President Roosevelt at this time say anything about Senator Truman's chairmanship of the Truman committee?

Rowe: I can't remember anything, although as I say, I wasn't following it because I was out in the Pacific. There had been, as you know, tremendous publicity, and everybody had a feeling, which even I, out in the Pacific, had a feeling, that the Truman committee was doing a very competent, careful job in which he was getting results. He was not smearing people, but he was not whitewashing them either. This was a constructive effort and it received a lot of publicity, so that by this time Truman was a very well known figure, and as well known as senators become, I guess.

Hess: Well, of course, Henry Wallace wanted to get the nomination again. What do you recall about the efforts that he made?

Rowe: I don't recall much because I was away. I think Francis Biddle was for him. I think Judge Rosenman was involved in this some way or another. Now that I think of it, Rosenman originally picked Wallace. He was responsible for Wallace in the first place. I think that the liberal crowd was sort of backing Wallace. But you see, we had run into this guru business. I don't know if you know about that.

Hess: The guru letters? [In 1940 Wallace was embarrassed when political opponents obtained letters that he had written to a White Russian mystic.]

Rowe: Yes. That had worried Roosevelt a great deal.

Hess: You say Rosenman was responsible for Wallace in '40?

Rowe: That is my memory, yes, that he came up with the Wallace name. And during the campaign we ran into guru letters, and they made us all nervous and they didn't break. I think the president was a little shaky about Wallace from that time on, but the other factor about Wallace was that he had been presiding over the Senate for four years and didn't have any allies up there. Rather odd fellow. Competent man. He was a great secretary of agriculture. But it was a fact that he didn't have any of these people supporting him.

Hess: Did you ever have occasion to work with the White House staff during the Truman administration?

Rowe: Yes, and no. I really did some work, mostly with Jim Webb, the budget director.

Hess: What was that work?

Rowe: Well, I did several studies. I did an aviation study for him. At that time, what had happened was — let me see — I've forgotten the period; I think it was '46 or '47. I had been in Nuremberg and had come back in the fall of '46 — the late fall of '46 — and I didn't quite know what I wanted to do. I think I was perfectly sure I didn't want to stay in Washington. I was thinking about practicing law in California and Montana — where I came from — and I was floating around really doing nothing. Then Jim Webb and I had got to talking somewhere or other about a few things, and before long I was helping him.

The airlines were in as bad a mess as they are now, and I think the president gave Jimmy Webb the assignment of taking a look at the whole thing and getting it straightened out. So, he put a task force together, and I remember the thing I was working on was the preparation of a paper. I don't know whatever happened to it. One of our concerns was the relationship between military and civil aviation, so I worked on that. I remember I came to the conclusion that civil aviation was not helping the defense program at all. It was all the other way around, as has been apparent pretty much ever since. This defense aid was one of the excuses for the airline subsidy and everything else.

Later, the other things that I did with the White House were really through Webb. I did two studies. I did one on jobs. I can give you a copy of both of them. Here's one. These are both political studies, and the first one I see is called "Cooperation or Conflict? The President's Relationships with an Opposition Congress." In effect, how does a president handle the Congress when you have both houses against him, as Truman did? It was a historical study, but really it was a realpolitik study. I see it's dated December '46, and was about twenty-three or twenty-four pages long when I finished. I spent quite a bit of time writing it. I don't know that it shows. I haven't looked at it for years. But I gave it to Webb, and Webb gave it to the president. Webb told me once — whether he was being kind or not I don't know — that the president told him that he kept it in a drawer of his desk and kept looking at it. But it was really a guide to techniques on how you handle the Congress. I think that maybe it might have been seed corn for the whole "do-nothing Congress" approach that the president took in the '48 campaign.

Hess: How important do you think that his handling of the Eightieth Congress matter was to his eventual victory?

Rowe: I think it elected him. But I don't want to suggest too much for this memo that I haven't read for a number of years —

Hess: Do you recall if he followed this suggestion?

Rowe: My memory is that he did.

Hess: What is the other memorandum?

Rowe: The other memorandum is called the "Politics of 1948." Now, this gets a little complicated. I wrote this and it went to Clark Clifford. It's really a memorandum on how to handle the political campaign of 1948. Clark and I have since discussed what happened to this one. I happened to read in the *New York Times* an article by Pat Anderson, which mentions this memorandum of Clifford's. Also, I think it's in a couple of books. I noticed some of the quotations at the time, and I thought they were very familiar; so I went back and looked at this memo, and they came from this one.

When I first wrote this memo, I mentioned it to a couple of people, and Clark heard about it and gave me a ring. I guess that is what always does happen. I gave it to Clifford, and I assumed that my name would be on it. What Clifford did — what he said he did — was that he took this memo and he took some other memos, and he put his ideas all together and then gave the president an overall memorandum, including, I think, most of this one.

Hess: Would you go so far as to say that the majority, or the largest part, of the memo that he turned over to the president was taken from your memo?

Rowe: All the quotations I saw that have been printed since, in the books or anything, came out of this memorandum. Now, this memorandum is about thirty-three pages. There have been references in the texts, somewhere or another, to a forty-three-page memorandum. So, I would guess that if he used all this, he probably added another ten pages and maybe took — I don't know. The problem was that Clark had sent his papers out to the Truman Library, so he didn't have a copy of his memo. So, the two of us never did sit down and look at it. It was the kind of thing that happens very often, as it did when I was in the White House. You get ideas from a great variety of people. You put it together, and you give it to the boss. You don't worry about who wrote what. I had had the impression from Webb that it was going under my name, and here I'll give you that.

Hess: There are two points there that the forty-three-page memo brings up that I would like to ask about. One, it mentions on page 29 that the president should take a trip, and he likens it to the inspection trips that President Roosevelt took. Do you recall if that was yours?

Rowe: Yes.

Hess: That was?

Rowe: I think you will find that these were very much the same. The beginning doesn't seem that way. You can take a look at it.

Hess: Another point that I want to ask about is on page 40 of the forty-three-page memo where it mentions setting up a small working committee to coordinate the political program in and out of the administration. Do you recall if that was your suggestion?

Rowe: It was, yes.

Hess: After suggesting that the small working committee be set up and it was set up, were you somewhat disappointed that you were not asked to be a member of it?

Rowe: I don't remember. I doubt it. I think I knew I had done my job. Frankly, I was never close to Truman, and at that time I was not a great admirer of his. I have become one since.

Hess: What has changed your mind?

Rowe: I think at that time the atmosphere was such that the New Dealers thought Roosevelt was perfect, and therefore no matter who went in — if God had replace him — he wouldn't have satisfied them. I think that is part of it. Truman didn't like New Dealers very much, and said so. I think it's only human nature that we weren't too fond of him. There are a number of the, oh, minor things like the refrigerators; I can't remember when that came. [Truman's military aide, Gen. Harry Vaughan, accepted an unsolicited Deepfreeze from an advertising agent, who sent other freezers to other administration officials and Mrs. Truman.] It was that sort of thing, too. I think, looking back on the tremendous things he did do, mostly in foreign affairs — the Marshall Plan, Korea — I think maybe those things, twenty-five years ago, have given us what you can't — peace, but at least not hot war, either. I think in the foreign field he was tremendous.

Hess: As a New Dealer, what do you think are the differences between the New Deal and the Fair Deal?

Rowe: There are none — except that the Fair Deal was not as successful in getting programs through. We didn't have the guns by then. I think the Fair Deal was a logical extension of the New Deal.

17

John W. Snyder

Kansas City   October 8, 1954, and October 9, 1954

Interviewed by Herbert Lee Williams, Francis Heller, and David Noyes

John W. Snyder (1895–1985), secretary of the treasury from 1946 through 1953, met Truman as a fellow army officer in World War I, and they became friends. Their wives and daughters were also close. The St. Louis banking executive played an important fund-raising role in Truman's early political career. When Truman became president, he chose Snyder as chairman of the Federal Loan Association and soon afterward promoted him to head the Office of War Mobilization and Reconversion. As treasury secretary, he was among the more conservative members of the Truman cabinet. Snyder's proudest accomplishment was the reduction of the federal debt by $10 billion.

Snyder: The president, unfortunately, — I don't think he clearly understood the difference between savings bonds and government bonds. Now, savings bonds have to be paid at par. I'd tell him, "You're talking about government bonds, not savings bonds," when he'd say he wasn't going to let savings bonds drop to 85 like Liberty Bonds. And they'd kid him about it, but it was just a confusion of terms. They sidetracked him, but he finally woke up to what they were doing to him, and he stood pat.

Q: Would you say the fiscal policy originated with the president?

Snyder: I certainly will say that; any member of the cabinet would. I always made it the president's program. The reorganization of the Internal Revenue was the president's program. I called it that. There was nothing that was my program. I wanted him to get the credit for it; some damned good things were done in the Treasury.

Q: In the councils of the president, your intimacy was on a closer basis than any other member of the cabinet —

Snyder: I don't say that.

Q: You were presumed to be the conservative . . .

Snyder: Yes, I got sick of hearing, "That's Snyder's banker attitude." In any group, in any White House group, I was immediately branded with the ultimate conservative viewpoint. The president might have felt that at times, but I think he paid a great deal of attention to what I pointed out.

I sensed that the treasury was a big job, and I knew that I couldn't try to run every other part of the government. Instead of building it up into a bigger, more powerful organization, I was one of the few who were willing to give up some. I gave up the procurement business and two or three other things, the labeling of whiskey, — and the RFC [Reconstruction Finance Corporation]; I wouldn't take it. I didn't believe that the Treasury had any business making policy for the supervision of banks, or to be in competition with banks in the making of loans. I told Mr. Hoover, when they wanted to put the RFC in the Treasury, that I believed the RFC should be preserved as an agency on a telescopic basis, to be able to expand in times of need, and that the framework should be kept for possible use. With an economy of our size and dynamic nature, you could prevent a recession or a depression if such an instrument were available to feed credit, or contract it if the need is no longer there. I testified on that in Congress, so it's on record. I didn't want the RFC, because as a lending agency it would be making loans in competition with banks, and I didn't feel, as secretary, that the Treasury at the same time should make the regulations for banks to follow in reference to loaning. It would be inconsistent for me to have under my jurisdiction a lending agency in competition with banks that we were regulating. And I didn't feel that it should go to the Federal Reserve Bank either.

Q: What was the function of the Treasury in relation to the conduct of foreign policy?

Snyder: I felt it was my role to bring to mind, in dealing with the State Department and with all the departments, that we could not commit our Treasury beyond what had already been prescribed by the Congress in appropriations. We had to see if we could afford to do some of these things and look to our revenue to see if we could raise the funds to do these things. And after passing Congress, I was holding the reins back to forestall commitments abroad beyond our scope. At the time of the Ottawa NATO meeting — the New York Times broke the story. Felix Blair wrote the story, how things were going high and wide until I made a speech — in full meeting, not an open meeting, but a full meeting so far as membership was concerned — that they could not expect the United States to go beyond what Congress authorized it to do. That was at the time they were discussing the support of the French and British armies. And I said the same things again at Lisbon and at Rome and Paris. I was not a popular fellow, yet they all seemed to get around to the fact that my safety valve was there. I was keeping financial operations within the scope of the president's policy. I expressed the policy of the administration, and the State Department took it from there.

Q: What was the relationship between the Treasury and the budget director — the Bureau of the Budget — in drafting the annual budget?

Snyder: Prior to Roosevelt the Budget was in the Treasury. Roosevelt took it out of the Treasury and made it a part of the Executive Office. Insofar as the Treasury is concerned, the Budget is the same as any other agency. As secretary, I was in an entirely different role. The budget director would consult with me on our capability to meet the demands made to operate the government, from a revenue standpoint. Even with Smith, and later with one of my boys, Jimmy Webb, and later Frank Pace and — Lawton, all of them constantly conferred with me on matters about policy in shaping up the various appropriations and interpreting the president's intent. I would talk it over with him. We worked very closely.

As a matter of fact, the Treasury Department never went as far as — the budget was set. They start initially in the spring to prepare the budget for the next year; they give a framework within which they expect the departments to live. I always kept within the budget. First, the overall policy was set by the president and the budget director as to what the level of operations was to be in defense, foreign aid, and so forth. Then that was patterned into the whole budget. Each department was told where to keep his budget, within a certain area. As for the overall picture, I would be as an individual working with the budget director and the president. We came together to see that we were all talking about the same thing.

Q: When the president talked to you about the budget, he said that by a process of taxation there was brought about a distribution of income throughout the country.

Snyder: He didn't mean that. Taxation is for revenue purposes only, and not to legislate. I stuck to that, and the president did, too. I do not say that we distributed wealth through taxation. I am definitely on record before Congress saying that taxation is for revenue purposes strictly. For any social reforms, it should be through legislation, not taxation. It was not to tax the rich to pay the poor. The purpose of taxation, as far as the secretary of the treasury is concerned, was for revenue purposes only. Social reforms had to be done through legislation, not through taxation. The amount of taxation depended upon ability to pay. You had to put it into a framework to get taxation without crippling the economy. You had to find out the weight that could be put on the various levels of income.

Q: When the Truman administration ended, what benefits were reaped by the following administration?

Snyder: I consulted with the president about it. I said we can run the cash position of the Treasury down very low and reduce the debt, but we will leave the economy in a very precarious position, because it will force the newcomers to go into the market to borrow money before they can get their balance. It is my intention, unless you tell me to the contrary, to leave a comfortable balance in the Treasury to shape up finances so they will have none to do for six or eight months after they get in, and to give them a full dossier on how the Treasury is run. The president said, "That's fine."

So, with his approval, we gave the new outfit the finest briefing any new administration has ever got. You have the booklet that spells out every department in the Treasury, how it functions, who knows what went on, etc. We held three briefing sessions. I fixed up offices and let them move their people in a month ahead of time so that they could get their feet on the ground.

We could have run the debt down five more billion dollars and turned over a smaller debt. We always overlook that — the newspapers, not me — when they talk about Eisenhower and his economies. Don't forget that Truman in the fiscal year 1947 had a balanced budget, and this after a devastating world war and a war economy. We had a surplus in the Treasury in 1947, and we had a surplus in 1948, an $8 billion surplus. For the whole six years to June 30, 1952, we took in more money than we took out. There was no deficit financing while I was there until after June 30, 1952. The Korean problem had welled up, and we had to get financing. Eisenhower is a long way from balancing the budget. Interest rates today are lower than they were except when I first took over, yet they accused me of forcing interest rates down. We were trying to hold them in position when the Korean War broke out. But these gentlemen forced them down, something I never did do.

The president and I had many battles and downright arguments, but once a decision was made by him, I always went along with him. At times he used to get annoyed with me. But I would tell him that he had to know both sides of any situation. I told him, "I don't want you to say later on, 'Why didn't you tell me about the other side.'" And I'd tell him everything. He got fretted with it sometimes, I know. But I quit going to those speechwriting contests, because there would be things in there I would raise sin about and would get them deleted. Then some half——would come along and slip it back in. It would make the thing sound silly as hell.

Williams: We have sections — one on how the budget is made up, then a section on general policy, financial policy or the theory of financing during your time in office, and a section on tax structure illustrating that policy.

Snyder: The president and I had spent many years talking about budgeting government here in the state and as senator. He was interested even back as far as when he was judge budgeting Jackson County. As a senator he kept an eye on the Missouri budget, and then he was plunged into the Appropriations Committee of the Senate. There was no senator who took a more keen interest in understanding what he was doing in the handling of budget matters for the United States when he was in office. He did homework on it, and he knew what he was talking about, which very few of them did.

When he became president, the first thing he did was to talk about the plan we were going to use in approaching the budgeting of the postwar period. V-E Day came on immediately; shortly after that, V-J Day; and he was plunged immediately into the heartbreaking job of financing the government in a reconstruction period and in a conversion from a wartime economy to peacetime, and, at the same time, with the objective of maintaining a high level of production and consumption in the country. We had built up a tremendous war economy — as near to an all-out war as there ever was in all history — only to be suddenly faced with a transition period converting our tremendous production plants, switching those plants along with the masses of people working in them, maintaining a high demand for goods and services. — It was a gigantic task facing him almost immediately after becoming president.

After V-E Day the president and I sat down together and started measuring how far we could cut back on commitments for defense and still preserve the assurance of victory in Japan. We were starting to move troops across the country to the Pacific, and we ran up against the problem of balancing revenues against expenditures and trying to cut down the expenditures of an all-out war program. The president courageously said that we must cut out all contracts for those types of materials not to be used in the Pacific but continue to maintain our position in occupied Europe.

Heller: In reaching this particular decision, the point that will recur is that this decision was reached on a basis of setting up the financial equilibrium of—

Snyder: Of the country, of the government. We aimed towards the assurance of victory and towards success in our victory. We were trying to maintain the assurance of that — the necessity for maintaining our position to win victory in the Pacific and aiming at the same time towards an equalized budget position domestically.

Heller: You define the goals of the government program then in terms of the necessary conquest of Japan, just as later it was defined in terms of the domestic . . .

Snyder: We did not put it down on paper or say that this was the program, as things were moving too rapidly. You must remember the timing of all this. The president took office in April 1945. V-E Day came shortly after that in May. He had to go to Potsdam to face the — unknown. He made the decision about the bomb. And then we had V-J Day and the rapid movement of events then. There was no time to say this is our program. It was a living, moving plan towards a certain goal. Even though the president had to leave after he became president — had to go to Potsdam — I was able to help carry through our policy by messages — and mutual understanding.

The plan was in our minds, which we can show by the actions we followed.

Noyes: But what was the motivation? Wanting to balance the budget? I would like to go back to Senator Truman — in terms of his interest in the budget. What actuated the president as senator to become interested in it?

Snyder: As judge, senator, and president — all through it — he had in mind a pay-as-you-go program except when the welfare of the nation became involved and courageous action was needed to face facts as they were. There is nothing sacred about pay-as-you-go, except as a principle of sound financing. The president had the integrity of the credit of the United States always in mind, even when, for the first time, President Truman and I were faced in 1952 with our first deficit financing. We didn't do any until 1952.

I communicated with the president at Potsdam, and I met him at Norfolk. A reappraisal looked inevitable. He had ordered the dropping of the bomb, and we knew that that would bring on something salutary. I said what are we going to do when Japan collapses? How are we going to move? And the president, there on the train, said the objective is, as early as possible, to start to bring the budget down to $35 billion and keep our tax situation as it is in order that we may reduce the debt as low as we can while things are in a prosperous position.

"If you will concede one point," I said to the president, "may we start in on a program to take out the inequities of it?" To meet the revenue demands for reconversion after the Depression and at the beginning of the war, we had to seek out revenue where we could find it. As a result, it was a bulky tax structure, and I wanted to try to pick out the inequities, iron them out while maintaining the bulk of the revenue. We made that a policy.

Japan collapsed, and we started our program of retrenchment. The president canceled $6.7 billion in war contracts. We immediately started a program of trying to prepare a program of financing, public and private, and assure ample working capital for the conversion of plants from war to peace, and we had the complete support of the banking fraternity of the country. We forced them to make a plan of their own. I laid it before the president to make sure we would have working capital in that transition period. The president then started a program of trying to reduce the debt, yet carry out other programs to maintain a high level of production and consumption. The war in Korea was a very small war. . . .

The president in his first year, after the cessation of World War II hostilities, in the fiscal year 1947, had a surplus in the Treasury and an $8 billion surplus in 1948. From June 30, 1946, to June 30, 1952, we had a net surplus of cash taken in over cash taken out. We actually did no deficit financing during that period. We did rollovers, as you know, but the debt got down to 252 billion from 278 billion. In those six years we had a surplus for three years and a deficit for three years, but the net overall was a surplus. That is very significant. If we had not had the Eightieth Congress, we could have gone through with the president's program of ironing out the inequities. But the across-the-board tax cuts of the Eightieth Congress were unjustified at that time. We could have taken half of that tax cut and ironed out the inequities of the tax program.

Q: Did these surpluses occur as result of sound tax structure, plus government agencies bearing in mind basic economies?

Snyder: Let's say a sound concept, rather than a sound tax base. It was not sound, because of the inequities involved. The first necessity was to bring in the revenue required to run the government. The president had many obligations to meet, commitments of the Democratic Party in the elections of 1940 and 1944, and later in 1948. He always had those in mind. He had to measure what his pledged program was, against the desire to do it within the framework of sound financing and government credit. Then your tax program became important. Our objective was that our tax program was for revenue purposes only, not for social reforms. We would place the latter before Congress for legislation. We wanted concrete legislation for such things as the minimum wage, Social Security, and so forth, but our tax program aimed at revenue only, and we were not going to slip social reforms into a tax program. In arriving at our tax program, we had to measure the capability of the taxpayer to pay. We didn't want to destroy incentives, yet at the same time we had those requirements for a big revenue program; we measured, with much counsel and advice, how much the traffic would bear — that's an unfortunate phrase — how much we could impose on the various levels during that period.

All it would bear and yet maintain the high level of our economy. We did not go to the limit of the capability of the country to pay, but only as far as we could impose it on a broad base to bring in the required revenue. Everyone was a citizen and should contribute to the welfare of the country, even though small. As we got the program better in hand, and if it had not been for Korea, we could have done good things — raising the exemption, spreading out a broader incentive, while still keeping the level of production and consumption high. The president and I just liked this program.

18

John R. Steelman

Washington, D.C.   January 15, 1963

Interviewed by Charles T. Morrissey

John R. Steelman (1900–1998), assistant to the president from 1946 through 1953, coordinated cabinet-level departments and agencies. An economics professor at the Alabama College for Women, he joined FDR's administration in the mid-1930s and became head of the U.S. Conciliation Service. With the nation facing postwar labor troubles, Truman named him a senior adviser. In the early months of the administration, the veteran mediator ran the Labor Department. Truman invented the title "the assistant to the president" for him. That made him first among equals. But in future administrations, it would not be unusual for a half-dozen senior staffers to be given this rank.

Morrissey: The first question, Doctor, is why did you move back to Washington to join the Truman administration after you left in April 1945 — is that correct? Then you came back, I think, later that year?

Steelman: No, I left immediately after the election of 1944. As a matter of fact, I had resigned. I'd been in the government about ten years, whereas I came to stay only one. I had resigned in July of 1944, and Secretary Perkins spoke to President Roosevelt about it, and he told her to ask me to stay on until after the election, that he was going to run again and he didn't want to be bothered with replacing me at the time. So, I agreed to stay until after the election; and so my resignation, although written in July, was accepted the third or fourth of November, the next day, I believe, after the election.

Morrissey: Then you went to New York?

Steelman: Then I went to New York and was there until the following October. I had a consulting office in New York at 70 Pine Street.

Morrissey: That's October 1945?

Steelman: Yes, in October 1945, I came back. In the meantime, however, immediately after President Truman succeeded to the office — pretty soon thereafter, at least — he appointed Judge Schwellenbach as secretary of labor. I had known the judge when he was a senator and had worked with him a

few times. So, he called me up in New York and asked if I could come back to Washington as undersecretary of labor and assist him in running the department. He stated that he didn't know much about it, but, of course, was very loyal to the president and very fond of the president and wanted to do a good job. He asked if I could come, and I told him no, I just couldn't. As a matter of fact, on one or two occasions, President Roosevelt had offered me this job, but I had turned it down thinking I could do better while I was in government where I was, as director of the U.S. Conciliation Service.

So, when I couldn't come down to join Judge Schwellenbach officially, he asked if I could come down and spend about thirty days helping him to go through and learn all about the various sections of his department, bureaus, etc., and then help him get it organized the way he thought it ought to be. I did that. I came down and spent about a month here with him. Then after I returned to New York, almost daily he and I were in telephone contact. He was the only one who had my telephone number in New York — my home number. Every night, or every few nights at least, we would talk on the phone. I assume that he told the president that I was working with him and that he had asked me to come down, and that I said I couldn't.

So anyway, sometime in October, the president's secretary called up and asked if I could come down to see the president. I believe he mentioned that Judge Schwellenbach had told him I'd been helping him. The president said he thought perhaps I could get leave of absence from my clients for a while, if *he* asked me to come to the White House. In those days, I thought you had to say yes when the president asked you something. I found out later you don't necessarily have to. At least, everybody doesn't say yes to the president. But I think if I had it to do it over, I would anyway. I said, yes, I'd see if I couldn't get leave of absence. He wanted me to come down for six months. He said, in effect, that "the war's over and everybody's leaving town and I can't get anybody to do anything, and I need your help." I didn't know it, but he said he'd sort of had an eye on me during the war, and he knew the job I'd been doing in the labor relations field. So, he wanted me to come down and help him, and I told him that I was sure I could arrange it. I went back to New York and talked to my clients and told them that he wanted me for six months. One or two of them asked me, "Are you sure it's just for six months?"

And I said, "Well, that's what the man said."

Morrissey: Do you recall meeting President Truman when he was Senator Truman and head of the Truman committee? Was there any actual meeting between you two, or he just had his eye on you from a distance?

Steelman: It was certainly mostly from a distance. I had never, so far as I know, never even seen him once. One time he was having a hearing on some subject that I was interested in, and I went up to the hearing room and I saw him there. I don't believe I actually met him even then. If I did, it's the only time I ever met him. I don't believe I'd ever met him till I came to the White House to see him, but naturally I knew a lot about him, and I didn't know he knew about me, but he said he did. Well, I think that is right, but as I say, the president had naturally been interested in all phases of war production, and labor dispute was a big part of it; and he said he'd had an eye on me through the war, and he knew I could be helpful to him.

Morrissey: Sam Rosenman was one of these old Roosevelt people who stayed on with Mr. Truman. Just what was his relationship with the White House staff?

Steelman: Well, Sam was very fond of the president, and it was mutual. They got along beautifully. I've forgotten how long he stayed, but he was certainly around for a while after I came in. He assisted in speechwriting and staff discussions. He was of general help rather than just a speechwriter. The president, I'm sure, depended on him just as much as anybody in those early days.

Morrissey: What went on in these morning staff meetings with the president? What was the usual procedure?

Steelman: Well, we would gather around the president's desk, and he would call on each one to see if he had any problem that ought to be brought to the president's attention; and at the same time, the president might have something in mind that he thought that a particular staff member could handle. In the early days, I was special assistant to the president and was interested only in labor problems, but in later days — as a matter of fact, when I first came, we weren't having regular staff meetings, as I recall it, but pretty soon, we began to have them. Later on, when I was the assistant to the president, he always called on me last, and he and I would exchange problems and files and so forth.

Morrissey: Could Mr. Truman depend on his staff to volunteer the type of things that he should know? That is to say, did he have a problem of staff members telling him only what they wanted to tell him? Or was he sharp enough and active enough to get around this problem?

Steelman: In the first place, I think in general, the staff had no particular reason for not telling him everything they knew. It was a very free and intimate give and take at all our discussions. The loyalty that he instilled in all of us — it would have been most unusual if anybody hadn't wanted to tell him everything they knew.

In the second place, however — and here is a very vital difference between President Truman and his successor — the successor didn't even read the newspapers in the early days, and it was generally known that he didn't read the newspapers. His contacts were very, very limited — limited to a few big-business people, and a very few staff people — whereas President Truman talked to everybody. He was all over the place; he talked to everybody, and he knew so much about all the things that were going on, that even if somebody had tried to fool him, they certainly would have gotten caught very soon. I've worked for thirty days on a problem, interviewing all the cabinet officers and staff people and everybody else, and he'd come in to tell me something I never heard of before. He was right on top of everything.

Morrissey: President Truman was careful, would you say, to follow up the decisions he had made to make sure they were implemented?

Steelman: Yes, he was very good at that, too.

Morrissey: Did the White House staff tend to push the president to approve some legislative proposals which were more liberal, let's say, than he wanted?

Steelman: I don't think so. Oh, there may have been instances. For example, when we were writing the state-of-the-union message, there would be a variety of opinions among the staff as to how far he ought to go in this, that, and the other direction, but he'd listen to all of us and then tell us what to do.

Morrissey: Probably a better question is this: Was it difficult for members of the White House staff to look at things the way the president was — that is, maintain the presidential viewpoint on matters and not go off on their own individual tangents and try to persuade him to see it their way?

Steelman: I think there was a minimum of that. Certainly, I had no difficulty in seeing things his way. He was so free in give-and-take discussions with us that I think he was much easier to understand than lots of people. I could tell just about exactly how he would react to any particular situation. I knew him that intimately. I think we all did. And of course, that's one of the great qualities of topside leadership and topside executive ability. I thought President Truman was one of the best — was the best executive officer that I've ever seen. Both before I went to the White House and during my time at the White House and even more particularly since I've left the White House, I've had dealings with many of the top executives of the land. I've had dealings with people who have a national reputation as an executive, and I've never yet found one that I would put up against him as an executive officer. He was very different in that respect, for example, from the man that he succeeded. President Roosevelt was probably the greatest politician ever produced in America, but I always thought he was one of the worst administrators. He wasn't in the league with President Truman as an administrative officer, as an executive officer of a group of people.

Morrissey: One reason I asked that question is that I've read that Clark Clifford wrote the message in 1946 to Congress recommending the draft of the railroad strikers with misgivings, and I was wondering if it was frequent for staff members to be involved in a situation in which their heart really wasn't in it; they were doing things that they weren't necessarily convinced were right or they would do differently if they were in the president's position?

Steelman: Well, that's entirely possible. I'm not sure Clark Clifford wrote that message. Many of us worked on it. He was there, but the president felt that it had to be done, and therefore we did it. After all, the president always knows some things that the rest of us don't know, and he has a different responsibility from the rest of us. So, once he definitely decided a course of action was necessary from his viewpoint, why, certainly, I never questioned it. I might question it until he had made a decision, but not afterwards.

Morrissey: I've heard other people say, too, that, let's say, contrasting the manner of writing speeches when FDR was president with the way they were written when Mr. Truman was president, that Mr. Truman used more of a team approach — that is, more people would be involved in the speechwriting process.

Steelman: That's right, absolutely.

Morrissey: Some people have criticized this as saying that it didn't encourage a distinctive style. In other words, it was too bland.

Steelman: Well, that's not the explanation for the style, I don't believe. For the most part, we ended up by saying it the way he would say it. It was just the difference in the two men rather than the system. However, I do have the definite impression — and I think I probably got it primarily from Sam Rosenman — that in the Roosevelt regime, not that one person always did the writing, but some one person would write a particular message almost exclusively and then go over it with the president and there it would be; whereas President Truman did use the staff approach always, but we knew about how he would say it, and if we didn't, when we met with him to go over it to make a final draft, we'd find out how he wanted it said. He was personally closer to his speeches, I think, than either Roosevelt or Eisenhower. In fact, I'm sure of that.

Morrissey: Did the White House staff, in your opinion, anticipate long-range problems, or were the staff members mostly preoccupied with day-by-day decisions and not looking forward, let's say, six months, nine months, or a year ahead of time in terms of diplomatic problems that might be emerging, or political problems or labor problems or something like that?

Steelman: Any White House staff would find great difficulty in finding time to look ahead because the pressure of the moment is always there so that it is very difficult to look ahead as far as we ought to. As a matter of fact, in our regime, the president did more of that than the staff, I'm afraid. In fact, I know he did, because from time to time he would remind us, "We've got to get to work on this, that, or the other problem because it's coming up six months from now or next year." Whereas, the staff, as I say, usually had their nose to the grindstone trying to solve some problem that had to be solved today.

Morrissey: Yes, your phrase "the pressure of the moment" I think is very good.

Steelman: Yes.

Morrissey: One thing that has intrigued me — and I think it's difficult to answer — while Mr. Truman was very concerned about getting all the information he could before he'd make a decision, in many cases he had no hesitation to ignore a lot of this advice and go ahead on his own steam and make a decision that might not quite fit the recommendations of so-called experts who supposedly would know an awful lot about it. From your vantage point, I imagine this is not only something courageous to see a man be willing to do this and go ahead and do it, but *why* did he do it?

Steelman: Well, that's again the kind of man he is. You're right. He would get all the information he could, and then he had what I came to think of as an uncanny sense of reaching the right conclusion, whether it's what the experts recommended or not. Time has told us that in the big things certainly, he was right. He made many of the great decisions of our age, and I'm sure he had expert advice in other directions on every one of them, for that matter. Perhaps the consensus in some of them was there, but whether or not it was, he had an uncanny way of reaching the right decision.

Now, one of the first things I learned about him — and I mention it in connection with his being a great executive officer — when I came, very shortly thereafter, something came up, and I've forgotten now what it was. He made some decision or some announcement late in the day, and the next morning I said, "Mr. President, I think you pulled a boner last night." I want to come back in a moment to why I spoke so frankly; don't let me forget it.

He said, "Well, you may be right, but if I spent today reconsidering and rehashing some decisions that I made yesterday, then all the decisions I've got to make today wouldn't be made at all, and therefore that would be wrong." So, he told me how he worked. He said, "When I make a decision, it is eternally right from there on, regardless."

The president told me that he got all the facts he could before he made the decision and after he made it, just to consider it right because he didn't have time to go back and reconsider because he had other decisions that must be made today. I came to realize that that was a much better theory than forever rehashing. In fact, his successor taught me a lesson on that. He either didn't make a decision at all, or if he did, then he often changed it the next day, and it made a lot of confusion.

So, long after President Truman had left here, some of the government officials down the line, particularly in the State Department, would say to me, "Well, when President Truman was here, we knew what the policy was. It wasn't changed every day." Now, some of these foreign officers would indicate to me, "We're over in Paris and London and Frankfurt, and we get the word that this is the policy, and by the time we get it over to our corresponding officials at the other side, that we're working with, why, the first thing we know, we read in the paper that it's been changed." They were just in a great state of confusion at all times. Well, under President Truman that was not the case. When he made a decision, that was that, and he didn't change it the next day.

Well, I asked you to remind me why I spoke so frankly to the president, even though I hadn't been here very long. I said, "Mr. President, I think you pulled a boner last night."

When I came to work with the president, he indicated to me that there is a great danger of people telling him what they think he wants to hear, and some of the staff, perhaps who had worked with him for years — maybe when he was a senator — he wasn't sure that they would always tell him just what they thought. He always urged them to do so, and I think they did as well as you can expect humanity to function, but he said to me, "Now, you're an outsider, so to speak; you're just here for six months, and the way you can be most helpful to me is to tell me exactly what you think, and we'll understand each other."

So, I felt perfectly free to tell him that I thought he pulled a boner, and he appreciated it, but that didn't mean he changed it. I won't say there haven't been times when he made decisions and changed them, but they were certainly very, very few. It was not his habit.

Morrissey: In a lot of your comments you've emphasized how you think a man who is a member of the White House staff can do a more effective job if he doesn't publicize himself — if he keeps what he knows to himself and keeps his name out of the newspapers. I would assume that you feel very strongly about this.

Steelman: I do. In the first place, just time alone. You cannot be in the press every day; you have to talk to all the boys that call you up about it, or they'll get mad at you. If you go in for publicity, you'll find that's about all you can do; that's one thing about it.

In the second place, if you talk, you lose your effectiveness anyway. If you talk, you have to tell them something that they don't need to know right then. I'm not for keeping things away from the press, and the president had somebody to tell the press what we were doing, but if all of us start being press agents, why, that's all we could do; we couldn't do our jobs. When I was appointed head of OWMR [Office of War Mobilization and Reconversion], I recall going in to see the president one morning, and I said, "Mr. President, you know, I find I've got thirty people in the information division, and I propose to fire all of them."

"Well," he said, "I don't know; I didn't know how many they had or what they do and so forth; that's up to you; you're running the place."

"Well," I said, "the only reason I haven't already done it without even asking you, Mr. President, is that I want to know if it's all right with you if Charlie Ross is my spokesman as well as yours?"

And he said, "Well, yes, if that's the way you want it. Talk it over with Charlie."

So, I went to Charlie and told him, "Here, right in the White House, here's an organization with a bunch of press agents, and I don't like it. Can't you make what announcements I want to make to the press?"

And he said, "Well, sure."

So, out went the press agents.

19

Richard L. Strout

Washington, D.C.   February 5, 1971

Interviewed by Jerry N. Hess

Richard L. Strout (1898–1990), political reporter for the *Christian Science Monitor* and author of the *New Republic*'s "TRB from Washington" column, followed presidents from Warren G. Harding to Ronald Reagan. Truman was among his favorites. When the United States entered the Korean War, the liberal columnist wrote that Truman had defied the conventional wisdom "even more than he did on Election Day, 1948." An early critic of Senator Joseph McCarthy's wild excesses, he defended the president's decision to fire General Douglas MacArthur. A graceful writer with an acerbic wit, this master craftsman set the standard for national political coverage and won a Pulitzer Prize in 1978.

Hess: To begin this afternoon, Mr. Strout, would you give me a little of your personal background?

Strout: Yes, I've been a newspaperman now for almost fifty years. I came down to Washington from Boston on the *Monitor* in 1923, I think it was, and I have been to practically every presidential press conference between now and then. I have been on the *Monitor* all that time, and the last twenty-seven years I have also, in addition, written a weekly column in the *New Republic* magazine called "TRB." I went to, I suppose, practically every press conference that Mr. Truman ever had.

Hess: Would you tell me a little about Mr. Truman's press conferences? Just in general, how skillful was he at fielding the questions that came up?

Strout: President Truman had the disadvantage, of course, of following a famous president, and we all tended to decry him and minimize him, and I think also certainly underestimate him, until in his own right in 1948 he won this amazing election.

The jokes that reporters usually make about presidents — they were a rather cynical group — I remember on one occasion we had to wait for about an hour to get into the press conference. In those days we stood around the desk just the way we had done under Franklin Roosevelt. And

I just remember an amusing little scurrilous remark: "What are they doing? Why do we have to wait?" "They are trying to get his foot out of his mouth." That was the comment. Well, you know, you have total recall of some absurd little thing of that sort. That sort of puts it in perspective.

Hess: Well, he was accused of "shooting from the hip."

Strout: That's right.

Hess: Did you think that was a fair accusation?

Strout: Yes, I think so. I think he did, and his personality has been pretty well identified and will be by others who will be interviewed by you.

Yes, that was a charm and at the same time the awe-inspiring personality that he had. He was perfectly direct like somebody driving a nail in a piece of wood, and you knew just where he was and he said what came into his head.

Hess: Is it always best for a president to be so forthright?

Strout: It certainly is not always best, but at the same time, I think under these circumstances in the great '48 campaign which I'm going to try to talk about, I think it was probably the thing that finally elected him, because I think the public — he established his personality, his character. That was Harry Truman, and Harry Truman was a man who said what he thought. He would always — there wasn't any credibility gap about him. I believe he was saying what he had in his mind.

Hess: Do you think that he used the press conferences in the most effective manner to educate the public and influence congressional action?

Strout: I think he did that as well as he could. He was not a past master as Franklin Roosevelt was, or later on perhaps as Jack Kennedy was. But yes, they came as I recollect, about once a week, and I think it was a magnificent method of carrying things over to the public.

Hess: You mentioned the location of the press conferences, and they were held in the Oval Room until April the twenty-seventh of 1950, and then switched over to the Indian Treaty Room in the Executive Office Building. All right, moving on to the events of 1948, what do you recall about that very eventful year?

Strout: Well, it begins with my going over to Union Station with my wife in June and waiting there. The sixteen-car special was waiting below, and it was kind of pathetic; there was no crowd there. There were about, oh, I guess maybe twelve people, mostly wives. I was talking about this to my wife just last night. She said it was — the mood she got was sort of the pathos of this little man who was — we all accepted the fact that he had insuperable obstacles; he couldn't possibly win, but he was going out in a game fight.

Then I'd like to say a thing about living on one of these special trains. It's like a traveling circus. The only thing is you can't take a bath; you get kind of high after the third week, you know, but it was a traveling circus. You knew everybody, and everybody was moving up and down. You got a feeling of intimacy with the president.

He worked awfully hard. No president has ever made as many speeches in a day as he did. He would make from twelve to fifteen appearances in speeches. He'd come out on the back of the — I think the train was called the Ferdinand Magellan, wasn't it? I think that was . . .

Hess: During those whistle-stops, did you ever have a chance to talk to the people who were there?

Strout: Oh yes, we'd always try to do that. There'd always be one squalling child, and there'd be a — people were friendly. They came out very largely to see the president, and everybody — that was — this thing grew. It was like a developing character, this whole — it was a drama; it changed as we went along. First it was curiosity and they came out to see the president, to show Johnny the president, and that sort of thing. And then he began this business of attacking the "no-good, do-nothing Eightieth Congress."

Now just at the start, a great issue was, was he going to — was he a spent bolt? Was he a burnt-out ember? Was he going to be able to attract people to come? And very early in the campaign — I don't have the date, but you have it here — he went to this Omaha, Nebraska — the Ak-Sar-Ben amphitheater, which held ten thousand people. And we went in there — let's see, these are the actual notes that I took on June 5, '48. I wrote, "amphitheater brick, cement, good functional arena stage, got American flag as backdrops sides of stage, and rather ugly wallpaper, sign from the top Ak-Sar-Ben." But the point was that nobody was there. The first — as I'm holding now in front of you a picture of this thing which is —

Hess: That appeared in Life magazine.

Strout: — taken from Life magazine on June 21, 1948. They were having a convention of Truman's old buddies from the army, and these boys didn't want to go down and hear a political speech and they were out on the town. And so we were right up here to the right — the press that is — the photographers were right here. The cameras were up here. He was halfway through his speech — here's his speech here — see if I can find the place where I noted it down. "Six great tables of press men were in front, then a gap of six empty rows, and then about a thousand people" — writer says two thousand; you couldn't possibly say there was two thousand people. "There was about a thousand people, and behind that emptiness." There were reporters — whispered to each other. We were kind of awed by this horrible flop.

Hess: All of the empty seats.

Strout: Here it is here. "A gasp of amazement as reporters entered the place and saw this thing and the spotlights were on Truman's face at first." In this picture you see they are on him. "Halfway through the speech the spotlights lifted from Harry Truman, and like a finger swept slowly all around this great amphitheater on the empty seats." And as I wrote down at the time in my black pencil, "There was a brutal — there was an affront." Harry was then reading his speech — I'm going to come back to that — in an uninspired voice with no resonance. He couldn't read his speech. "The audience is frozen," and so forth. Well, that's about the point. Well, that was a horrible beginning.

I think nothing has ever been as bad as that. The Life magazine on this June 21, 1948, has this article "The Truman Train Stumbles West." It was a very sharp piece in which they just said, "The most impressive thing last week about Mr. Truman's trip to the West was his incredible ability to pretend that nothing at all was wrong."

Then you go to Cheyenne — that was the next day as I recollect it. And this was the picture in Life. This was a series of pictures that irritated me. The crowd — he had a good-sized crowd and they had all gone up to the mansion up here, and so this was just a fraud. I took it upon myself . . .

Hess: That shows a soldier, just standing there and no one around.

Strout: Yes. No — yes, yes, his back is toward us, and he is looking up toward the mansion. The trees hide the crowd, so it looks just empty and it says, "A lonely soldier faces outwards towards what should have been crowds along president's route in Cheyenne. Crowds were small nearly everywhere." And the fact is that there was a fairly big crowd there.

I took it upon myself — I suppose the reporters tended to identify themselves. I sent a — I wrote to Life magazine and two weeks later they published an apology, which I have the date, but I — oh yes, my letter to Life appeared on page 7, July 19, 1948, and there was an explanation by Life that they had been able to cover it only half of the trip and were not aware of the good crowds and, "*Life* regrets that the time element caused a one-sided picture of the tour as a whole." Well, that was, I suppose, a reasonable enough explanation. There was no question about resentment. We were just — I tried to speak, as I say, for forty or fifty reporters on just that one particular item.

Ah, let's see, then he — then he went on and what he did was he dropped — with the thick lenses of his glasses, he could never read a speech successfully. He finally dropped the speech reading and took up his famous direct speech, in which he was utterly himself, and he had a short jerky right-hand motion up and down —

Hess: Just a chopping motion.

Strout: A chopping motion. And he got it over, and I look back through my notes, and I say this at my own expense, because we were all utterly convinced that he didn't have a prayer. And the great question that we all asked ourselves was, "Does he know it?" And we never really knew whether he knew it or not, and we don't know it to the end.

Another untoward occurrence — which is terrible funny — at the Carey, Idaho, airport, where he — I don't blame that on Charlie Ross, and Charlie Ross was my dear friend, and how he did it I don't know. Maybe he had stayed up too late the night before playing poker; maybe he had one or two too many, although he was not a drinking man. But anyway, he had been told by long-distance telephone about the circumstances, and he gave the circumstances.

Truman was out to dedicate an airport. He thought the airport was for a brave soldier who had lost his life for his country, and when he got there he began by saying, "I'm honored to dedicate this airport and present this wreath to the parents of the brave boy." Somebody told him that it wasn't a brave boy. Wilma was a girl. And then he went on, wandered on; he said it was someone that gave — she had given her life for the country, and she died in an ordinary airplane accident. Well, that was a horrible thing to happen to anybody, and when you think of the — really of the disadvantages of the problems that he had when he started out to — of course, we all know he won, but he overcame this hideous beginning.

And I look back over the pieces I'd been sending to my paper, the *Christian Science Monitor*, and I — just in glancing through them — October 8: "The politicians are baffled. They cannot figure it out, and some places registration figures are the highest in history; in others they are low to the point of apathy." We thought the apathy later on was, "Well, we know who is going to win, so why spoil the record?" There was a great deal of apathy, and it was obviously his job to go out, try to break that up, and get them — there were more Democrats in the country at that time — I think there still are — if you could just get them to come out. And his job is to get out some liveliness and excitement.

On October 14 I wrote to my paper — oh no, I switched over to the Dewey train at this time and I wrote this — then I say it with blushes — "October 14: It is now as certain as anything can be in the course of American politics that Governor Dewey is elected and the nation knows it, and yawns over the final three weeks of the campaign, whose outcome was certain before it began."

I've jumped as you see from June. I'm coming back to June, and to October, because that was what we were writing. We're a respectable, reputable paper, just sort of taken for granted.

On a little later, October 15, I said, "Governor Dewey on his side is blandly continuing his chosen course, which is apparently carrying him straight for the White House."

And that was what really apparently ruined Mr. Dewey, because he accepted that he was going to be elected, so he — was not a — Dewey was a sort of an artificial person. He was — the famous story about his was that he was like a little bridegroom on the wedding cake, you know, and he was rather cold. He had a sonorous, beautiful voice. He had been trained one time — I think he had thought of going into the opera — and a beautiful voice, but he didn't have any passion, nor did he feel that he needed to elicit any passion.

Hess: How did the crowds react to Governor Dewey as compared to the crowd reaction to President Truman?

Strout: Every newspaperman watched that, and that's why you switched from one train to another. At first I would say there was not much difference between the two. At the end though, without any doubt — and I'm going to come to that — the Truman crowds had just changed in the last three weeks. They had changed enormously and part of — reading through this to me is like a Sherlock Holmes story. I had all of the evidence here in my own writing as to what was happening, and yet I was — like everybody else — I was so mesmerized by what everybody was saying that I didn't take the logical conclusion of the evidence that I was writing about.

Hess: Just why were you convinced that Mr. Truman was going to lose?

Strout: Well, I think probably it was due to the polls. I think the polls hadn't — I don't know that they have perfected it now — but they had — they were not merely the Gallup poll, but the Crossley poll and all the other polls, and they all unanimously said that it was all over. And what can you do? What can a reporter do if the polls say that it is just — it's all happened? And yet here as I'm coming down — this is again from the Dewey trip: "Dewey's speeches are so generalized that accompanying newsmen 'find difficulty in picking out a salient news item for the lead in the stories.'" Every newsman has to say in the first sentence the lead of his story, but you'd get these speeches where there wasn't any lead.

Hess: You have to head your story with something.

Strout: Yes, you have to start with something.

Then October 21. Now see, this is about three weeks before the election. "There's no doubt about it any longer, that shuffling you hear is the sound of the wide Democratic hopes over their prospects in House and Senatorial election contests." See, I was coming closer to it, but I wasn't quite getting it. But, I said, "A combination of recent evidence indicates that a mild 'trend' may be developing in many areas for Democratic congressional and state candidates and if any such result actually occurs it may complicate the problems of interpreting the 1948 election. Your reporter notes a slight increase in Truman sentiment in one of the national opinion polling groups."

Of course, "he was defeated," but he was coming up a little bit — they were subtle enough to catch that — "But nothing that would give them a chance at capturing victory," I add.

Well, what a relief it was to get away from the Dewey artificiality and get back into the bubbling, hard-hitting naturalness of this little Harry Truman's campaign. I mean I would defy anybody, even people who were ardently for Dewey, not to find it more entertaining to be with Truman because he put on a better show.

And I want to make the point that what Truman said in a way made sense. To Congress he had presented a plan for — way back then — for nationalized health insurance; they just turned it down and a whole series of things. And, oh, so that he was to — he had some basis for attacking them in the campaign.

Now, if I can switch back to this first initial June trip. One of the jokes about the Truman trip was that the further West he got the more his western vernacular increased. He started out for California. They wanted a good reason for a "nonpolitical" trip to go out to California. And some-body—[Dr. Robert G.] Sproul, the president of the university—offered to give him a degree if he came out there. You can tell little, in their corni-ness that today would—well, there's no cornier than Lyndon Johnson when he tells about his grandpas! All the way across the West as his ver-nacular got thicker, he told the grandpa's covered wagon trip to Oregon and produced an historical relative or two in virtually every area where he spoke. Furthermore, as he advanced, denouncing the Eightieth Congress with more brilliant flights of language he would just—he would fetch out these grandpas.

Now, if you will permit me, I'll glance through a piece that I wrote for my paper at the time. As you can see, we were having just a wonderful time on this picnic. I will say in all my almost fifty years of traveling, I never enjoyed a trip more, with one exception, and that was going across the country with the Russian, Mr. [Nikita Sergeyevich] Khrushchev, and that was very much like it. It was a burlesque. Anything would happen and it practically did.

I say in this piece that "President Truman carried the savor of his two grandpas through the West with him on his recent trip." This was written in past tense, because—"there seemed to be hardly a rear stop some-times when Grandfather Young or Grandfather Truman weren't brought up. Generally they had an adventure in the vicinity." The incident was told in semihumorous, intimate fashion, and the rear platform audience seemed to like them; the president getting up and telling about Grandpa, you know, and as I say, you couldn't help loving the little fellow . . .

"Generally they linked Mr. Truman up with the neighborhood, by inheritance anyway. It was maternal grandfather Solomon Young who popped up in the introductory remarks of the president in the Mormon Tabernacle in Salt Lake City." Now, that was hardly a place for Grand-father to come in. "The president's grandfather he said had been a trader"—trader apparently was a technical word—"and he had come up to Salt Lake City with a consignment of merchandise which the con-signee refused to accept. His grandfather appealed directly to Brigham Young." He wouldn't have said "grandfather." "Grandpa." He'd reached the grandpa stage then. "Mr. Truman told the audience Brigham Young had helped him get justice. This pleased the big crowd a good deal. It was another score for the Truman grandfather."

"It was down at Shelbyville, Kentucky, that the grandparents really went to work, however; it was here that a love interest entered the story. Nobody could tell a romantic affair better than candidate Truman himself. And so let it be recorded that at 8:45 A.M. on October 1st, Mr. Truman greeted several thousand Shelbyvillers from a rear platform of his special train, with the customary friendly good mornings, and went on from there." And then I'd tell it. Anyway . . .

And then I go on, "Well, that was the Shelbyville incident as Mr. Truman told it. He added that he was proud of his Kentucky ancestry, naturally, and the audience seemed flattered and pleased."

Lyndon Johnson did just the same thing as this when he was running as a vice presidential candidate with Mr. Kennedy. He went right through the South telling in a very Southern accent —

Hess: Relatives all over the place.

Strout: —very, very slow.

"As the train pulled out of Shelbyville, the reporters could hear Mr. Truman on the loudspeaker, which they had forgotten to cut off, good-naturedly challenging his daughter, Margaret. The people of Shelbyville were well-acquainted with her he insisted because she had come up here to make certain investigations of her own as to the validity of his runaway grandparents' marriage lines.

"Later on Charles, Charlie Ross, hurried back into the press car" — that's where we had one big car where the typewriters were — "with a self-conscious and anxious expression on his face to make sure the reporters understood the president had been facetious in his remarks."

I hadn't read this thing, for heaven's sakes, for twenty-five years or so. This is written from Washington. "What is causing correspondents aboard the presidential train some anxiety as to what is going to happen to the grandparents when Mr. Truman leaves the West and starts an intensive drive of the East. He has made a preliminary trip to Philadelphia, through upstate New York this week . . . no grandparents. Correspondents had grown familiar with the group and wanted to hear more about them, but what will happen when he gets to work, say, in New England? Is President Truman running short of grandparents? In this genealogical crisis it is believed, however, that Mr. Truman has virtually untapped stores of great-grandparents, almost certainly one or more of them came from the East. Then again, from Mr. Truman's own admission, Grandmother — Grandma Young — was one of thirteen children. If one of them doesn't turn out to have settled in Roxbury, Mass., and made the long trek home to Freeport, Long Island, before the campaign is over, this correspondent will be surprised and disappointed."

The Republicans I think had started out a truth-squad special — I'm not sure whether that had been invented yet or not — anyway, they were denouncing Truman vigorously and naturally, up and down the country. And Truman at one point said, "They can't prove nothing; they ain't got a thing on me."

Well, my dear friend and one of the finest newspapermen I ever knew in my life was the syndicated columnist Thomas Stokes. He had written many songs and parodies for Gridiron Clubs, and he got us together one time. He said, "We've got to have a song for this trip." And he sat down in somebody's cubbyhole. Each one of us had a little room we sat in, and I remember he began pounding on the table to get the rhythm, and he said, "'Oh! Susannah'—that would be a good tune." And then just by a flash of genius, it came to him right all of a sudden. Tom Stokes — and I'm not in a singing voice today and I can't carry a tune, but you can get —:

They can't prove nothin', they ain't got a thing on me
I'm goin' down to Berkeley fur to git me a degree.

If you've got a chorus like that, why don't — *anything* falls into place. Well, then it began:

Old Grandpaw went to Oregon, the dough was on his knee
Grandpaw went to Oregon, the west coast fur to see
He got himself a partner in Californiay
They bought up Sacramento on a lovely summer day.

Now actually Grandpaw was no businessman, and he went right on the rocks. Just the way Harry's haberdashery store went bankrupt.

Grandpaw warn't no businessman, he went right on the rocks
So grandson went to old KC to peddle drawers and socks
The curse was strong right down the line, no profit could he see
So Harry quit and folded up his haberdashery.

And then you go on that same one:

They ain't got nothing . . .

The next line:

> I went to work for Pendergast, he made a judge of me
> Before I knew what happened I was picked by Franklin D.
> I got my boots and saddles on and started for the sea
> I made a lot of speeches and I plugged for Sun Valley.

It all comes back to me as I recite it, the gang—and then somebody would want to—we all felt this was going to be an immortal song, so each would compose a little quatrain to go into it. And you'd kid above the bounce of the train and the smell of cinders and the rattle of the typewriters and so forth. And some people were taking drinks and holding beer and singing a new stanza that somebody had just written. Yes.

Hess: Did you write sentences yourself?

Strout: I don't recall. I don't recall that, but Tom Stokes probably did. One would think of a precious line and then try to make it rhyme with something. And you kind of went in with the sound of wheels, you know, going around below. Truman talked at one point about "a light-foot Baptist," and none of us had known what a "light-foot Baptist" was. I think he had gone out to —what was it?—yes. Oh yes, this immortalized that.

> One Sabbath bright he campaigned right through Texas' bonny
>   breast.
> He laid a wreath at Alamo that there the heroes blessed.
> He met Rayburn, a Hard Shell man, a Baptist to the root.
> And there revealed, though on himself, he claimed to be light foot.

> They can't prove nothin', they ain't got a thing on me.
> I'm goin' down to Berkeley fur to git me a degree.

Well, I think that's . . .

Hess: How many verses were there to the song?

Strout: I think I've got the whole thing here.

Hess: Also on the June trip at one of his stops in Eugene, Oregon, he said, "I like old Joe." Do you recall that?

Strout: Oh, yes, that caused him a lot of trouble. It had a qualifying phrase to it. "I like old Joe; the only thing, he's . . ." or "you can't believe a word he says" or "he's a terrible liar." But first he said, "I like"; yeah, that was just poison to say a thing of that sort.

Hess: And also on the June trip, in Irwin Ross's book *The Loneliest Campaign*,

Ross quotes part of an article that you wrote. He said, "The bombast made effective political vaudeville," and then he quotes you: "His reception has been uniformly cordial, Richard L. Strout recorded in the *Christian Science Monitor*. Most reporters on board feel that his warmth has increased as the journey progressed. Just why is a matter of speculation, but it may be that word had gone around that a scrappy fighter is making an uphill fight."

Strout: Well, that — yes, I would say it colloquially a little bit more. First he made his attack on Congress and that caught on. Then he abandoned the prepared speeches for colloquial speeches. He hit his stride, and then it got closer to the election. And first you get through the World Series, you know, and then you get through something else, and then finally they come to the last three weeks. I think I have a little about this right here. As I went through my notes, I noticed that in my own correspondence that it got more and more so. October 22, I say that "hardly a week exists before election day." Now that was — you see it was warming up now; he had got hold. Oh, and I think, too, that Dewey realized that he had — that he wasn't coming over, and that it was too late for him to change. I think that was another thing.

October 25: "Mr. Truman had a spectacular turnout in downtown Chicago, and today Mr. Truman is storming over the big cities of the East." He had won confidence and we had won confidence. No, I should not say that; we still knew that he was "defeated." There was no question at all though, that he was coming up.

October 27 — this I remember rather vividly as my paper's published in New England and I accompanied him up into this New England trip there looking for his grandparents — "President Truman has swept into New England for a two-day campaign tour breathing hope and confidence. Accompanying reporters are sufficiently impressed by big crowds, the enigma of the trade union vote, and the last-minute Democratic appeal to minority racial and religious groups to revise earlier estimates, and reappraise the whole situation."

Well, that seems almost as though I were going to come out on the right side there, doesn't it?

Hess: Yes.

Strout: Then I immediately add, "While correspondents, almost to a man, believe that Mr. Truman's uphill fight will be unsuccessful, an upturn of Truman stock generally is felt to be underway." In other words we sensed it; we saw it; if it had not been for the polls, we would have — might have touched it. "There seems to be no question that Mr. Truman generally has outdrawn Governor Dewey, whatever that may mean in the final vote. The Democrats obviously feel that they are gaining ground. The upturn of Truman stock might change the result from a rout to a mere defeat."

I think I came to him — well, I answer my own question here — to be October 30. October 28: "He, Truman, has shown much ability so far as this writer can judge, to communicate emotions of fear, rage, and similar political passions to his audiences that have appeared in horrendous charges."

October 29: "The agile Mr. Truman was moving about almost every instant" — that was in New York City — "and made fifteen speeches after leaving Boston the day before, six of them in New York City."

October 30: "Mr. Truman went to New York after being seen by 2 million to 3 million people."

And here is one comment that was made to me — this was back, way back in the June speech — it was out in Idaho, and as you say, the reporters talked to people in the crowd: "Say, what do you think of him? What do you think of his speech?" And people would all smile in a friendly way. And one Idaho editor I talked to who was evidently a Republican and who I was absolutely sure would vote for Dewey, observed to me, "He's a spunky little cuss." He said it in a very friendly fashion, and I've always had the feeling that — or at least how they were going to vote until election day, and then they got into the polling booth and they said, "This poor little guy is going to get beaten so badly that I'm just going to give him a vote to show I —"

Hess: Just because he's spunky.

Strout: "— I like him." Yes. I'm not sure; he didn't win by very much. The speeches that I remember are those hard-hitting —

Hess: The whistle-stop speeches.

Strout: — whistle-stop, off-the-rear-platform speeches, yes.

Hess: Did he seem more relaxed and more able to deliver that type of speech than he was a full-fledged, standing-behind-the-podium type of speech?

Strout: Of — quite — yes, I'm glad you brought that up. Yes, he was obviously ill at ease. I don't think he could see his copy very well. I think the man who could read a speech like that best I've ever known is Franklin Roosevelt. You really couldn't tell whether he was extemporizing it or his eye was moving ahead and he was — it seems to be coming right from the —Truman's glasses were a great handicap and then his great — he didn't have the capacity to do that. He wasn't that type of man.

Oh, yes, after that horrible Ak-Sar-Ben thing, his self-confidence you could see coming back. He always claimed that he knew he was going to win. And Jack Redding in his book offers some evidence to that effect. I don't know, I never — I don't know, I think in his heart of hearts he thought he was going to be defeated and he was — that would have been my estimation.

Hess: Now let me ask you a question about some of his White House staff members who were on the train. Did you at times have occasion to talk to the staff members other than Charles Ross, other than the press secretary? Charles Murphy, Clark Clifford, and George Elsey for instance?

Strout: Yes, I think they thought he would be defeated. I think almost certainly they did.

Hess: Did they tell you?

Strout: When I say that — no, naturally not, that would be heresy or would be — it would be treachery to say such a thing as that. No, purposely they had to create this confidence and so forth. I'm sure from other witnesses you've got the record of the public opinion polls. I have them here, which just simply seem to be overwhelming.

Well, this is from the *Washington Post* after the event. This is the Thursday after the election. It's dated November the fourth. There's the famous photograph of "Dewey Defeats Truman" from the *Chicago Tribune*, and there are three columns of excerpts from different newspapers. One that I recall appeared in *Life* magazine by Joe and Stuart Alsop, who said, "What kind of a president will Mr. Dewey make?"

Hess: Another photograph in *Life* magazine showed Mr. Dewey — I think it was in San Francisco — on a ferry boat.

Strout: Yes.

Hess: And it was captioned, "The next president travels by ferry boat over the broad waters of San Francisco Bay."

Strout: Broad waters of San Francisco Bay, yes. That was from *Life* magazine.

The columnist Drew Pearson was caught flat-footed with a prospective lineup of the Dewey cabinet.

I mentioned this Joe and Stew Alsop; I think that was in *Life*.

Newsweek. Oh, this was — this came to him while he was on his trip. A copy of *Newsweek*; they polled fifty top political writers who predicted, without a single exception, Dewey's victory. That was — discouraged them enormously when that thing came aboard. Well, now, look at these polls. The *Post*'s Elmer Roper — I guess they don't have the figures here, or do I?

Hess: Let's see; that mentions Roper.

Strout: "Nothing but a political convulsion would save him."

Hess: And Roper quit polling on September the ninth.

Strout: Yes, that was his farewell. *Fortune* magazine. Gallup and his last report, his final prediction: "Dewey will get 49.5 percent; Truman 44 percent." Well, now, that doesn't seem very big, but most presidential elections, that's comparable to a landslide. That's five percentage points.

Archibald Crossley: "Governor Dewey and Governor Warren were sure of election," and so on, and so . . .

Hess: Now, this clipping mentions Henry Wallace and Strom Thurmond.

Strout: Yes.

Hess: What effect did you think it would have on the Democratic Party, splitting into three wings; Mr. Truman and then Henry Wallace moving off on the left, Strom Thurmond moving off on the right? What effect did you think that would have?

Strout: My belief and recollection was that both of them would injure Truman because Wallace, whom I knew pretty well and was writing for the *New Republic* at the time when my TRB column was appearing, would have taken away a lot of the militant intellectuals and Thurmond would help split the solid South. So, from both wings — the extraordinary thing was it didn't go into the House of Representatives with four parties.

I have to say in fairness, too, and I say this blushingly, in my TRB column I had to write it in advance, and I mentioned "President" Dewey in the column, and it's a terrible feeling for a newspaperman to know that that thing is in the works when —

Hess: And can't be stopped.

Strout: —when the election — nothing on earth — nothing on earth can stop it.

And then I say, "We think, moreover, that the Republicans are underestimating Truman as a campaigner. There's gratification in watching a rather mild, temperate, long-suffering man finally blow off steam against a reactionary Congress" — as I regarded them — "and what a record he has to work on. The ore is practically inexhaustible."

This is written for a liberal magazine; it represented my view: "This election may be more entertaining than we had supposed." So, as I say, the evidence was all there; only you needed a Sherlock Holmes to put the thing together.

And then I paid my respects to Mr. Dewey: "Dewey, we guess, is at a quiet place. We honestly tried to put aside all bias, but when he came to the front to receive the vigorous ovation after his nomination" — that was at the Philadelphia convention of course — "and we saw again his bottle brush mustache, and his toothy smile, his dimples and mannequin face, we couldn't love him. His fine resonant voice soared out, and there wasn't any warmth in it. The words were appropriately humble, but the speaker seemed to us cool, calculating, and supremely self-confident."

Well, he was self-confident.

Those were the biased words of a young man who was so liberal. And I might not have written them today.

I don't know how I would approach it, but — and then finally on July 24 I wrote — this was just before the Philadelphia convention, but you remember both conventions were held in Philadelphia that year — "Harry Truman may not have given his party victory in Philadelphia, but he gave it self-respect."

That was a time, if you recall, where he came in by train. It would have been terribly gauche for him to appear before he was nominated. So, they put him down in a little room in the cellar of the amphitheater, and they kept him there. Hot, humid — it was before air-conditioning — and he stayed there I don't know how many hours and then finally at 1:30 or two o'clock in the morning, he came out and he let go. And again, it was this sense that the fellow had more power than we had supposed, and it was evidently on the — I must have written it right after hearing him when I was elated by what he had done. It surprised me, just I suppose as a theatrical critic, I thought this was going to be a lame and dull affair and had a feeling that, "Gee, this fellow may show them something after all."

Hess: What had been the mood of the convention up until that time?

Strout: Dispirited. Oh, it was the most dispirited convention I have ever — that I can recall, until Alben Barkley made a speech.

Hess: The keynote address.

Strout: He made a splendid speech in which he got at the line where somebody had attacked the — how did that go? Somebody had attacked the birds — oh, the blue eagle, wasn't it, the blue eagle or something of that sort?

Hess: The old NRA blue eagle.

Strout: Yes, I think when he — he said when he came to — when the Democrats came to office the poor creature was so emaciated they were so poor and emaciated. They loved it; they laughed.

Well, let's go back and just finish this thing off. "Harry Truman may not have given his party a victory in Philadelphia, but he gave it self-respect, and it was fun to see this scrappy little cuss come out of his corner fighting at two o'clock in the morning, not trying to use big words any longer, but being himself, and saying a lot of honest things that needed to be said. Unaccountably we found ourselves on top of a pine bench cheering." That's a terrible admission for a reporter to make a violent statement . . .

Hess: Reporters are not supposed to do that, are they?

Strout: This was an anonymous column, you see, so I could do that. "We have always thought of Mr. Truman as Mr. Average Man himself. Nice and likeable and commonplace, mediocre. These attributes made something of a problem when one is president, but it is the hope of salvation for the average man that you find in him a touch of the divine if you jab around long enough. And there was real splendor in the way Truman took over that convention. As we wrote last week, 'He is a stronger campaigner than a lot of people realize.'"

Well, that just about covers it, I guess.

Hess: All right, one question on that particular speech: At the end of that speech he said that on Turnip Day he was going to call Congress back into special session.

Strout: Yes, that's right. He was a sensation. That's a — there again, lest I be thought overwhelmingly biased — that was a *pure* political ploy. He knew *perfectly* well that Congress, the lame-duck Congress, was not going to pass anything. It was pure and simple politics. He got them back, and he dramatized the situation, and the country needed — he wasn't running against Mr. Dewey; nobody can run against Mr. Dewey; Mr. Dewey wasn't saying anything. But he had an antagonist, and the nation, it was like the end of the World Series; he was this man versus all of the powers of Congress and of — well, the newspapers I think — the newspapers of the country in that election, 75 percent of the papers — or 75 percent of the circulation — was on Dewey's side. After all, the Democrats had been in office, I think, sixteen years, and people thought it was time for a change, and it may have been time for a change. It might have been better for the country. I don't say that it wasn't, but Truman's next four years weren't very successful.

Hess: Mr. Truman, as you say, had called the Congress in to set them up as a straw man to attack them during the campaign and to run against the Eightieth Congress.

Strout: That's right.

Hess: But the Eightieth Congress had given him the Greek-Turkish aid bill, which became known as the Truman Doctrine; the Eightieth Congress had passed the Marshall Plan. They had cooperated with Mr. Truman in the foreign field.

At the time that you were traveling on the Truman train, did you ever have occasion to speak with Mr. Truman and pass the time of day with him?

Strout: Yes, we passed the time of day and said, "Hi," and so forth, but no, I don't think we had any deeper personal contact. I did with Margaret sometimes.

He would introduce Mrs. Truman, the First Lady, as "my boss," and then Margaret. Always with very evident pride, and he conveyed to the audience the warmth of a typical American family. They were very closely knit.

Hess: Where were you on election night?

Strout: Right here in Washington.

Hess: What do you recall about your feelings when the election did not go your way, or did not go the way that you thought it would?

Strout: I kind of hate — that's a painful subject. Well, I'll be frank about it; there'd been a — at some great rally; oh, let's see, first of all we went to friends', and the ambiguous returns began to come in, and I was superior and I said, "Yes, oh yes, he's winning these, these big — some of these big stages, but wait until you hear from the small towns."

Hess: Fundamentally the same thing Mr. Kaltenborn was saying.

Strout: Yes. Oh, quite — yes, we all said the same thing. And then I told my wife, "Why, I'm going down early and write the story, so I'm going to bed early and I'll write a story about Mr. Dewey in the morning. I'll get down to the office about six o'clock — the wire would open about eight o'clock," and then he didn't win.

Well, I had mixed motives. I had the feeling that this piece of mine in the New Republic coming out — but then a kind of snobbishness developed. We were all so badly fooled that we all began boasting. That was eating crow; we all had our own various types of crow to eat. And I was in there with everyone else.

Hess: As you are TRB, what is your evaluation and opinion of Mr. Truman's commitment to liberal policies?

Strout: I rate President Truman pretty high. In retrospect, he grows rather than diminishes, which is a fine thing to say about anybody. In my writing twenty years later I come back to things he did. Yesterday I was writing about the Subversive Activities Control Board. Truman vetoed the bill setting it up and was overridden in the McCarthy era. He said it wouldn't work. It didn't. Eisenhower was an idol of many, but in retrospect his eight years were rather commonplace — on the economic side he got three recessions in eight years. It was the cliché of the times that Truman did the hard things better than the easy things; he made some poor appointments and was overloyal to second-rate friends — unlike FDR, who could sever relations skillfully and perhaps with suave brutality.

Truman could make decisions. "The buck stops here," his desk motto said; he meant it. He was not the father figure of many presidencies; people felt he was one of them; they liked him; his simplicity and naturalness came through. His enemies derided him as being too little for the job, which probably meant that he was not pompous or sententious; but there was no credibility gap; people felt he was honest, maybe too honest, in shooting from the hip. A trait recalling Jackson. People felt, too, I think, that he was courageous, a scrapper, "a brave little cuss." There was deep, though not always recognized, feeling by masses of people of identification with him; like them he had limitations, but like them he was doing his best — maybe working at it, in fact, harder than they were.

I try to look back. He handled the Douglas MacArthur period boldly and effectively when a smaller man would have tried to compromise.

It is interesting to recall how he tried to get a national health insurance system about thirty years ahead of his time and was defeated, of course, by the conventional wisdom of his day, mobilized politically by the American Medical Association. On foreign affairs I think he did better than average, though I have never been sure it was necessary to drop the atom bomb on crowded Japanese cities. I thought so at the time; reporters knew that it was to be done and were quite powerless to intervene. The Greece-Turkey interventions seemed wise; at any rate, they were successful. The Marshall Plan was splendid. He helped create NATO.

My, the U.S. was lucky to have a spunky little chap just when he came, when he was overshadowed by the glamour of the late FDR.

Hess: In your opinion, what are Mr. Truman's major accomplishments?

Strout: Oh, the foreign affairs things I think. I would have to stop and think. You can't spring that one on me all of a sudden. It's been a long time ago.

I would just take the conventional view. He did a lot of good things, and then he pointed the way, too, to a lot of welfare proposals that will ultimately be accepted, but he was tapering off the New Deal and obviously the country wanted time to consolidate what it had done.

20

Roger Tubby

Washington, D.C.   February 10, 1970

Interviewed by Jerry N. Hess (Harry S. Truman Library)

Roger W. Tubby (1910–1991), Truman's last press secretary, was a newspaperman before and after his governmental career. He began working for the federal government in 1942 on the staff of the Board of Economic Warfare. From 1945 until 1948, he was press spokesman for the State Department and in 1950 became assistant White House press secretary. In the fall of 1952, he became the chief presidential spokesman after the death of press secretary Joseph Short. After the Truman years, he was the publisher of the *Adirondack Daily Express*. Truman sent him advice on how to run a successful newspaper. The veteran spokesman returned to the State Department as assistant secretary for public affairs during John F. Kennedy's administration and later served as ambassador to United Nations organizations in Geneva.

Hess: Ambassador Tubby, to begin, would you tell me a little bit about your background: Where were you born, where were you raised, and a few of the positions that you've held?

Tubby: Well, Jerry, I was born in Greenwich, Connecticut, in 1910 — December 30, 1910. I went to Yale University. I worked in Vermont for the Bennington, Vermont, *Banner;* I was a reporter and then editor. My main achievement there, I think, as I look back, was getting town manager government for Bennington. During the war I was in the Board of Economic Warfare, and when that became the Foreign Economic Administration, a combination of BEW and Lend-Lease, I became assistant to the administrator, Leo Crowley. Subsequently, I went to the Department of Commerce as director of information of the Office of International Trade; and after that to the Department of State in 1946 with Mike [Michael J.] McDermott, who was then the chief spokesman of the Department of State and had been for a great many years before. In 1950 I went to the White House as the assistant White House press secretary under Joe Short.

Hess: We will come back to a few of those and ask some further points on them. But to get back in time, just how did you come to be a member of the White House staff?

Tubby: Well, my understanding is that Charlie Ross and the president asked Joe Short, who was then with the *Baltimore Sun*, and Bill Hillman, who was then with *Collier's*, and I think one other, to make nominations for a possible successor to Charlie Ross, because Charlie had indicated that he would like very much to retire and to get a country paper and edit it during his last years.

Hess: About what time was this that Mr. Ross was thinking of retiring?

Tubby: My recollection is that this was maybe as early at 1949. Anyway, Bill Hillman called me one day at the State Department and said he would like to have a meeting with me at the Carlton Hotel, and I did meet him there with Matt Connelly. They told me what they had in mind — would I be interested in coming to the White House? They didn't say exactly what date. I had been nominated to go to the National War College for the following year, and I was very much interested in doing so and continuing my career in State, but naturally, when you get an invitation to go to the White House, you drop everything else.

Then Charlie Ross had his heart attack and died, and Mr. Truman, very wisely, I think, chose Joe Short as Charlie's successor. Joe had been covering the White House for a number of years for the *Baltimore Sun* and had the complete confidence of HST.

Hess: Do you recall when you first met Mr. Short?

Tubby: I had known him slightly over the years, but I don't think I really met him or had a talk with him until around November of 1950.

Hess: How would you compare the two men, as to the way that they handled the office: Charles Ross and Joe Short?

Tubby: Well, I didn't know Charlie Ross enough — I rarely saw him in action. My impression is that he had an easier personality, more relaxed personality than Joe Short, that he enjoyed a *very* long friendship with HST over many years, and that there was complete confidence, rapport between the president and Charlie, and the president held Charlie in very high regard. He had been former editorial writer for the *St. Louis Post-Dispatch* and chief of the bureau for the *Post-Dispatch* in Washington.

Joe enjoyed the president's confidence likewise. He was, by nature, however, quite tense, very conscientious as was Charlie Ross, but very much aware of the possibility of error and of consequences of error in anything that was said to the press, and so I do think that Joe was more wary and therefore, perhaps, in some ways, not quite as successful as Charlie was. Somebody else really ought to make a judgment on that.

Hess: Were there any members of the press that seemed to have Mr. Truman's special favor?

Tubby: Well, I think, of course, Joe Short himself before he came on board. Eddie Folliard of the *Washington Post* — Mr. Truman was very fond of him and vice versa, I think. Tony Vaccaro of the Associated Press. Pete Brandt of the *St. Louis Post-Dispatch*. I'm not sure about Merriman Smith, of that relationship.

You did have a question that you were going to suggest that I would like to comment on, and that is my first meeting with HST. When I did go in to see him, I reminded him that I had a rather dark background: that in Vermont in the thirties, I had been on the Republican town committee and I had campaigned for a liberal Republican for Congress, who was beaten by Congressman Plumley in the primary; and that I had been the one editor of a daily paper in the state who had supported George D. Aiken for the Republican nomination when he first ran for the Senate. Mr. Truman said, "Well, if you're okay with George Aiken, you're okay with me, and I understand you *are* okay with George Aiken."

I think that he was interested in — although he was very partisan — but he was interested, really, in what people could do.

I remember once a young nephew of mine showed up from the state of Washington, and he came in kind of old clothes, and I said, "Would you like to hear a presidential press conference?" He said he would and so I took him along, and afterwards I introduced him to the president, and the boy, who was about eighteen or nineteen, apologized for the look of his clothes.

And the president said, "Son, I don't go by that. I go by the look of a man, his eyes, his general bearing, etc., and I can see that you're okay!" putting the boy very much at his ease.

Hess: I have one question about the pre-press conferences, or the sessions that went on before the press conferences: After the time that you instituted using the briefing books with the information from the various agencies, did they still have a discussion group?

Tubby: Yes, they did, right before the conference.

Hess: Who usually sat in on that, and how was that conducted?

Tubby: Well, usually, the president and Joe Short — whoever was the press secretary — John Steelman, usually the military attachés, Charlie Murphy, Dave Lloyd; I think Dave Stowe was usually there; five or six, maybe eight or nine. It was rather like morning staff conference.

Hess: Do you think that they conducted those at that time much as they had before you had instituted the briefing books?

Tubby: Yes, I think so.

Hess: Just trying to figure out what subjects might come up that day?

Tubby: Well, what subjects might come up that day. I think it gave the president a chance to double-check with some of his top staff aides on a recommended answer.

Hess: Did Mr. Truman usually use the recommended answer, or once the press conference was going, would he come up with something that would surprise you as well as . . .

Tubby: No, he usually used a general line. He didn't read it, but he usually talked pretty much along the line of what had been recommended. There were surprises in the press conferences.

Hess: What do you recall?

Tubby: Well, I recall particularly the day that he said — that was on April 24, 1952 — the day he said that he had sent an ultimatum to Joe Stalin directing him to get his Russian troops out of Iran by a certain day, and as soon as the president said this — I had never heard of an ultimatum to Stalin — and I whispered something to him, "Was he sure?"

And he said, "You know, Roger's asked whether I sent an ultimatum or not; I sent Stalin an ultimatum."

When the conference was over and as we were going down in the elevator, he said, "If you've got any doubt about it, you check over it, you check the records, and if I'm wrong, why, set the record straight." I did check the State Department very carefully, up and down the line, and Defense, and the White House records themselves, and there was no indication of an ultimatum having been sent to Stalin, though there was a pretty strong letter sent on March 6 making our position very plain. The Russians did, in fact, withdraw their troops from Iran in May 1946. The note to Stalin was sent to the Russians by the State Department at the direction of the president.

Hess: Do you recall if you came out with a clarifying statement at this time?

Tubby: Yes, I came out with a clarifying statement in the afternoon on August 24.

Hess: Do you recall the president's reaction when he was told that a clarifying statement would have to be issued in this case, or did you see him?

Tubby: Oh, yes, I saw him. I told him what I thought we might say about it.

Hess: What was his reaction?

Tubby: It was, "Well, go ahead and say it." Naturally, he still felt, though, that we — "we" in the press — were being too technical. The important thing was that a pretty strong note was sent to the Russians, and the important thing was that they got out.

Hess: There were other times during the administration when clarifying statements had to be made to cover over or to explain something that the president had said in an interview. Was that much of a problem? Did you have to watch for that?

Tubby: Yes. We watched for it. I think that, in my time, this was the most difficult situation. He did speak rapidly. And, of course, one other more celebrated case, and I think it was his acceptance of the word *red herring*. He didn't dream up the word but was simply replying to the use of the word by a correspondent in such a way that from that time on — I think in the '52 campaign — during the '52 campaign it was alleged that it was really Truman who thought up the use of the word *red herring*.

Hess: Did he have a tendency to accept the phrasing of some of the reporters rather than taking their question and rephrasing it himself?

Tubby: Well, I wouldn't say he always did it, but this was something that we watched for.

Hess: Is there any particular news conference that stands out in your memory?

Tubby: Well, naturally, for my small part in it, the ultimatum stands out. I think his last press conference, when he sort of summed up his years in the White House — and did it in a very effective way, I thought — I think that stands out.

Hess: Mr. Truman was often accused of "shooting from the hip." Did that cause any particular problems, or, indeed, do you think that he did?

Tubby: Well, I think at times he did somewhat.

Hess: Was news leaking out of the White House offices through unauthorized sources much of a problem during the Truman administration?

Tubby: Well, there's likely to be always some leakage from any government office. And I think one of the most troublesome leakages — I think the one you've referred to in another context — and that was this business on Wake Island. The Truman-MacArthur meeting on Wake Island which Tony Leviero of the *New York Times*— and incidentally, Tony Leviero was certainly one of the people that HST liked very much — and how that got out, I haven't any idea. But stopping news leaks is almost an impossibility. Really, one has to depend on the loyalty and the sense of responsibility of individual officers.

21

Earl Warren

Washington, D.C.   May 11, 1972

Interviewed by Jerry N. Hess (Harry S. Truman Library)

Earl Warren (1891–1974), chief justice of the United States, was governor of California when he first met Truman. In 1948, as the Republican nominee for the vice presidency, he was Truman's opponent. Yet it was a cordial rivalry. The president quipped that Warren was "a Democrat but didn't know it." In making racial equality the law of the land, the Warren Court aligned itself with the civil rights revolution launched by Truman. Dwight D. Eisenhower, who favored a more gradual approach, regretted his choice of Warren. Truman thought he was a great chief justice and in 1957 was honored that his former opponent delivered the main speech at the dedication of the Harry S. Truman Presidential Library and Museum.

Hess: All right, Mr. Chief Justice, to begin this afternoon, what are your earliest recollections of Mr. Truman?

Warren: I believe the first time I met President Truman — at least as far as I can recall — was when he came out to the United Nations convention in nineteen hundred and forty-five, very shortly after he became president. I was the host governor of the convention and made the first speech at that convention welcoming it to California. And when President Truman came to town, I met him at the airport and rode in his car with him to the St. Francis Hotel where he was staying during the convention. There I visited with him in his quarters and so on.

Hess: It is well known that you and Mr. Truman are good friends. Now, just what is the basis for that friendship?

Warren: Well, as far as I am concerned, it came from admiration of his forthright qualities. To me he was a man of no guile, a man who was forthright in his positions that he took. I believe not only from what he said, but the manner of his actions, that he was acting from his own inclinations and was not being pressured into any positions that were alien to his nature; and I always felt that he felt highly toward me, too. And as time went on,

my regard for him grew, and I came to consider him a most valuable man in the public service.

Hess: As you know, Mr. Truman has said that you are "a Democrat and don't know it."

Warren: I suppose. I know when he would come out to California, as usual he would just give the Republicans the heck; and it got to be ritualistic. Someone in the crowd would say, "But how about Warren?"

He would say, "Oh, Warren is just a Democrat and doesn't know it." And of course, he couldn't have said anything better for me, talking to a Democratic crowd, and me being a Republican with our cross-filing system out there. It was that kind of a relationship all the way through.

I remember once I was back here when he was having real difficulties with the Congress; it was quite bitter, and —

Hess: Was this the Eightieth Congress that came in in '46?

Warren: I'd have to look that up. I don't recall. It seems to me it was later than that, but I won't be sure. Anyway, the Republicans, most of them didn't show up, and the House of Representatives room wasn't filled by any manner of means, and I came in there when he was speaking. I was here on a committee of the Governors' Conference, and I suggested we adjourn and go down and hear the president and his state-of-the-union message. We went down there and I was standing in the back, and when he was talking, he apparently saw me; so when he concluded his speech and had gone out, the first thing I knew a young man came in and said to me, "The president would like to see you outside."

I said, "Oh, yes?"

He said, "Yes, that's true; he's out at the elevator and he'd like to see you."

I said, "Very well. I'll go out."

I guess it was a Secret Service man; and I went out and there was the president standing at the elevator, and he said, "Well, I just wanted to know how you are getting along and how your family is and so forth."

I told him I thought he had made a good speech and so forth, and we visited a little and he got into the elevator and went away. I was the only one he spoke to out of the whole crowd. You know, I never had any close association with him in which to really become sociable. We didn't have a relationship of that kind, but I admired him greatly and still do.

And I remember another time, not so long after he became president, I was on a committee of the Governors' Conference to see the president about some matters that involved federal-state relations, and we had a date with the president. And the day we had set for the date was the day *after* the Japanese surrender. It was in the morning, and I remember we came in and this city looked like it had been hit by a tornado, papers and everything — you know what a wild night they had that night. We went and he was there waiting for us, and we went in and visited with him.

As I recall it — I've been doing a little thinking about it — my recollection is he told us that the pressure was already on to bring the boys home. And I won't be sure, but I believe he told us that he had already canceled some war contracts. Now, this was about ten or eleven in the morning, and it was in the evening of the preceding day that the surrender was announced.

Hess: Did he give any indication, either by word or tone of voice, that he thought bringing the boys home at that time would be premature?

Warren: Well, I wouldn't want to say that he said that, but I just had the idea that he thought it was pretty hasty, you know, and that he could feel this pressure building up. Now, that's the impression that was left with me from the visit that we had.

Hess: All right now, as you stated, your first meeting with President Truman was in San Francisco at the United Nations Conference.

Warren: Yes.

Hess: When did he first come to your attention, if you can think back?

Warren: As far as I can recall, he first came to my attention as the chairman of the war committee.

Hess: What came to be known as the Truman committee.

Warren: The Truman committee, yes. I thought that was a very important committee, and it received a good deal of publicity, you know. I thought it was serving a very, very good purpose. I thought it was a great service that he rendered in the war effort through that committee. But I didn't know him at that time.

Hess: What was your opinion when he was selected in 1944, in Chicago, as the vice presidential nominee on the Democratic ticket? Were you a little surprised?

Warren: Well, I don't think that I was tremendously interested in that, because —

Hess: You were looking from the other side of the picture.

Warren: . . . that was the year that they tried to force the vice presidential nomination on me at Chicago, and I had run for governor just a little over a year and a half before on the theory that I wanted to be the war governor of California, that our incumbent governor wasn't giving it the attention that it should have been given; and the people had accepted that, and had elected me and we were still in the war, and I just felt that I couldn't honorably do it then. They just took it for granted that I would do it; they wouldn't believe me. Tom Dewey talked with me for upwards of an hour, the day of nomination, but I told him that I just could not do it, and so I didn't do it.

Well, as far as I can remember, I didn't know anything except about his work on that subcommittee, and also whatever I heard about the convention when he was nominated for the vice presidency. I think that's about all that I knew about him at that time.

Hess: All right, now moving on to the 1948 election. As you were the vice presidential nominee of the Republican Party, would you give me your assessment of that election and why Mr. Truman and the Democratic Party were supported in 1948?

Warren: Well, I think one reason, the main reason, that he was elected was because he *was* such a plain and simple man, going out on his own, on a whirlwind trip to talk with the people, whereas Governor Dewey was talking *at* them, and there's a great difference. I don't believe it was because the people were satisfied with all the things President Truman had done in his administration, but I think it was largely a matter of personality between him and Governor Dewey.

Hess: Support for the underdog?

Warren: I think that played a part in it, I think the Eightieth Congress played a great part in it, and I think his carrying the Midwest, by going out for the farmers, had a lot to do with it. I don't know that I could describe any one thing that would be responsible for his election other than that.

Hess: Do you think that part of it could have been that many Republicans thought that Mr. Dewey's election —

Warren: Oh, yes.

Hess: — was a foregone conclusion and therefore they didn't have to go vote?

Warren: I sure do. They started me out on a train on — I think it was the fifteenth of September — from Sacramento, and I was on this train for thirty-five days, never got off of it; and we went to thirty-eight states around the country. When I came home about ten days before the election — and I was entirely out of touch with what was going on at home while I was on this train — and talked with some of my friends there, they told me that the Republican office in San Francisco was closed, and some others told me some other city headquarters were closed. I said, "Closed? What do you mean by that?"

They said, "Well, there isn't anything to fight, nothing to fight. The Democrats aren't making any fight out here, they have no offices running, and there is just no money available; people think there is just no contest."

I wouldn't take that, and I went around the state right up to midnight before the election giving talks and so forth; but they were just lackadaisical; everybody thought it was all over, you know.

Hess: The vote in California was extremely close.

Warren: Eighteen thousand that day.

Hess: If there had been a shift of 8,933 votes, California would have gone for Dewey.

Warren: Yes, that's right; that's about half a vote a precinct.

Hess: What could have been done? Was it just lackadaisicalness —

Warren: Oh, yes.

Hess: — or was it overconfidence at that time?

Warren: Oh, absolutely, they didn't work; they didn't work at it at all. They just thought it was in the bag and let it coast, and how people who have been through campaigns can *ever* get that idea, I don't know, but it seems to be human nature for a lot of people to do it.

Hess: Now, according to some statistics I have, if Illinois, California, and Iowa had changed — and it would only have taken 29,294 votes to swing all three states . . .

Warren: Yeah.

Hess: That's the final page there that I have given you.

Warren: Yes. And Indiana was very close, too — 870 to 821.

Hess: Yes, and there's one — Mr. Truman took some states that it was very unusual for a Democrat to take — Iowa for instance, a farm state.

Warren: Yes.

Hess: Do you recall the issue of the Eightieth Congress rewriting the charter for the Commodity Credit Corporation and leaving out the provision to buy and to provide government storage for corn?

Warren: I believe that that was a vital thing in the campaign, his speeches on that. I remember reading about them when I was on this trip around the country, and I thought it was vital. I remember at the Republican convention I had a press conference, and I remember they asked me what I thought of the Eightieth Congress. I told them I thought it was a liability.

Hess: You did?

Warren: Yes. They didn't like it, but I told them I thought it was a liability. I just thought they hadn't performed.

Hess: Why did you view the Eightieth Congress as a liability?

Warren: Because they did very little if anything, that I could see. They didn't satisfy the farming community; they hadn't done anything on reclamation out our way. I know that their attitude and Tom Dewey's attitude toward the water and power issue wasn't at all satisfactory, and he wouldn't discuss it further with them out there either.

Hess: Now, all of those are domestic issues. If you will recall, the Eightieth Congress passed the Truman Doctrine for aid to Greece and Turkey; the Eightieth Congress passed the Marshall Plan, one of our largest foreign aid things. The Eightieth Congress did, with the help of Arthur Vandenberg, come through and carry out Mr. Truman's request in foreign aid matters.

Warren: Yes, but there were domestic affairs.

Hess: Yes. Do you think elections are settled more on domestic affairs than foreign affairs?

Warren: Normally I do.

Hess: In the absence of a shooting war.

Warren: Yes, normally I do. At least I did out in my part of the country, out in California. It may be different back here in New York, Pennsylvania; I don't know. But I think out there people are more concerned the way the government is functioning domestically than it is internationally. If there is no crisis, I mean.

Hess: As you well know, after the election Governor Dewey received some criticism, by the benefit of hindsight, of taking too high a plane during the campaign and not coming out with a hard-hitting speech. Do you think that he should have taken a stronger stand in some of his speeches in '48?

Warren: I think the big mistake he made was to have all those speeches written before the convention. And you just can't be oriented to a campaign if you're stratified, and I know that he had these speeches scheduled for — let's say for conservation in Oklahoma City — and that would be his talk on conservation; he wouldn't talk about it other places, or answer any questions on it, refer to any speech he made at that place; and Social Security down at Los Angeles, and so forth. I don't believe you can structure a campaign that way. I believe you've got —

Hess: Not that rigidly.

Warren:— to meet things as they arise, and that's what Mr. Truman did.

Hess: Did you discuss political strategy with Governor Dewey during the campaign?

Warren: No, I never —I was on this train, and I only talked to him a couple of times.

Hess: Do you find that a bit unusual, that the man —

Warren: I think so. It would be for me.

Hess: Why weren't you called upon for your advice?

Warren: I don't know. I don't know, but I wasn't. I was in second place, and I took whatever they asked me to do. I went about and did it, but I didn't force myself on any counsel. No, I had nothing to do with their deliberations at all.

Hess: In the 1952 campaign you met President Truman in Davis, California, and introduced him to the crowd. What do you recall about meeting with the president on that occasion?

Warren: Well, he was coming down from Oregon, I think; he wasn't coming into Sacramento. He was going through to Davis — a little university town there — and then going right down to San Francisco. So, again, the chairman of the Democratic Party wired me and inquired if I would like to come out to Davis and greet President Truman. I wired him and said, "Sure I will."

So, I went out there and went into his car, and there was just he and Margaret there — I don't believe Mrs. Truman was there at the time, but if she was I didn't see her. But anyway, Margaret was there with him and we visited him in his car a little while, and he said he appreciated me coming out. After we had been there awhile, somebody came in and said, "Governor, would you mind standing out here on the rear platform and being photographed with the president?"

The president hearing said, "Now, here, you let that man alone. It's very kind of him to come over here," he said, "and I'm not going to embarrass him."

I said, "Well, Mr. President, there's no embarrassment to a governor greeting the president of the United States. Of course, I'll go out there with you, and if you want, I'll introduce you."

"Would you do that?"

I said, "Of course, I'd do that." I went out there, and I saw a lot of young Republicans they had out there. They all had signs, you know, that hadn't been disclosed yet, and they had them behind them and were —

Hess: Going to say, "I like Ike?"

Warren: — going to bring them out when it was the right time; and so I told them that one thing about Californians and particularly Sacramentoans, that we're always happy to have a president of the United States there; and when he came we always showed him the courtesy that his position called for, and I was sure that on this occasion no one would think of embarrassing the president, and so forth. I talked along those lines for a little while, and then I said, "Now, Mr. President, you and the Democrats can do your own job," and I left, but they never brought those signs out.

Hess: Good. Now, Mr. Chief Justice, in recent years, historians and other writers have set forth various theories on the theme that when the United States employed such programs as the Truman Doctrine, the Marshall Plan, and Point Four, that to marshal public support behind those programs the government purposely set out to frighten the American people by invoking visions of Communist world conquest; and that basically the reason we wanted to restore Europe and the other countries of the world was only to restore our prewar markets for our products. If Europe failed, our markets would dry up and unemployment and depression would result, and self-interest was our only, or basic, consideration. What is your opinion of that general line of thinking?

Warren: Well, I think it's an aggregation of half-truths. I think, of course, when he advocated the Marshall Plan, and aid for Greece, and the Truman Doctrine, he — of course, we were anticipating to make a better world in which we would have a chance to prosper; that's human nature, and to do otherwise would be silly almost. There might even be some people whose only interest was that, but I think the Marshall Plan was basically a humanitarian plan, and I think America is entitled to get credit for it. I think his Point Four Program was a very, very sensible program and if used to better advantage by succeeding administrations, would have made it much more viable than it has been. So, the only interest of our government was a selfish one to help ourselves. It isn't a normal reaction to help humanity to that extent just for personal benefit. There are other things that they could have done, without that expenditure of money and so forth, if that was their only interest. But I think they were good programs and the best programs that we've had, and I think they are not only whole-some, but I think that they were humanitarianly conceived.

Hess: Where would you place President Truman on the scale from a liberal to a conservative, and what would be your thumbnail definition of those terms, "liberal" and "conservative"?

Warren: Well, I don't like either of those terms; I think they are misnomers. I think they have been made epithets rather than philosophies of govern-ment. I think that there's no irreconcilability between being a liberal and a conservative, according to my concept of those two things. I think some people by instinct want to walk more slowly than others, even though they are going in the same direction; and I think that both conservative and liberal thought in this country can accommodate to each other, and we have to do it to have a viable government, because neither of them can be satisfied with the status quo, or to turn the clock back. We have to go forward, and any movement toward the general welfare of the coun-try and all of the people in it, to my way, is a liberal thought, and I think Mr. Truman thinks very much like that, too. I'm not an ideologist and I don't think he is either, but he's been more of a pragmatist than other-wise, and I don't believe . . .

Hess: In your opinion, what were Mr. Truman's views on the subject of in-dividual human rights and the striving by minority groups for a place in society?

Warren: Well, I think that his position — at the time that he was in there — is a perfectly reasonable one, and I think the platform on which he ran in 1948 spelled that out in very good form. Spelled it out better than, I think, the Republicans have.

Yes. So, I think his record was good. As I recall it, he was the first one to integrate the armed forces, wasn't he? And he ran on that civil rights platform, and it was tougher then than it has been in recent years even to assume that position, because it was newer.

Hess: Now, there were times when Mr. Truman had a good deal of difficulty getting his civil rights measures through Congress. What's your view on that? Was it just at the wrong time? Was it a little too early? Was the Con-gress too conservative?

Warren: Well, the times had a lot to do with it; it's a long story, but the ero-sion of civil rights started with the old Tilden-Hayes affair. [In the com-promise that settled the disputed election of 1876, Republicans abandoned their support of civil rights and allowed Democrats to restore white home rule. Federal troops were also withdrawn from the South.]

Hess: Now, during Mr. Truman's administration, of course, there still was the separate but equal . . .

Warren: Well, yes. But I will say this, that during the years of the Vinson Court, the separate but equal doctrine was eroded to the point where it only took one more step to put it entirely behind, and that was the step we took in *Brown v the Board of Education*. Now, those things were done during the time Vinson was in the Court.

Hess: You know there were several things civil rights people were calling for, a permanent Federal FEPC, Fair Employment Practices Commission —

Warren: Yes.

Hess: — which is sort of an on again, off again, sometimes by law, sometimes by executive order. That was not put through. That was one of the things that civil rights people would have liked to have put through. In other words, were there things that Mr. Truman could have done but he did not do in the field of civil rights?

Warren: Well, I don't think I could answer that because I don't know. But I'll say this, that President Roosevelt with all of his popularity couldn't put it through, as a law; he put it through as an executive order.

I know how hard it is to get those things through. When I became governor, I started out my first session in the legislature asking the legislature to set up a commission to determine what we could do in that area. I think New York at that same session enacted its Fair Employment Practices Act, but there was no state in the union that had it. But I thought that the thing for us to do was to pave the way with a commission to say it was all right, and I got nowhere from *either* side. Those that were extremists and wanting, like today, an FEPC, were against it; and those who were against any form of FEPC thought this was just the camel's head in the tent and they wouldn't go for it, so I just left there without practically any support at all. In the next two years I studied the matter, and I came to the conclusion that we ought to have one, and I introduced it in our legislature and advocated it. And again, I lost the support of both sides, because the extremists wanted to put such powers in it that no one would stand for it and the other people who were against it, of course, were against it in any form. So, I lost that one, too.

Then the extremists put their bill on the initiative ballot and drove everybody who was in favor of the movement away from it; they lost it by an *enormous* majority — just didn't go at all. So, I have some knowledge of how difficult it is to do those things.

Hess: That's right, you know what it's like to work with the legislature, don't you? One that won't go along.

Warren: That's right.

Hess: In your opinion, what were Mr. Truman's major accomplishments, and what were his major failings?

Warren: Oh, I think only history can determine that. I think that generally speaking you can say that in all his most important decisions he made good decisions, and some of the smaller ones, why, you could disagree more about them. But I think he had to go to Korea and do what he did, and I think he was wise in doing it with the United Nations. I think, as I've said before, his Point Four Program and his Marshall Plan were very forward-looking programs, as the present condition of Europe would testify to. I don't think of any great failures he made in his administration. We all have weakness, you know, and some things you would like to do you can't do; you can't get support for them and so forth; but I think his instincts were all good, and things he did put through were good.

HARRY S. TRUMAN TIME LINE

May 8, 1884	Born in Lamar, Missouri
Summer 1890	Truman family moves to Independence
May 1901	Graduates from Independence High School
1902–1906	Works in mail room of the *Kansas City Star*, as a timekeeper on a Santa Fe Railroad construction project, as a clerk for the National Bank of Commerce, and as a bookkeeper for Union National Bank
1910	Begins courting Elizabeth Wallace
1915–1917	Invests in and works in zinc mining and oil drilling ventures
1917–1919	Serves in the 129th Field Artillery, rising to become captain of Battery D during World War I service in France
June 28, 1919	Marries Elizabeth (Bess) Wallace in Independence
November 1919	With partner Eddie Jacobson, opens men's haberdashery in Kansas City; store failed in 1922
November 7, 1922	Elected eastern judge of the Jackson County Court
February 17, 1924	HST's only child, Mary Margaret Truman, born in Independence
November 4, 1924	Defeated for reelection as county judge
1925–1926	Works as membership salesman for Kansas City Automobile Club
November 2, 1926	Elected presiding judge of Jackson County Court
November 4, 1930	Reelected presiding judge
August 7, 1934	Wins Democratic nomination for U.S. Senate
November 6, 1934	Elected U.S. senator from Missouri
August 6, 1940	Defeats Governor Lloyd Stark to win renomination for Senate
November 5, 1940	Reelected to the Senate
1941	The Senate Special Committee to Investigate the National Defense Program, called the Truman committee, organized
July 21, 1944	At the Democratic national convention in Chicago, HST nominated for the vice presidency

November 7, 1944	Elected vice president as Franklin Roosevelt wins fourth term
April 12, 1945	FDR dies; Truman sworn in as his successor
May 8, 1945	On his sixty-first birthday, announces the Allied victory in Europe and surrender of Nazi Germany
June 26, 1945	United Nations charter signed
July 17–August 2, 1945	Summit at Potsdam with Churchill and Stalin
August 6 and 9, 1945	Atomic bombs dropped on Hiroshima and Nagasaki
August 14, 1945	Japan surrenders
September 6, 1945	Presents twenty-one-point address to Congress, outlining domestic agenda
September 20, 1946	Fires Henry A. Wallace as commerce secretary
November 5, 1946	Republicans win both houses of Congress
March 12, 1947	Delivers Truman Doctrine speech in response to the threat of Soviet aggression
June 20, 1947	Vetoes Taft-Hartley Act; Congress later overrides
April 3, 1948	Signs the Marshall Plan to rebuild Europe from ashes of war
May 14, 1948	Recognizes the state of Israel
June 26, 1948	Berlin airlift begins; Russian blockade of Berlin not lifted until May 1949
July 15, 1948	Accepts Democratic presidential nomination in Philadelphia's convention hall
July 26, 1948	Issues executive order ending racial discrimination in the armed services
November 2, 1948	After a hard-hitting campaign, defeats Republican Thomas E. Dewey in an astonishing political upset
April 4, 1949	Signs the North Atlantic Treaty
June 30, 1950	In his most difficult decision, responds with force to North Korea's invasion of South Korea
April 11, 1951	Removes General Douglas MacArthur as commander of U.S. and United Nations forces in the Far East for insubordination
March 29, 1952	Announces that he will not seek another term
July 26, 1952	Endorses Adlai E. Stevenson for the presidency at the Democratic national convention in Chicago
November 4, 1952	Dwight D. Eisenhower wins presidency

January 20, 1953	After attending Eisenhower's inauguration, Trumans move back to Independence
1955–1956	HST's memoirs published by Doubleday
July 6, 1957	HST Library dedicated in Independence
1957–1966	Works daily in his office at the Truman Library
December 26, 1972	Dies in a Kansas City hospital at the age of eighty-eight; buried in the courtyard of the Truman Library

Harry S. Truman is the subject of more literature than all but a handful of American political figures. Since the research room at his presidential library opened in 1959, more than ten thousand scholars have explored its vast collections that include 14 million pages of primary source material. These documents have made it possible for future generations to gain a better understanding of the man and his times. The four most comprehensive and insightful biographies are Margaret Truman, *Harry S. Truman* (New York: William Morrow, 1972); David McCullough, *Truman* (New York: Simon & Schuster, 1992); Robert H. Ferrell, *Harry S. Truman: A Life* (Columbia: University of Missouri Press, 1994); Alonzo L. Hamby, *Man of the People: A Life of Harry S. Truman* (New York: Oxford University Press, 1995).

Of Truman's own books, his memoirs *Year of Decisions* (Garden City: Doubleday, 1955) and *Years of Trial and Hope, 1946–1952* (Garden City: Doubleday, 1956), and *Mr. Citizen* (New York: Bernard Geis Associates, 1960) are essential reading. *Truman Speaks* (New York: Columbia University Press, 1960) is a delightful collection of lectures that the former president delivered at Columbia in 1959. *Off the Record: The Private Papers of Harry S. Truman*, edited by Robert H. Ferrell (New York: Harper & Row, 1980) is a superb collection of diaries, letters, and other selected writings from the beginning of his presidency through his retirement years. The eight volumes covering the Truman years in *Public Papers of the Presidents* (Washington, D.C.: U.S. Government Printing Office) were published because the man from Independence led the way in obtaining congressional support for the documentation of the entire American presidency. The first volume covering the Truman years was published in 1961, and the final volume appeared in 1966. *Dear Bess: The Letters from Harry to Bess Truman 1910–1959*, edited by Robert H. Ferrell (New York: Norton, 1983), is an illuminating portrait of a marriage that does much to explain how this uncommon man would surprise the world. Monte M. Poen's *Strictly Personal and Confidential: The Letters Harry Truman Never Mailed* (Boston: Little, Brown,1982) and *Letters Home by Harry Truman* (New York: G. P. Putnam's, 1984) are among the frankest letters ever written by a president.

Richard S. Kirkendall, a leading authority on Truman and the Bullitt Professor of American History at the University of Washington, edited *The Harry S. Truman Encyclopedia* (Boston: G. K. Hall, 1989), which includes more than three hundred essays about nearly every major personality and policy question of the Truman era. *The Truman Administration: A Documentary History*, edited by Barton J. Bernstein and

Allen J. Matusow (New York: Harper & Row, 1966), is a good starting point for any student of the postwar era. A revisionist historian, Bernstein is critical of the administration's policies but is eminently fair.

The Presidency of Harry S. Truman by Donald R. McCoy (Lawrence: University Press of Kansas, 1984) is the best single-volume study of the administration. The Truman Presidency, edited by Michael J. Lacey (Washington, D.C.: Woodrow Wilson International Center for Scholars; and Cambridge: Cambridge University Press, 1989), is a collection of essays on Truman's foreign and domestic policies by reputable scholars, including Barton J. Bernstein, John Lewis Gaddis, Alonzo L. Hamby, and Robert A. Pollard. Robert J. Donovan's two-volume history of the Truman years, Conflict and Crisis (New York: Norton, 1977), covering the first term, and Tumultuous Years (New York: Norton, 1982), which chronicles the second term, is well written and based on primary sources. Donovan, who covered the Truman White House for the New York Herald Tribune, is among the few Truman scholars who had first-hand acquaintance with the subject. Cabell Phillips, The Truman Presidency: The History of a Triumphant Succession (New York: Macmillan, 1966), is another highly readable study by a White House correspondent who lived through this history. Even though Phillips wrote this book before Truman's private papers were opened, he did extensive research and showed why this presidency mattered more than most.

Memoirs by key participants in the Truman administration include Dean Acheson's Present at the Creation: My Years in the State Department (New York: Norton, 1971); James F. Byrnes, Speaking Frankly (New York: Harper, 1947) and All in One Lifetime (New York: Harper, 1958); Omar N. Bradley with Clay Blair, A General's Life: An Autobiography (New York: Simon & Schuster, 1983); The Forrestal Diaries, edited by Walter Millis with the collaboration of E. S. Dufield (New York: Viking Press, 1951); Lucius D. Clay, Decision in Germany (Garden City: Doubleday, 1950); Matthew B. Ridgway, The Korean War (Garden City: Doubleday, 1967); Dwight D. Eisenhower, Crusade in Europe (Garden City: Doubleday, 1948) and At Ease: Stories I Tell to Friends (Garden City: Doubleday, 1967); Henry L. Stimson with McGeorge Bundy, On Active Service in Peace and War (New York: Harper & Brothers, 1948); Alben W. Barkley, That Reminds Me: The Autobiography of the Veep (New York: Doubleday, 1954); W. Averell Harriman with Elie Abel, Special Envoy to Churchill and Stalin, 1943–1946 (New York: Random House, 1975); Clark M. Clifford with Richard Holbrooke, Counsel to the President (New York; Random House, 1991); The Price of Vision: The Diary of Henry A. Wallace, edited by John Morton Blum (Boston: Houghton Mifflin Co., 1973); Charles Sawyer, Concerns of a Conservative Democrat (Carbondale: Southern Illinois University Press, 1968); Ken Hechler, Working with Truman: A Personal Memoir of the White House Years (New York: G. P. Putnam's, 1982); and Truman in the White House: The Diary of

Eben A. Ayers, edited with commentary by Robert H. Ferrell (Columbia: University of Missouri Press, 1991).

Truman's role as commander in chief is analyzed in J. Robert Moskin, Mr. Truman's War: The Final Victories of World War II and the Birth of the Postwar World (New York: Random House, 1996); Richard F. Haynes, The Awesome Power (Baton Rouge: Louisiana State University Press, 1973); Charles L. Mee Jr., Meeting at Potsdam (New York: M. Evans, 1975); Richard B. Frank, Downfall: The End of the Imperial Japanese Empire (New York: Random House, 1999); Robert Jay Lifton and Greg Mitchell, Hiroshima in America: Fifty Years of Denial (New York: G. P. Putnam's, 1995); Thomas Parrish, Berlin in the Balance, 1945–1949 (Reading, Mass.: Addison-Wesley, 1998); Don Cook, Forging the Alliance: NATO 1945 to 1950 (London: Secker & Warburg, 1989); and Clay Blair, The Forgotten War: America in Korea, 1950–1953 (New York: Times Books, 1987).

The great upset of 1948 is chronicled in Irwin Ross, The Loneliest Campaign: The Truman Victory of 1948 (New York: New American Library, 1968); and Zachary Karabell, The Last Campaign (New York: Knopf, 2000). Choosing Truman: The Democratic Convention of 1944, by Robert H. Ferrell, is the definitive account of how the Missouri senator emerged as FDR's heir. Sean J. Savage, Truman and the Democratic Party (Lexington: University Press of Kentucky, 1997), and Robert Underhill, The Truman Persuasions (Ames: Iowa State University Press, 1981), are useful studies of the president's political style.

Franklin D. Mitchell, Harry S. Truman and the News Media (Columbia: University of Missouri Press, 1998), is a solid treatment of the president's relationship with the Fourth Estate. Andrew J. Dunar, The Truman Scandals and the Politics of Morality (Columbia: University of Missouri Press, 1984), is a first-rate history of the controversies that plagued Truman throughout his administration. Though Truman was a man of great character, Dunar shows that not all of his associates lived up to the president's ethical standards.

William E. Leuchtenburg's "The Conversion of Harry Truman" in the November 1991 issue of American Heritage is the best account of Truman's evolution into a civil rights hero. Quest and Response: Minority Rights and the Truman Administration, by Donald R. McCoy and Richard T. Ruetten (Lawrence: University Press of Kansas, 1976), was written while Truman's private correspondence was still closed to scholars. But it is based on exhaustive research and shows how Truman set the stage for the civil rights movement with his bold leadership.

Among the better histories of the United States during the Truman years are James T. Patterson, Grand Expectations (New York: Oxford University Press, 1996); John Patrick Diggins, The Proud Decades: America in War and Peace, 1941–1960 (New York: Norton, 1988); Cabell Phillips, The 1940s: Decade of Triumph and Trouble (New

York: Macmillan, 1975); David Halberstam, *The Fifties* (New York: Villard, 1993); Eric F. Goldman, *The Crucial Decade* (New York: Knopf, 1956); Geoffrey Perrett, *A Dream of Greatness: The American People, 1945–1963* (New York: Coward, McCann & Geohegan, 1979); and Joseph G. Goulden, *The Best Years, 1945–1950* (New York: Atheneum, 1976). David M. Kennedy's *Freedom from Fear* (New York: Oxford University Press, 1999) is a study that spans America from Herbert Hoover's presidency through the beginning of the Truman era.

The Truman Library's oral history program is described and more than 460 interviews are listed in *Guide to Historical Materials in the Harry S. Truman Library*, edited by Raymond H. Geselbracht and Anita M. Smith (Independence: Truman Library, 1995). They are also listed and many transcripts are available on the Truman Presidential Museum and Library Web site: www.trumanlibrary.org.

CREDITS

INDEX

Page numbers for photographs are in boldface type; for interviews, in italic.

STEVE NEAL is a political columnist for the *Chicago Sun-Times*.

His most recent books include *Eleanor and Harry: The Correspondence*

of Eleanor Roosevelt and Harry S. Truman (2002) and *Harry and Ike:*

The Partnership That Remade the Postwar World (2001). His earlier

Rolling on the River: The Best of Steve Neal (1999) is available from

SIU Press.